"Ever dream of running an inn? With lively prose, 3-D detail, great humor and strong honesty, *Inn Mates* is a fascinating visit to one such dream, told from the perspective of a 15-year innkeeper who's a delight of a guide...Anderholm tells it all in a story still as delicious and memorable as the creme brulee French toast she once served..."

—SUZANNE STREMPEK SHEA, author of *This Is Paradise: An Irish Mother's Grief, an African Village's Plight and the Medical Clinic That Brought Fresh Hope to Both*

"Teri's beautifully crafted memoir reads like a novel; a young couple in love who risk all to pursue their dream of opening an inn in Bar Harbor, Maine. Both witty and deeply personal, *Inn Mates* describes the joys and sorrows of the hospitality business from extensive renovations to zany guests, ethereal ghosts and scrumptious gourmet meals. I was swept away!"

—MARGARET JONES, author of *Walking Sacred Sites: Listening to their Story*

"Teri Anderholm's *Inn Mates* is, at its core, a love story. She and her partner changed their lives; with no clue what they were doing, they quit their jobs and put their life savings into a dilapidated inn on the coast of Maine. Unlike most of us, they did not end up broke and divorced and with bitter acrimony, but somehow created a hearth, a welcoming beacon for travelers in the night. This is their journey; every floorboard that had to be replaced, every fixture, every setback, and the larger triumph as well."

—CHARLES BOCK, NYT bestselling author of *Beautiful Children, Alice & Oliver,* and *I Will Do Better*

INN MATES

An Innkeeper's Memoir

TERI ANDERHOLM

Inn Mates: An Innkeeper's Memoir
Copyright © 2024 Teri Anderholm

ISBN: 978-1-63381-384-7

All rights reserved. No part of this book may be reproduced in any form or by any electronic or mechanical means, including information storage and retrieval systems, without permission in writing from the author, except by a reviewer, who may quote brief passages in review.

Designed and produced by:
Maine Authors Publishing
12 High Street, Thomaston, Maine
www.maineauthorspublishing.com

Printed in the United States of America

To Jeff…always

CONTENTS

Author's Note xi
Prologue: A Bar Harbor Classic Is Reborn xiii

PART ONE

CHAPTER ONE 3
   Late Arrivals 3
   Inn Our Dreams 8
   Innovators 13
   Inn Trouble 17
   Birthday Wishes 20
   Wake-Up Call 21
CHAPTER TWO 27
   Inn Décor 27
   Door in the Floor 32
   Countdown 40
   Running on Empty 45
   Breaking Glass 47
   Inn Quest 49

PART TWO

CHAPTER THREE 57
   Family Affair 57
   Meet Your Innkeeper 59
   Internal Affairs 61

CHAPTER FOUR..74
   Opening Day..74
   Breakfast Is Served 77
   Help Wanted..79
   Doctor in the House.. 80
   Family Matters 83
   Double Vision 86
   Holiday Letter...89

PART THREE

CHAPTER FIVE...93
   Front Desk Notes 93
   Meet Your Innkeeper 94
   Inn Mates..101
   Work Release... 108

PART FOUR

CHAPTER SIX... 115
   Front Desk Notes 115
   Early Riser 115
   Duty Calls.. 119
   Show Time.. 120
   Heated Encounters... 123
CHAPTER SEVEN 126
   Life's Rich Pageant 126
   Rad Dad... 126
   Springtime in Maine 128
   Privacy Please..131
   Frisky Business.. 134
   Golden Moments 136
   Last Call... 138

Coffee To-Go 142
Paradise Bound 143
Holiday Letter 149

PART FIVE

CHAPTER EIGHT 153
   Front Desk Notes 153
   We Do Weddings 153
   Here Comes the "Bride" 164
CHAPTER NINE 182
   Innkeeping Academy Redux 182

PART SIX

CHAPTER TEN 209
   Front Desk Notes 209
   Innkeeper Wellness Program 210
   Medical Leave 213
   Family Leave 220
   Work/Life Balance 222
   Holiday Letter 224
CHAPTER ELEVEN 227
   Front Desk Notes 227
   Exit Ramp 227
   Paradise Tossed 235
   Holiday Letter 250
CHAPTER TWELVE 251
   Swan Song 251

Acknowledgments 257
About the Author 267

AUTHOR'S NOTE

*This is a memoir of my life and my experience
as an innkeeper in Bar Harbor, Maine.
The events and stories are true, but some names
of the characters have been changed.
Others are composites of various people,
experiences, and conversations.
Innkeepers like to maintain high standards of discretion.
In this regard, memoirist innkeepers make cozy companions.
Someone once wrote, "God is in the details."
And as all innkeepers know, it's all about the details.*

PROLOGUE

A Bar Harbor Classic Is Reborn

During the nineteenth century, Bar Harbor, Maine, was known as Eden, a quaint coastal village located on Mount Desert Island and situated on Frenchman Bay along the banks of the Atlantic Ocean. Once inhabited by indigenous communities, it was discovered by Samuel de Champlain in 1604, and incorporated as the Town of Eden in 1796.

Eden then, as now, boasts a beautiful, rustic landscape, pristine granite shorelines carved by glaciers, dramatic seascapes, and pine-scented mountains. The rocky coastlines are bedded-down among wild gardens of cinnamon fern, sheep laurel, and blueberry alongside mountain ponds and spring-fed kettle lakes that were etched by glaciers at the end of the last ice age.

During the summer months, warm bands of sunlight collide with the ocean's cool water vapor, creating billowing banks of fog across Frenchman Bay. Such atmospheric conditions often give way to spritzy rain showers resulting in single and double rainbows, or occasionally the heavens erupt in icy crystalline sun dogs, a phenomenon of halos that appear to encircle the sun.

Eden was an idyllic destination for rusticators—people "from away," in local parlance. In other words, people who had idle time to stay in boardinghouses and simple cottages, often for weeks and months. The visitors spent leisurely summer days in active outdoor pursuits: early morning hikes along winding streams, boating, fishing, swimming, and lounging on warm granite ledges while sketching. Later they joined their hosts for simple suppers of chowders, stews, and blueberry pie, followed by a good night's sleep in spartan rooms.

In the 1840s, artists from the Hudson River School of painters created iconic masterpieces which publicized Bar Harbor and Mount Desert Island. By the 1870s, there were fifteen hotels. By the 1880s, the cottage era was in full swing as the pre-income tax fortunes of industrial magnates built grandiose mansions, also called cottages, edged with formal gardens and tennis courts and boasting a cadre of servants. These fashionable cottages rivaled those in Newport, Rhode Island, ushering in an era of elegant social gatherings held by wealthy summer residents, satirized by Mark Twain and Charles Dudley Warner in the novel *The Gilded Age, A Tale of Today*.

> For many years…[Bar Harbor] had been frequented by people who have more fondness for nature than they have money, and who were willing to put up with wretched accommodations and enjoy a mild sort of "roughing it." The notion spread that it was the finest sanatorium in America for flirtations; and as trade is said to follow the flag, so in this case real estate speculation rioted in the wake of beauty and fashion.
> —"Their Pilgrimage" by Charles Dudley Warner, *Harper's New Monthly Magazine*, June 1886

In 1885, a summer cottage was built in a field near the center of the village overlooking Frenchman Bay. Like many visitors during that era, the owners came to escape the heat of the city and to enjoy the forests and salt air. The 26-room estate was built by local craftsmen with loving attention to detail. In the early 1890s, it was purchased by a prominent politician and newspaper publisher, Joseph Parker Bass from Bangor, Maine. Sometime around 1930, the property first began to be operated as an inn by a new owner.

Accounts of Mr. Bass's life paint him as a shrewd businessman who never failed to speak his conscience. "He roused the slothful and prodded the stupid, while he admired the clever, even if he was careful not to spoil them with praise." Perhaps this eulogy was intended for the future innkeepers.

Inn Mates

On March 3, 1918, Eden was renamed Bar Harbor, after a sandbar that connects the village with Bar Island. Bar Harbor and the surrounding communities of Northeast Harbor, Southwest Harbor, and Bass Harbor were greatly admired by summer and year-round residents, leading to the establishment of Acadia National Park in 1919. It's now one of the most beloved and popular vacation destinations on the East Coast of the United States. In 2022, Acadia National Park recorded more than four million visits. Lodging reservations are highly recommended.

Check-in time is 3:00 p.m.

PART ONE

CHAPTER ONE

When I am with you, we stay up all night. When you're not here, I can't go to sleep. Praise God for those two insomnias. And the difference between them.
—Rumi, 13th-century Persian poet

Late Arrivals

My guests from Chicago called. Their flight is delayed due to a fire started in the terminal by airline employees. Oh, the joys of travel in the 21st century! They said they'll be landing at Boston's Logan Airport at 11:00 p.m., and rather than playing it safe and booking a hotel near the airport, they plan to drive to Bar Harbor, a five-hour trip, in the middle of the night. Not a wise idea.

Night driving in Maine can be hazardous going. The interstate highway consists of long stretches of forested area prone to moose and deer appearances. The night sky is illuminated only by the headlights of oncoming cars and spangled starlight, with few if any streetlights. It's easy to succumb to sleep or miss an exit, especially after midnight. I'm having trouble staying awake myself, sitting here in the cozy embrace of my warm leather chair. After a long day, I was looking forward to a restful night's sleep; instead, I've set my alarm for 3:30 a.m. to await their arrival.

I figured if the guests made good time, they'd arrive around 4:00 a.m., effectively staying one night out of the two-night booking for which they've already paid. I offered to release them from their reservation, offering a full refund due to the extreme circumstances, but they insisted on coming. Now I'm waiting in the inn's library under dim light. In an effort to stay awake, I thought a good book would be a fine companion. I flipped to a bookmark and found a poem written by Rumi more than 700 years ago.

Teri Anderholm

The Guest House

This being human is a guest house.
Every morning a new arrival.
A joy, a depression, a meanness,
some momentary awareness comes
as an unexpected visitor,
Welcome and entertain them all!
Even if they're a crowd of sorrows,
who violently sweep your house
empty of its furniture,
still, treat each guest honorably.
He may be clearing you out
for some new delight.
The dark thought, the shame, the malice,
meet them at the door laughing,
and invite them in.
Be grateful for whoever comes,
because each has been sent
as a guide from beyond.

Such wise words, as relevant now as then, even in Downeast Maine in the middle of the night. And despite the late hour, and the march of time, hospitality remains the generous and cordial reception of guests provided by caring innkeepers. A noble tradition stemming from ancient history, focused on the relationship between host and guest.

For Jeff and me, it was a joy and always a privilege. Sure, sometimes we'd have to work at it, if we were tired, cranky, or if one of the guests was a troublemaker. But our goal was to quietly witness, read, and understand what guests wanted. To anticipate and to delight them, each interaction a meaningful experience, a lens on humanity we laughingly dubbed "Life's Rich Pageant."

Growing up, I never considered entering my family's restaurant business or the hospitality field. My dream was to be the first member of my family to earn a college degree, graduating from Boston College, rather than attending the University of Michigan, the academic centerpiece of my hometown.

It was during my return to Ann Arbor a few years after high school that I met the sun in my solar system, my future husband, Jeff.

I was 21, still a fledgling college student, a green-eyed brunette, a third-generation Romanian on my mom's side, with German heritage from my dad's. I was a music lover and long-distance swimmer. Jeff was 23, tall, handsome, a darkly humorous bookish type, with Irish-Swedish roots and tweed scally cap. He was a budding tech writer who sported a trim beard, his blue eyes framed in round wire-rimmed glasses. Both of us were working retail gigs until we could plot our life's course.

As teenagers, Jeff and I ran around the block of hospitality and restaurant jobs as student workers. Sprinting up and down the staircases of inns and restaurants many, many, many summers ago, flipping pancakes, pouring coffee, chatting with tourists. Even then, we were fed up with fusty hotels, inns with poor plumbing, shared bathrooms, and uncomfortable beds. Our bosses, stressed-out inn or restaurant owners, constantly looking over our shoulder. Or yelling at guests.

In 1982, we traveled to Jeff's home turf, Kennebunk Beach, Maine, for a short summer break, staying at a beachfront inn steps from his childhood summer home. As a high school student, Jeff worked at that very same inn playing an all-hands role in the hospitality symphony—breakfast cook, dishwasher, laundry sorter. His job description included hazardous duty hanging upside down out of the upper windows painting the building's exterior, his boss holding him by his ankles. All for a flat salary of $110.00 a week.

During our visit, we had a front-row seat in the theater of innkeeping. Sitting across from visitors from Quebec, we learned they were repeat guests who stayed at the inn every year. They loved the accommodations and the beach, but somehow they didn't like the coffee that year. It wasn't the same as last year, and it was too weak. The innkeeper breezed past the table and caught wind of their complaint. She stopped short, table-side. "What do you expect me to do, freeze the coffee from last year so it tastes the same?" The couple gently withered, eyes fixed on their coffee cups.

"Yeah, I remember, she went nuts!" Jeff laughed. "Why the bad attitude? How hard can an innkeeping gig be?" Oh, the echoes of our hubris. Our naive, ill-informed egos grabbed on tight, lacing us into straitjackets of delusion. Some might have said we deserved what was coming…to the second power.

Two decades later, our career balloons burst somewhere over Boston Common. When we landed on the ground, we dusted ourselves off and jumped into our Aventurine Green Porsche 911. Heading north on a highway of dreams, windows rolled down, we popped in a CD and sang along to classic hits from Boston, searching for some "Peace of Mind." But with our view fixed in the rearview mirror, waving goodbye to the life we had, we missed a key lyric change. And instead of taking a look ahead, Jeff and I looked at each other: "We're energetic and creative, let's do something entirely new. Let's become innkeepers!"

We thought innkeeping would be an easy career choice after being discouraged by corporate reversals and executive shenanigans and jaded by disappointments. Meanwhile, head-hunters circled overhead, sending job leads and asking for CVs, then ghosting us. Jeff said, "Let's take a break and travel before making any rash moves."

While working as a marketing executive in the software business, Jeff's extensive business travel was a perk: He was in regular rotations through Hong Kong, India, Japan, France, Italy, Malaysia, London, Singapore, and South America, but his time was often spent in airless hotel conference rooms, international departure lounges, planes, trains, and taxicabs. And my business trips presenting to investment managers in Bermuda and London were much the same. Crisscrossing the skies on business excursions left bite marks from the travel bug all over us.

We figured we should see the world while we were young and able-bodied. Since we didn't have children, we dived headlong into adventure travel as a cure for our wanderlust. Coveting vacation days, accumulating travel points, finding analgesics to blunt the aches and pains from the burnout of 60-hour weeks, we sweated the math like actuaries, tallying up our allotted vacation and personal days, and maxing out our time budgets every year. Weekends were spent researching ideas and destinations for the next trip, then the one after that. We created a string of travel commitments, a lifeline we would throw to one another if our moods were flagging or one of us needed a pick-me-up.

During the rough patches, we'd float away, drifting into our imagination of summer vacations cycling or driving the country roads in New England, Ireland, Italy, or France. We pictured renting small cottages, strolling outdoor markets, visiting museums and historic sites. Warming up from frigid New England winters, we would imagine tropical destinations in the Caribbean. Each trip we planned offered opportunities to lap up new experiences and flavors, and we found ourselves feeling relaxed and buoyant as soon as our plane touched down in a new destination.

We treasured snorkeling in dreamy underwater coral gardens, bathing in warm, blue lagoons amid schools of parrot fish, red snapper, and turtles, watching swirling formations of damselfish, or sergeant majors striped with golden and black military insignia. Glimpses of barracuda or shark were grim underwater reminders of lurking danger amid paradise, best drowned out with a tropical rum drink or a Dark 'n Stormy, fine antidotes for deferring thoughts before returning home to the real world.

We agreed we needed a new direction, a fresh start. The trip down memory lane got us thinking about buying an inn. Combining our hobbies of cooking, entertaining family and friends, and caring for our home and garden, we decided to get out there, learn more, build our inn credentials. And with the clock loudly ticking, we needed to find new employment or buy an inn, and soon…

A sunrise foghorn blast shook me out of my reverie. I glanced at my watch—5:45 a.m. My guests are still a no-show; *Where are they?!* I tried again to reach them by phone; it went straight to voice mail, but they called me right back. They said they had stopped at a motel for the night and planned to arrive in time for breakfast. I should have known better.

Yes, some innkeepers wouldn't bother staying up to greet their guests. They'd leave a key in an envelope taped to the inn's front door. But the envelope greeting often results in guests ringing bells and knocking on doors and windows if they need assistance—if they can't open the door or find their way around the inn, or if they want ice or an extra pillow. And God forbid a late check-in knocks or bangs on another guest's door by mistake. In my book, safe is always better than sorry.

Now my morning meditation is interrupted by the mind-numbing *beep, beep, beep* of tour buses jockeying for position in advance of today's cruise ship arrivals, and I worry the noise will wake my guests. Soon there will be rafts of day-tourists, visitors disembarking on our quaint village, all hoping to take a walk in Acadia National Park. I have a feeling it's going to be a good day to sell ice cream cones.

Inn Our Dreams

After we had a laugh remembering our good old days as student workers, we began our inn search by attending inn seminars conducted by real estate agents, usually former innkeepers who'd kicked the innkeeping habit. Many continued to hover around the edges of the hospitality scene, selling or investing in B&Bs or inns. Or teaching innkeeper wannabes like us.

Jeff and I found ourselves in groups with people just like us, with stories similar to ours, all looking for a new life purpose. We watched hilarious videos of innkeepers riding around on horseback, strolling along garden paths while whisking eggs in a bowl, sitting on porch swings drinking iced tea, surrounded by adoring guests.

Real innkeepers know the scenes depicted in seminar videos are far from the truth. Innkeeping is a serious business requiring handsome commitments of time and money, all for the opportunity to offer hospitality to people who are mostly deserving and appreciative.

One real estate agent/facilitator sent a questionnaire asking us to complete the material and bring it with us. A few of the questions were intended to tease out requirements for each participant's ideal property profile or dream inn. The *dream* nomenclature clanged in our ears. We didn't consider ourselves dreamers! We were hard-nosed business types! We called our search criteria "Inn Property Wish List." Yet again, egos were wide awake, chattering in our ears. We said, "We're looking for something special." As for our dream inn, "We'll know it when we see it." Looking back, we can offer wannabe innkeepers tips about ego suppression and realistic expectations.

We were asked to read the "Inn Property Wish List" from our business plan. (Yes, we had one!) In addition to requesting a copy of our business plan, we were asked to submit a personal financial statement to the brokers as well.

Jeff and Teri's Inn Property Wish List
A grand, shingled New England cottage, near the ocean, a lake, or a stream. Beautiful wood furnishings, whispering candlelight, handmade pottery, fresh morning coffee, blueberry jam, morning muffins, a delicious hot breakfast, spending days waking leisurely, walking in the woods, making friends and apple pie. Enjoying warm sunny days, crisp evenings, crackling bonfires, wine, cheese.

Our plan was to meet or exceed the wonderful experiences we had at our one-time favorite inn in Bar Harbor, which had a contemporary vibe, clean décor, and a relaxed attitude. We would have purchased it in a heartbeat, but at the time of our search it was not for sale.

The brokers and bankers looked over our financial disclosures and quickly sized us up: "Wow—you two have great innkeeping potential! And your tidy sum of retirement savings may come in handy, but only as a last resort. In case you have a soft season or you spring a leak." After our egos were thoroughly massaged, we hit the road with teams of brokers to find the inn of our dreams.

We were scheduled to view inn listings across our chosen three-state New England region: Massachusetts, Vermont, and Maine. The typical real estate listing read:

Inn for Sale. Charming Details. Good Business Potential.

Our broker scheduled stays in a few inns that had been on the market for years. All were listed at top dollar by owners who'd recently died, or were literally dying to sell. Soon, we'd learn why.

We checked into an inn in southern Vermont, in the shadow of the Green Mountains. Late winter was melting into "mud season," and our car tires bit into the soft slushy driveway as we slid into a parking space. Walking up the front steps into nearly dark conditions, we saw few lights on in the building. Not a good sign. Later, we learned we were the inn's only guests. We stepped into the entry hall.

Silence.

No staff.

No guests.

Eventually the innkeeper peeked around the corner. "So, you're the folks Heidi sent." Our reputation preceded us.

"Yes, we drove up from Massachusetts."

"Feel free to take a look around. Can I fix you a drink?" He filled a rocks glass with ice and poured a healthy four-finger pour of bourbon, topping it off with Diet Coke.

"No, thanks. We're OK; going out to dinner and taking a walk around town," I said.

He turned on the TV, a massive screen sitting in the middle of the historic, lonely inn. "My wife's not here right now; she works in New York. We have another inn down in Florida. We don't see each other that much."

"What type of guest do you have here at the inn?" Jeff asked.

"Mostly parents of college kids, a few tourists; it's pretty quiet around here."

Jeff and I looked at each other with raised eyebrows. His response wasn't encouraging.

The innkeeper gave us a room key, leaving us to find our way to the guest room. "Go up the staircase, take a left at the landing, then head up to the second floor."

I paused at the railing, looking down into the beautiful cavernous space below. Spookily dark, few lights burning, I felt woozy looking at the blood-red carpeting on the stairs and landing. It was a haunted house. The guest room wasn't much better—two old twin beds pushed together and covered with bed linens that resembled a plaid dog blanket. The bathroom had been updated sometime in the late 1970s. A chipped cast-iron tub with a floral plastic shower curtain, next to a small pedestal sink with a mirror and a bare light bulb with a pull-chain. We left our overnight bags on the bed and left the inn to find a restaurant for dinner.

"God, I'm so glad to be out of that place!" Jeff said. "That guy looks like a prisoner in his own private hell. Why are so many inns so decrepit? We need a place that feels like home. We've got to keep looking."

In reality, many of the inns we toured were architectural and décor nightmares. Mismatched, stained wallpapers crawling up walls and across ceilings. Shared bathrooms, musty, sour smells, fusty old furniture. Twin beds, sagging mattresses, dust bunnies and frou-frou at every turn.

The next morning, we skipped breakfast (to the relief of both parties), got back in our car, and raced home. Meanwhile, in the midst of our search, our residential broker was working hard to sell our house—our most valuable asset—a beautiful renovated historic waterfront home sitting on the banks of a tidal river near Newburyport, Massachusetts. The sale proceeds would be the golden-goose egg we needed to finance our transition to innkeeping.

We had bought our home a decade earlier. It had been languishing on the market for more than a year, quietly falling apart. The home's fine architectural details were tarnished by a failed septic system spewing sewage near the waterway. The reasonable price, combined with our inspection report, supported our offer, which was submitted at a steep discount. The seller didn't bother to counter. He accepted the offer in relief and didn't bother moving out.

We loved antique homes and thought nothing of living amid chaos, all for the thrill of spinning gold thread from time-ravaged cloth. We thought about converting our home into an inn, but we were told there would be obstacles—zoning, licensing, and potential building modifications. In hindsight, the obstacles would have been minor nuisances compared to the gut-busting route we chose to innkeeping. So a few months after our home was listed for sale and actively marketed, offers started coming in. We began to get jittery. We were unemployed, changing careers, our home listed for sale. A few weeks later, our broker called. "We got our number. Pack your bags!" We were on edge taking the offer since we had nowhere else to go. Fretful about our transition to self-employment, Jeff and I consoled one another. Relax. It'll all work out. We had a knack for trading up, and reminisced about our first home.

On Black Monday, October 19, 1987, the global stock market melted down, and a Greek revival schoolhouse came to market, the seller in a panic. Located in a charming village north of Boston, the home wasn't fully renovated, but it was livable. Three stories tall with a large cupola, it had first- and second-floor classrooms and slate blackboards. An open staircase led to the second floor, and a circular stair to the third. Two of the three levels were heated with woodstoves. It was a historic charmer, albeit chilly.

We spent our first Christmas thawing frozen water pipes with a hair dryer, as ice dams sweated over our heads. Early Christmas morning, we celebrated the holiday chipping logs from a frozen wood pile buried in slush and snow, while a hot bowl of rice pudding was cooling in a nearby snowbank. Inside, two Jøtul woodstoves were chugging out heat while the windows steamed up, like a Currier & Ives photograph, smoke curling from the top of the chimney.

Wood was a fine way to heat the house and keep it cozy three out of seven days a week, but midweek, we were unable to keep the stoves stoked during the day. We'd arrive from work to a frigid, freezing icehouse. Inconvenient on weekdays—yes! Impossible to live with—no! Still, we were smitten with our beautiful schoolhouse. So, after years chipping away at DIY projects, and a few added polishes by local contractors, our home emerged as an awesome traffic-stopper. Cars slowed as they passed into town. People took photographs from car windows.

Thus began our extracurricular home-school coursework to earn PhDs in edifice complex. Now we were back on the road, in the midst of a search for our dream inn. A warm, relaxing place to rejuvenate paying guests, which would help us repair our bruised egos and possibly find ourselves.

Innovators

We were scheduled to move out in three months, not enough time for two choosy people to fritter time away looking for perfection in a new home and inn business. Traveling with brokers across New England, we covered a lot of ground but found nothing of interest. Eventually our search led us to Mount Desert Island, home of Acadia National Park. We loved the rocky granite coastline, rolling seascape, and robust visitor stats.

Our broker called. "There are a couple of inns for sale in Bar Harbor; come up and take a look." The inns were strong seasonal businesses open May to October, and the innkeepers took downtime over the winter to recharge their batteries. We liked the sound of that. We drove to Maine and stayed at an inn in Bar Harbor, later taking tours of listings on the island.

At one inn, we followed the broker and the innkeeper from the kitchen downstairs to a basement. We took a look around. Stacks of 50-pound bags of flour were resting on the floor; a thin mist of wheat and dust motes drifted in the air. A curtain was pulled back to reveal a group of student workers sleeping on mattresses on the floor. Living in a damp basement was not what we had in mind for ourselves or our future staff.

Since Bar Harbor inventory was tight, our broker urged us to make an unsolicited offer to buy any inn we wanted. "Everyone has their price," he said. We decided to approach an owner in Southwest Harbor. We booked a room for two nights to spend time researching the property and the neighborhood. Staying incognito, we asked our broker to prepare an offer. We were hopeful, but the owner rejected the offer outright, then countered our offer, which exceeded the inn's valuation. We smugly crowed to ourselves, "We're smart enough not to fall for *that* deal!" We returned home to continue packing boxes for our move-out to storage, uncertain where we would be going, only knowing for certain we were moving out, and soon.

A few weeks later, the phone rang. It was our broker calling to tell us there was an incredible cottage in Bar Harbor that was newly listed for sale. "It hasn't been on the market in over fifty years," he said. "It's furnished, but run-down. It could use your talents."

Naturally, we took the call, loved the flattery, and rose to the bait. "Wow—tell us more!"

The "cottage" was a 26-room Victorian mansion with ten guest rooms. Once a grand home, it had become a scruffy, historic inn landmark, a down-at-the-heels boardinghouse. But according to the brokers, the property had it all: location, location, location. A few hundred yards from the harbor and an easy walk to Main Street, Shore Path, and the town dock.

The inn had been run by an elderly woman who had recently passed away. It remained under the ownership of several extended family members who didn't plan to continue running it. The heirs were eager to sell, and here we were: two crazy potential buyers. Our broker sent us the real estate listing, photographs, and property disclosure. The inn showing was scheduled. We drove from Boston to Bar Harbor to meet with the broker and tour the property.

The four-story, 16,000-square-foot building was once beautiful, with glorious stained-glass doors, windows, and skylights, carved oak details, coffered ceilings, and grand oversized common areas. But the photos sent to us could not capture the blighted, worn condition of the inn. The guest rooms were quaint, stale, and heavily dusted with deferred maintenance. The ceilings were water-stained, and plaster walls were cracked floor to ceiling. Walls were covered in dramatic, dark marine-blue wallpaper with red peonies on it, and had been mended with Scotch tape, offering a mysterious feeling of melancholy and days gone by.

Several large collapsed cardboard refrigerator boxes separated two of the grand sitting rooms to create a privacy divide for an improvised family-sized suite. The flimsy, makeshift wall was covered with water-stained velvet draperies. Such magnificent potential in near shambles: electrical, plumbing, heating, and infrastructure all nonconforming to modern building codes, the rest in disrepair.

The building was stacked to the ceiling with furniture from a half century of habitation, with rooms full of twin beds, old mattresses, small, uncomfortable chairs, racks of old clothes, cardboard cereal boxes and plastic bags stuffed with tea bags. And the inn was offered for sale unfurnished; the sellers were asking for another $100,000 to deliver the inn with FFE—furniture, fixtures, and equipment. We balked at paying so much money for so little. Sure, we were people "from away," as locals say (perhaps to brand an easy mark), but a hundred grand was far too much money for a plethora of saggy twin mattresses, headboards with Brylcreem stains, and chairs with sprung seats.

Walking around the exterior, we were surprised to see garlands of orange extension cords strung from rear windows between the second and third floors, then down to the first level. A tour of the basement revealed a warren of squalid, illegal housing, mattresses on dirt floors, used crack pipes and syringes. A massive torpedo-sized brassiere was strung across the prewar fuse box. Screw-in fuses were missing, stuffed with pennies and sawed-off copper pipe. A firetrap. An accident waiting to happen.

The inn hadn't been painted in years, and many of the roofs were suspect. The first order of business would be removal and replacement of electrical and plumbing to provide robust sanitary systems, heating, and air-conditioning for a four-story hotel. Then repairing the roofs to keep the rain out, adding an ADA-compliant guest room for visitors, and, finally, conforming to all local building codes.

I stepped into the working kitchen where the deceased innkeeper had lived during the winter, occupying a single room with a small bed and bathroom mere steps from the food prep area. The room was heated only with a mammoth Ben Franklin wood-burning stove with clotheslines and wire hangers crisscrossing above it. The toilet privacy door and curtained stall shower opened out to the old refrigerator and range. As a chef, I couldn't imagine the kitchen had ever passed fire inspection, let alone a health inspection. Shaking our heads, we reread the listing:

AS-IS CONDITION

Even now, nearly two decades after entering the fray, we still ask ourselves: Why didn't we stop right there? Why couldn't we see past the stars in our eyes, when the grim reality was right under our feet? Why? I guess we were a couple of smarty-pants know-it-alls, having restored old homes before. But a distressed hotel? Never.

Keep in mind, we had sold our home, we were unemployed, we had nowhere to go; in short, we were *motivated*. We negotiated an offer for the million-dollar property pending an inspection report. Jeff and I encouraged each other, joined by a chorus of enthusiasm from our broker, who kept telling us how much money we would make.

We made an offer, inspected the building, then withdrew the offer. The inspection was thorough, nailing down the obvious condition of the building. Decrepit. The business records and tax returns revealed bookings were negligible. We finally understood the reasons the abutting neighbors wanted to knock it down and build a parking garage. With the building facing possible demolition, the beauty of the broken, once-grand inn compelled us. We were the right people to restore it to its former glory. And we'd developed a sweet spot for the place, the founding family lore, and the inn's legacy in Bar Harbor history. We obtained construction bids, reduced our offer, and proceeded to the closing table.

Weeks later at the attorney's office, we gathered with the extended family owners for the closing. Cold spring sunlight was glancing off the windows, and in such brightness, we had to squint. Under the harsh light of reality, we'd thought more than once of walking away from the deal. We'd lose our deposit, of course, a pittance compared to the investment the restoration would require. Still, our emotions clouded our better judgment as dreams for the inn, as well as for ourselves, floated in our heads. A couple of dreamers…yes indeed, we certainly were.

Quietly, the aunts, son, and cousins filed into the office, all taking turns talking about the inn's glory days. The son of the deceased innkeeper was a kindly gentleman of fifty years or more, dressed in a crisply starched pale-blue button-down shirt. Tears were streaming down his face, and he pulled out a handkerchief. "Mom used to serve lamb chops with frilly bows on silver platters. I slept in a room on the second floor, listening to a transistor radio playing the Beach Boys."

I was seated next to one of the grand dames of the family, a charming, talkative woman. "My family lived and worked fifty-four years in that Inn!"

"Will you miss it?" I asked.

She turned squarely to face me. "Honey, not on your life!"

Other younger family members were more upbeat, perhaps hopeful about the prospect of a payout. And so goes the pattern of many family businesses. The first generation sacrifices, usually, to start it. The second generation is recruited to work there. By the third generation, no one wants anything to do with it.

Inn Trouble

They gave us the keys. Jeff and I walked around the building and found the inn's old sign stuffed in the bushes. An aged, rough-hewn yellow pine panel, with black painted trim, it was a rustic piece of art. We covered the sign in plastic and stashed it in a storage bin.

Over the next few days, Jeff and I and our feisty black-and-tan Airedale terriers, Dooney and Archie, set up camp at the inn. Since the property was uninhabitable and scheduled to undergo significant work, we had to line up alternative living arrangements, which in Bar Harbor doesn't come cheap, even off season. We moved into a nondescript modular rental house close to the inn, later buying a small cottage mid-island, which was cheaper than renting.

Our new work schedule consisted of meeting with the construction draftsman on plans to redesign guest room layouts so every room had a private bath. Jeff and I agreed all guest rooms had to be "en suite," a private bedroom and bath. The hall bathroom concept was obsolete and wouldn't work for the guest experience we contemplated. Such thoughtful design amenities were simply icing on the cake, already half-baked, compared to the nuts-and-bolts work needed to provide safe, adequate systems to the inn.

The list of structural deficiencies mounted as the crew began exploring the building. Water incursion from leaky roofs on two floors. Chimneys in states of near collapse. The dirt-floor basement leaching moisture up and into the walls. Single-glazed windows, some broken, offering no insulation from gales coming onshore from Frenchman Bay.

One of our first visitors was the Bar Harbor Fire Marshal. He handed us a yard-long punch list. "Here you go guys. I've been waiting thirty years to get into this building." And he didn't mean as a paying guest.

He meant the entire building was unsafe, and had been for decades. The inn's code requirements were "grandfathered," until or unless the inn was sold or renovated. As a result, it was now required to conform to ALL modern fire/safety codes. This translated into the installation of sprinkler systems top to bottom, exit lighting, automated fire monitoring with ear-splitting sirens, and strobing lights for the hearing impaired. Not to mention fire escapes.

Walking out with the inspector, Jeff attempted to schmooze the chief. "My grandfather and great-uncles were all firemen in New Haven, Connecticut."

"Ha! And you still bought this place?" he said dryly. His taciturn Maine humor unfurling reminded me of Jeff's Grandma Edie. We called her Nan, a sweet, plucky woman who didn't suffer fools. She'd have told us, "Go ahead, you two, laugh at that!"

Days later, Jeff and I were removing wallpaper in the entry hall. One of the foremen saw us spraying the walls with solution and scraping the paper off in sheets.

"Don't waste your time doing that. We're gonna rebuild this place from the inside out."

Nonetheless, we continued our work—it was cathartic; we had to do *something*. We'd received acceptable construction bids from a reputable company, but The Builder had a reputation of working for deep-pocket clients from away. We weren't people with deep pockets. We were dreamers from away with stars in our eyes, who'd scrimped and saved to own a home, and we were plowing all of the equity into the purchase of the inn.

Our new neighbors owned the two inns next door. They spotted us in the parking lot and walked over to introduce themselves. "Hi, I'm Roy, and this is my wife, Helene. It's nice to meet you."

We noticed a trace of Roy's New York accent. He and Helene had met while living in New York City; she hailed from Quebec. Their inns were beautifully restored and popular with guests. We later learned from other innkeepers in town that Roy and Helene were amazing innkeepers. It felt good to have two innkeeping pros to talk to for encouragement.

Roy said, "We were approached by the family to see if we had interest in buying the inn, but we decided to pass. Helene and I have enough on our hands owning the other two inns next door."

Jeff apologized for the inconvenience about to ensue. Roy said, "Jeff, I don't care how long it takes, how dirty or noisy it gets. Just make it beautiful."

"We will, Roy. We promise."

Within days, the construction tubes arrived, tumbling from the fourth-story windows to clusters of Dumpsters below. A duo of Porta-Potties, scaffolding, trucks, construction trailers, and work crews arrived shortly thereafter. The crew was setting up for a long haul, obstructing the driveways and water-side views, cluttering up the roadway, and inching close to Roy and Helene's parking area.

Early-spring onshore breezes blew in from Frenchman Bay, billowing clouds of plaster that dusted the neighborhood. Meanwhile, basement excavation was a riotous spectacle of heavy earth-moving equipment, whirling and spiraling like circus elephants across the yard, cartwheeling into, then under the building, dragging out debris from the basement, unearthing tree roots and tangled masses of rusted pipes. Front-loader buckets dragged along the ground, hoisting up gobs of wet, rotten clapboards, shingles, and sodden under-layers of insulation, all destined for waiting Dumpsters in the parking lot.

Despite the massive inconvenience, teams of work crews, dump trucks, car traffic, and "looky-loo" tourists wandering around, there was never a word of complaint from Roy and Helene. Not once. Ever. We were dredging the inn's basement, dirt heaped high, debris hanging in the trees. Our full-tilt demolition and mining effort had struck pay dirt: two amazing, wonderful friends with hearts of solid gold. Right next door.

Birthday Wishes

As a new inn owner, I bade farewell to past birthdays enjoyed in quiet remote farmhouses in New England, Italy, and France. I was a fraught, fledgling business owner, and I shelved my fond memories, knowing they would not return soon.

My forty-third birthday was spent diligently working as midwife in anticipation of the inn's rebirth. Now electrified with 50,000 feet of new electrical cable, the lights were safely shining inside our Victorian-era beauty. Shrouded in dust, the crews hoisted twin steel I-beams between floors to strengthen the structure. New plumbing, boilers, and sprinkler systems waited for fresh transfusions from the town's public water supply.

By August, the construction pace was picking up, as fall was fast approaching. The plan was to get the heavy, open-air work completed and the inn's roofing repaired before winter set in. Still, the crew wanted to celebrate. Someone bought a large sheet cake: "Happy Birthday, Teri!" I was surprised and touched by the thoughtfulness. Often, I was the only woman on-site, but the guys knew their salty language and dirty jokes didn't faze me much.

As we gathered on a makeshift deck behind the inn, one of the guys mentioned that a chimney had partially collapsed as the masons worked to repoint the bricks, threatening to take the crew and scaffolding along for the ride. The men held on tight, finally jumping to the ground before the massive wall of bricks collapsed on top of them. No wonder The Bank insisted on two builder insurance policies. The safety meetings and insurance policies were additional layers of icing on the cake, and the use of candles on the job was not permitted. Still, I was touched by the sweet impromptu party and the cake decorated with birthday candles. I made a birthday wish as news of the chimney near-disaster sank in: "Complete the work safely, and on time." I blew out the candles. Kent, a curly-haired master carpenter, cut the cake with a Sawzall.

Jeff and I passed around slices of birthday cake with bottles of water, watching as my birthday and our dream had grown into an eccentric's folly requiring a monarch's purse. With our gaze fixed on the project's timeline, stacks and stacks of change orders, a dwindling budget, a veritable taxi meter running in our heads, Jeff and I both thought, *Please, do not charge us overtime for this party.*

Wake-Up Call

Maine winters are long, offering few steady employment opportunities for builders, carpenters, and painters, unless jobs are lined up ahead of time. With winter turning to spring, after more than 200 workdays, we were sweating for details. Would the builder have sufficient crew? When would the job be completed? And, with so much work still to be done, how much would it cost to bring the project to successful completion?

The Builder, a former accountant, was the quiet, fidgety type, quietly managing the restoration from his office, offering information if asked, frustratingly not forthcoming with details. Flummoxed by The Builder's lack of transparency, seemingly indifferent to our timetable and budget, Jeff inserted himself into the fray as the bills piled up, our funds drew down, and there looked to be no smooth road to project completion.

We faced stunning monthly invoices of $25,000, $50,000, $75,000, each bitterly rhythmic and formulaic in multiples of $5,000, to the tune of five figures. The financial metronome was terrifying to observe and impossible to ignore. A ringing, *ding-ding-ding* pinball effect of numbers and flashing lights sung to the tune of the inn's new front door chime: "Hail, Hail, the Gang's All Here."

Jeff said, "Yesterday, I counted twenty-nine men at the site. I asked one of the foremen when the drywall was going up, and no one knew the answer or could tell me whether we'd be able to open on time."

Yet, reality was painfully obvious to us: the inn was a cavernous shell. No interior walls, only framing and toolboxes sitting on makeshift sawhorse tables. Looking up through the open ceilings, we had a clear view to the fourth floor, where an old copper gravity cistern was scheduled for removal to make way for a new guest room. All forms of trim, woodwork, and doors had been pried off, tagged, stacked on racks floor to ceiling across the common areas, sunroom, porches and dining room. Stained-glass panels had been removed and were bedded down, hidden from swinging hammers and drills. Hallways remained a latticework of exposed new wires and plumbing. We were miles from the finish line.

Jeff said, "Teri, I think we're in the path of a juggernaut. The expenses are through the roof, change orders are stacking up, but the walls aren't up, and the crews can't begin painting. We've gotta open in May—our loan commitment is at stake." Meanwhile, the website had been launched, announcing opening day just after Mother's Day. We were already taking reservations. And we'd made many, many promises we had to honor.

Looking for a few answers, we turned to Marco, a family friend, for the scoop. A boatbuilder by trade, he had moved to Maine from Massachusetts, and The Builder hired him early on. Marco spent months doing demo, crawling around the ductwork installing insulation, attending the weekly safety meetings. Then, out of nowhere, he was laid off. We put him on our personal payroll to help with painting and to keep him on site, our insider for the inside story.

Marco met us for a few beers. "Yeah, the foreman told me the lazy guys are doing the shitty jobs, stacking trim, busting up bathtubs and old toilets. One of the guys said I'd never worked construction before, only boatbuilding. So I just did what I was asked to do. The Builder told me, 'Don't worry about it; building a house is like building an upside-down boat.' Still, I'm pretty sure I got laid off because they know we're friends. I'd seen and heard too much."

Marco didn't hold back. "I hate to say this, but The Builder thinks you guys are a bottomless pit of money." With that, we'd finally heard enough; we would demand answers.

On Monday, Jeff called The Builder, who didn't seem to know what it would take to finish the job. Terrence, a young project manager, spent a week compiling a set of wild-ass cost estimates, going room by room. The information was to be reviewed with Jeff that Friday afternoon in The Builder's office, and finally all the cards would be on the table. Jeff and I had a feeling we were in for bad news.

A numbing chill was wafting in from the shore, seagulls circling overhead to stay warm. Jeff attended the meeting with The Builder by himself, in a modest shingle-style building. He wanted to focus on getting the answers to our questions: What is going on? Why is the work taking so long? Will the restoration be completed by opening day?

Jeff climbed the stairs to the office, his imposing six-foot-four-inch frame towering, and he took a seat, dwarfing the small desk and two Windsor chairs. The Builder, a slight, balding man, removed his glasses and attempted to wipe away the streaks of sunlight and stress that were leaking into the room.

Jeff opened the meeting: "OK, guys, what's it going to take to get this thing done?"

"Not sure, Jeff. It's a really big job."

Jeff was thinking, *They don't have a grasp on the numbers or project status. I knew it.* Meanwhile, he had been tracking progress and expenses to the penny.

The Builder said, "Jeff, I'll work the numbers and give you an answer by the end of the week."

Jeff shook his head at this unsatisfactory report and was stunned to learn The Builder didn't have a handle on his company's only job that winter.

Friday rolled around, and Jeff arrived early to meet The Builder, who got right to the point. Perhaps wishing he were somewhere else, as if to get it over with, he told Jeff, "We've done the numbers—this is what it looks like." His hands shook as he slid a piece of paper across the table with nail-bitten, slightly chapped hands.

Jeff reached across, scanning the page for the bottom line. More than $900,000 over budget.

He drew in a breath and paused, taking a moment before responding. Gripping the table, he looked The Builder in the eye. "I don't know which makes me more fucking angry. That you would show me a number this out of whack, or that you think I would accept it! Sharpen your pencils and reduce this number!"

Jeff called from the car to give me the bad news. I was home making minestrone, slowly sautéing onions, carrots, and celery. I stirred the simmering contents over increasingly high heat, trying to focus. Jeff returned home as I was setting the table for lunch. I was despondent. Both of us were afraid and frustrated, puzzling whether this was a runaway project or whether we were hapless victims of a construction Ponzi scheme. Either way, it would have been impossible to back out of the commitments we'd made without facing financial ruin.

We'd made a huge bet buying the inn, staking all of our home equity in the deal, somewhere north of a million dollars, and we were on the hook for the fixed terms of a million-dollar commercial loan. With the inn broken into pieces, it couldn't be sold "as built." And it was too late in the game to hire another construction company.

A few days later, an early-morning meeting was held to review the revised budget. A financial plan was hatched with The Bank as we swallowed this bitter pill of the construction project. The wild card we'd drawn blew our three-year business plan right off the track—and we'd landed in the whirlwind of a Restoration Vortex.

We'd misread the warning signs, and now we were completely underwater. Covering the financial overages and relaunching the inn was going to be tough.

A cold February rain was falling while we were driving along Mount Desert Street, Jeff behind the wheel. Taking our usual route to the inn, we were hot and bothered, venting anxiety at each other until the car windows fogged up. Jeff said, "I can barely see the road in this rain. This project was such a stupid idea. I wish we'd never bought it."

I agreed. "You're right, and whose stupid idea was this, anyway?" We looked accusingly at each other. The inn was taking a toll on both of us, and our marriage.

"I'm sorry Hon, that was unfair. I didn't mean what I said, and it doesn't matter. We've just gotta get through it." I glanced out the side window.

"JEFF, STOP, STOP, *STOP!*" I shouted.

He jerked the car to the side of the road. "Yeah, I saw it, too." Both of us had caught sight of the same thing, at the same time, in front of the Episcopal church. Glancing at the sidewalk, we watched an elderly man striding along—then, in an instant, he slammed face-first to the pavement with nothing to cushion the impact of his fall. He was felled like a tree cut down by an axe, his limbs dangling by his side.

Jeff hit the brakes, threw the car into Park, jumped into the rain as it rushed along the gutters, and raced to the man's side. Jeff and I tried to assist. The man's nose was crushed, he was bubbling blood in a puddle as pink rainwater roiled into the gutter. It took two of us to carefully flip him over, fearing he'd drown where he landed. As we rolled him onto his back, blood and rainwater gushed from his mouth and nose. He couldn't speak.

The parish priest ran out, seeing the three of us on the ground. An RN commuting to MDI hospital stopped at the scene, called 9-1-1, and rushed over to administer CPR. Within seconds, the ambulance arrived, and the nurse climbed aboard with the injured man. Jeff was ashen and I was in tears alongside the priest as the patient was rushed the four-block distance to the emergency room. Standing there in stunned disbelief, I cried, my tears mixing with the raindrops. The priest asked, "Are you two going to be OK? Would you like to come into the church for a little while?"

Jeff answered, "We're late for a meeting. Thank you, but we have to leave."

We turned and solemnly walked back to the car. Climbing back in, we shook off the rain and cleared the steamy windows with tissues. Jeff sharply turned the wheel of the car, backing off of the curb, and slowly pulled forward, turning left onto Main Street. The two-minute drive felt like slow motion as our car of dreams scraped the guardrail of reality. The windshield wipers kept time as we drove past the shops; Windowpanes, C&J's Big Dipper, Cool as a Moose, the Clock Shop. We drove in silence.

The universe had sent us a wake-up call—and we were wide awake, as if for the first time. Finally, we were immersed in the present—instead of bogged down by past regret, ambition, or hubris with our vision fixed on the future and the stars in our eyes. It no longer mattered how, why, or when the project had gone off the rails, along with our careers, our dreams, our investment. The $500,000 we'd need to finish the job. Our earthly concerns and problems suddenly seemed manageable. We were grateful to be alive.

A day or two later, both of us visited the hospital due to personal mishaps. Stress was getting the better of us. We were clumsy and distracted. Jeff suffered a nasty cut from a box knife. I nearly amputated a finger in the kitchen. We asked a nurse about the man we had found on the ground in front of the church. She said she couldn't tell us his name, but the patient had been admitted code blue, and he didn't make it. Hearing this sad news, Jeff and I looked at each other, humbled. We were bloodied but alive, and we had only one option: Keep moving forward.

CHAPTER TWO

Start a huge, foolish project, like Noah…it makes absolutely no difference what people think of you.
—Rumi

Inn Décor

By early March, parts of the inn still resembled a large jigsaw puzzle. Doors, windows, trim were stacked on racks or lying in pieces on the ground. It was difficult to imagine how or if the pieces would fit back together. "Demolition was the easy part; the hard work is still ahead," I said, still churning my way through décor decisions: wallpaper or paint; window treatment choices—blinds, shades, or draperies; and furniture placement.

During my investment career, I was a strategic, big-picture person, Myers-Briggs personality profile ENTP: Extraverted, Intuitive, Thinking, Perceiving. I loved the spontaneous, fast-paced, volatile environment of the trading room. Periods of boredom, punctuated by drama, sometimes panic. Sometime later, I was bumped up to management, and I pivoted to strategic planning, program management, and motivating people. Leaving the fine print and details to others, I was fond of delegating.

But designing and installing décor for a 16,000-square-foot, ten-guest-room luxury inn is challenging at best. At its worst, you have no formal interior design training, a dwindling budget, and less than 90 days until opening day. Our success in renovating other historic homes caused me to assume the project would be a piece of cake. In reality, it took nerves of steel.

Jeff and I were determined to restore the inn's original floor plan, which had not only been spacious, but was open and flowing on the ground floor. This was unusual for Victorian-era buildings, but it offered ample porches and several gathering places, as well as a dining room, butler's pantry, library, and living room. Large windows framed views of Frenchman Bay, welcoming fresh ocean breezes.

Jeff did his homework. "I read that Mr. Bass was an erstwhile socialite who liked to hobnob with his more rich and famous neighbors from away." This seemed to explain the building improvements made during his ownership—the addition of rooms, gables, and an entire wing on the west side of the building. The renovation uncovered reused timber from older Bar Harbor buildings, as was the practice, and the graffiti of paperhangers and carpenters dating back to the dawn of the twentieth century.

Our plans were to reinvigorate the inn, happily blending old with new, period details coexisting with modern comfort and convenience. A style fresh and clean, with a nod to history without being overwhelmed by kitschy clichés. We dubbed our style "Un-Victorian-Victorian." An atmosphere that was creative and comfortable, a place that allowed guests to kick off their shoes and feel at home.

To achieve this, it meant no busy floral wallpapers, dark forest-green or brown wall-to-wall carpeting, or Early American reproduction furniture.

I worked up the ten guest room motifs, each designed with a friend or family member in mind, purchasing at least one heirloom from the inn's founding family for each guest room for good luck. The ten rooms would be refurnished with original art and fine linens, the walls touched with creams and pastels. Each room, uniquely decorated, would have a story of its own to tell.

We looked forward to welcoming paying guests from away who would enjoy relaxing in wicker rocking chairs on the glassed-in sunporches, one of which would be converted to an atrium dining room. Guests would enter through four ten-foot French doors leading into a bright, warm, sun-filled area set for twenty guests.

Unlike traditional B&B's, our guests would be seated at tables for two, an emerging trend at the time, now commonplace. We learned that most guests preferred dining with their significant other, rather than sitting with strangers seated shoulder-to-shoulder banquet-style.

The dining room was shaping up nicely, soon to be furnished with white wooden tables, Nantucket red painted dining chairs, matchstick woven window blinds, and printed linen drapery panels decorated with blossoms, scrolling vines, and leaves.

The soothing décor, colors, and textures framed views to the newly planted river birch trees, beach roses, and oak-leaf hydrangeas in the garden. The windows framed tender spring buds promising white-cluster blossoms by July, a leafy haven for birds and bees frolicking and buzzing amid the flowers, far from the bustle of Main Street yet only a few steps away. A serene atmosphere with windows on the natural world for guest enjoyment during a splendid breakfast which we hoped would keep them coming back to the inn. This was a non-negotiable goal—repeat guests—and our financial lives depended on it.

Jeff remembered the inn's former street sign, which had spent the winter sitting in storage. After cleaning it, we hung it in the dining room as folk art, a step up from its former location, stuck on a stake in the bushes by the driveway. Jeff nailed a 50-pound picture hanger into the wall and hung it up, flipping a tab so the sign would read "No Vacancy." Good karma. Or so we hoped.

Passing visitors often strolled by hoping for a quick tour, knocking on the plywood panels covering the front door and porch windows. All of which had been replaced, since they were previously painted and nailed shut, impossible to open or repair. But the inn was a hard-hat construction site, and it wasn't possible to play show-and-tell just yet. We remembered Roy from next door, his words echoing in our ears: "I don't care how long it takes, just make it beautiful."

From the front door, it was a few steps to the entry hall with soaring ceilings and a grand staircase. We purchased hand-blown Venetian glass pendants in colors of plum and apricot to complement the magnificent inner doors outfitted with stained-glass panels evocative of translucent butterfly wings. The hallway was anchored by a massive pier mirror that would cast reflections of the contemporary art and photography we planned to hang, creating an interesting juxtaposition of light, art, and historic architecture. Further down the hall, an elaborate, carved red-oak-paneled staircase led to three more floors.

A single queen room on the first level. Three king and two queen rooms on the second floor. Two queen and one king room on the third floor, and a spacious king-size penthouse suite. All guest rooms with private baths, and some with fireplaces, all converted from wood-burning to propane.

Jeff and I took to roaming the halls, both of us dressed in blue Carhartt coveralls, he sporting a LOTUS baseball hat from his software days. My dark curly hair was tied in ponytails topped with a pink Red Sox cap. After stopping for steaming cups of gas station coffee, we paced with our morning joe up and down the staircases, poking our heads into the new bathrooms as whirlpool tubs were installed, glass shower doors put into place, floor tiles and surrounds grouted.

All bathroom floors had been laid with the same sea-foam-blue glazed tiles, a natural choice, evoking shallow tide pools under a clear blue sky, accompanied by white, glossy subway tile surrounding the new tubs and shower areas. Fresh as cotton, an easy palate for housekeepers to spot dirt, cosmetic stains, or stray hair. The clean simplicity of the guest bathrooms was intentional, planned to minimize complexity for the crews and to complement the interior design plans I had worked out for each room.

As the interior walls were going up, I was tossing and turning nightly over nuances of paint colors—Flower Pot, Bee's Wax, Dove Wing, or Barn Owl—with scattered paint chips in my dreams. My resting hours were tinged with colorful anxiety, and insomnia became chronic. Somehow—remarkably—Jeff slept soundly.

I was also focused on fabric selection for bed covers, draperies, and window shades for our grand hotel. The building crew chipped in a few decorating ideas of their own, stapling Playboy centerfolds behind kitchen access panels. A few of the guys spent their break time on hands and knees, drowning in cleavage behind the dishwashers.

So, with pieces of the inn scattered on the ground, Jeff and I worked from computer-designed floor plans, while the crews were working flat-out completing construction of the redesigned guest rooms. As the new spaces emerged, it looked like the ten guest rooms and commodious common spaces were forecast to be sparse and incomplete. We were light on furniture.

Initially, it seemed unlikely that we'd need more furniture and furnishings, since we had socked away the contents of our former large home in storage. We thought we had enough. Enough artwork, chairs, tables, rugs, all boxed or otherwise packed up. Each item was labeled and color-coded by room, scheduled for delivery eight weeks before opening day.

Jeff and I worked out room-by-room lists detailing what furniture would be needed to ensure guest comfort. Bedside tables were in short supply, as were comfortable chairs for the lounge and the larger guest rooms with sitting areas, and we needed full-length mirrors for each room. Still, we were on a tight budget, and we couldn't afford to pay top dollar at antique stores for quality furniture with patina. Instead, we climbed into a white 1999 Dodge panel van equipped with two bucket seats, a massive cargo bed strung with bungee cords and milk crates, and got back on the road. The next destination: New England's antique trail, heading south on I-95 from Bar Harbor to the Mass Pike to Sturbridge, home of the Brimfield Fair, held three times a year.

Wandering the miles of aisles at the fair, we knew we were on the right track, spotting fellow MDI cottage owner Martha Stewart during one of our buying trips. I'd read in the *Boston Globe* that she'd purchased Skylands, a magnificent Tudor estate in Seal Harbor, Maine. The historic home was built by Edsel Ford in 1925. The article said it was one of the most beautiful coastal properties in the United States.

With our own van for transport and with the last stash of cash from the sale of our house, we drove a hard bargain with dealers during our twelve round-trip excursions. Our van became the inn's shuttlecraft, transporting us from Maine to the Berkshires, returning on the round trip with a jog to Essex, Massachusetts, and Wells, Maine. We logged more than 6,000 miles.

The road trips were a pleasant distraction from reality back at the inn. We found it easier to keep eyes on the road, rather than on the financial metronome at the job site, keeping time for the crews' frenzied performance of "Flight of the Bumblebee." After all, we'd already been stung over and over, and the bees were looking for fresh victims.

After completing the floor plans, fabric storyboards, and color schemes, Jeff and I dedicated ourselves to scheduling deliveries with the moving crews. Within weeks, four tractor-trailers were primed for deployment. Steadying myself, I channeled my inner *generalissima* and crossed my fingers. Staying ahead of the landing parties was the name of the game, as vendor deliveries started rolling in, along with a thousand questions. "Hey, lady, where is all of this stuff going?" It was a good question.

Eleven mattresses, 11 box springs, 80 cases of bed linen, bathrobes, towels, mattress pads, pillows, pillow protectors, 20 cartons of dishware, glassware. A wide array of kitchen tools and silverware. Hospitality 101 had taught us we'd need a lot of teaspoons. Everything (and I mean *everything*) was scheduled for Drop Shipment, or "DS." DS means the delivery crews "drop it" outside the threshold, requiring Jeff and me to either pick it up and carry it inside, or schedule local moving crews to assist with the heavy lifting. Soon mattresses were stacking up in the work areas, an impediment to painting. Towers of cartons, rafts of tables, heaps of teaspoons, were moved inside the building. The king and queen mattresses, unboxed, were carried up the staircases and fire escapes, some folded and contorted to fit into narrow hallways, finally unsprung and released into their final resting places in each guest room.

Door in the Floor

I was focused on coordinating the moving crews when I was reminded that we'd be needed on the painting team. I bumped into Jeff, who was carrying a roller tray and pole. "Hon, I know you're busy, but it's crunch time." The painting company had slightly underbid the job to get the contract and told us we needed to get busy.

Since the project budget was stretched beyond thin, Jeff and I were responsible for painting most of the inn's interior walls and ceilings on three of the four floors by opening day. The professional painters were taking on the exterior, the first-floor areas, and Room 1, the ADA-compliant room located off the front porch.

Our relentless moving activities would be complemented by eight-hour painting shifts to complete the nine guest bedrooms and bathrooms. By this point, Jeff and I were too exhausted to bicker, and it was no use. We'd had plenty of practice painting, and at times repainting, walls and ceilings in our other homes. The difference was that the clock was ticking, and opening day was five weeks away.

The painters were primed and ready to get to work on the first-level walls and ceilings of the porches, hallways, dining room, large living room, library, and lounge. Hanging on my every word, they awaited decisions as they aimed paint guns into the air. The enormity of the decision-making was overwhelming. Did I make good selections? What if I picked the wrong colors? Who will repaint the inn if I get it wrong? I fretted constantly and Jeff tried to reassure me.

Then, early one morning, sometime after 3:00 a.m., I awoke from a dream inspired. All the work was done! The guest rooms were completed, landscaping installed, gardens in full flower, each and every detail in full technicolor. More beautiful than I'd dared to dream. I interpreted my night vision as a sign to have faith, to keep going. I was ready with fresh inspiration.

Mornings, before painting rooms, Jeff and I would wander around the inn, referring to our clipboards and binders—which were bulging, fit to burst. Crammed with the tattered pages of the floor plans, room-by-room punch lists, detailed delivery schedules, and invoices, the binders were our gospel. We created a daily work plan, donned our coveralls, and jumped up onto ladders. Fortunately, we found another painter and Marco to round out our team of four. Jeff and I took breaks from painting to open cartons of linens, coordinate furniture deliveries, organize the inn's office, and answer the telephone, as reservation activity was picking up. I was continually sleep-deprived.

Jeff had his hands full managing front office, design and installation of building alarm systems, phone and computer cabling, scheduling the code inspector, licensing and health inspectors. He installed the reservation and payment system software himself, along with writing brochure copy and designing and finalizing the inn's new website.

I took over décor installation and back-of-the-house operations. I figured my skills juggling stock, bond, and option trades, then compliance programs for hundreds of mutual funds, myriad layers of state and federal regulations, and managing a team of analysts for a firm with millions of clients would make this project seem like a piece of cake. "I GOT THIS!" I developed flow charts of activities outlining the who, what, where, and when of every key deliverable; of moving crews and carpet and window treatment installation. I was constantly on the lookout for competing priorities and overlapping deadlines, all in an effort to head off any potential "single points of failure," aka SPF, that might derail our goal of opening the inn on time.

My comical mantra with the vendors, crew, and contractors was: "Hey, guys, no single points of failure on this project, please!" Despite the disarray and chaos of the inn, I was strangely energized. I also considered myself an expert in single-point-of-failure avoidance. And I believed that with proper planning, most single points of failure *were* avoidable. Anything else was a sign of poor planning, lack of attention to detail, or ignoring obvious obstacles. With the SPF thing settled, I'd worked out a décor installation plan using a phased approach to avoid problems.

Starting at the top of the inn in Room 10 on the fourth floor, my plan was to work down toward the first level, then out of the building, thereby eliminating unnecessary foot traffic up and down the staircases and permitting the uninterrupted installation of a magnificent stair runner. The carpet, a richly woven mosaic in deep blues, plum, and jewel tones, complemented the elaborately carved oak staircases, wainscoting, and, overhead, three large stained-glass panels in the stairwell.

The carpet required expert installation and several hundred feet of stair runner, which was trucked from Boston to Bar Harbor along with a youthful installation pro who had old-world skills working with carpet. He casually spoke a language we'd never learned—"pattern loop, pile crush, pattern repeat"—while he hand cut and carefully pieced the rug together. Corners were not only cut, but each turn of corner was mitered, stitched together with its matching piece, and sewn into place. No pattern breaks, all of the edges perfectly square. A walkable work of art. The light pouring down from the artful stained-glass windows transformed into kaleidoscopes as sunlight was bent into shimmering purple, violet, and azure rainbows, spilling color across the rich, warm carpet, wood-carved balustrades, railings, and walls.

Luckily, I was able to source several drapery makers, and counted in my good fortune finding upholsterers open during Bar Harbor's off-season to work on the project. This was unexpected, as most island businesses operate only six months of the year. However, given the demands to measure, pattern, cut, sew, and install window treatments for more than 100 windows, I leaned into my Myers-Briggs skills and insisted that no single curtain maker would be getting the full order.

As *Generalissima*, I also devised plans to delegate the window treatment projects to the contractors by floor, fabric, and type of window treatment. The teams got my design directions, measurements, fabrics, and initial deposits as I aimed my project gun high in the air: "Ready, get set, go!"

While double-checking paint colors, fabrics, and furniture measurements outside of the library, I was stretched between priorities. Walking back to the kitchen, I heard a carpenter yell out, "TERI—BE CAREFUL!" The floor grates had been removed from the rooms on the first floor, soon to be covered with plywood.

Maybe fifteen minutes later, Jeff and I bumped into each other painting Room 6. He reminded me, "Don't forget, the guys removed the floor grates in Room 1."

"OK, thanks for the info, Jeff." I hurriedly brushed him off, thinking, *Why does everyone keep telling me this?* "You don't need to keep reminding me."

The phone rang. "Hello, it's your favorite Yankee Gentleman! We have the draperies, valances, and hardware ready for Room 1." Hot tears sprang to my eyes: We were two weeks ahead of schedule. "Would you like us to install today?" he asked.

A short time later, Yankee Gentleman's van came down the lane, turning into the roundabout. He and his helper stepped onto the sunporch, finally cleared of cartons, with the window treatments for Room 1. Both men were wearing charged cordless drills in their hip holsters.

The dramatic eight-foot-tall windows begged for a soft treatment. I designed draperies nearly floor to ceiling, with flouncy valances cut from soft polished cotton, decorated with petal-pink and ivory checks, pillow-ticking lining, and white fringed cotton pompoms.

The guys brought in the draperies, covered in plastic wrap, along with custom rodding, hooks, and hardware. I couldn't resist peeking, but before jumping in, Yankee Gentleman asked, "Do you mind if we take a look around? Everybody's talking about what's going on here." He had deep ties to the island and a love of historic buildings, so naturally, he was curious.

"Sure!" I said. "The guys are wrapping up work on the second floor, so let's check out the first floor."

While strolling around, we took care to avoid sawhorses supporting doors that were being rehung, stacks of trim work, ladders, and paint buckets. Yankee said encouragingly, "This place is gorgeous! It's going to be booked solid once the word gets out. Do you think you'll hold a reception for the local community?" Earlier in the week, the Bar Harbor Chamber of Commerce had asked us to host a "business after hours" event at the inn. We were honored, but concerned whether the work would be completed. Nonetheless, we had said yes, applying more external pressure to plow through the maelstrom. "Yes, we're hosting a Chamber of Commerce event in May. Our doors will be open!"

Yankee and I popped into the kitchen to check out the commercial kitchen build-out. Jeff was wrapping up painting Room 6, coming down the service staircase, a private passageway between the kitchen and the basement, and the Inn's other floors.

"Hiya, Jeff, whaddya think of those Red Sox this year?" Yankee asked. The topic turned to the team's preseason opener and prospects for the 2004 season. "Do you think this will be our year to win the big one? Think the Sox can reverse the curse of the Bambino?" We certainly hoped so, but history told us not to hold our breath.

The baseball chatter struck a chord from my childhood, and I slipped into reverie. I'm a Midwesterner, transplanted to New England. Growing up in Ann Arbor, I had rooted for the Detroit Tigers. As the guys enjoyed trading stats and prospects, my thoughts drifted to summer nights sitting between my grandparents, Doris and Henry, in a pale-bronze Buick La Salle, on our way to our family cottage near Chelsea, Michigan. Snugged-in between them, warmed by the golden glow of the dashboard, catching glimpses of the metallic semicircular horn ring on the rim of the steering wheel, I watched Grandpa tune the car radio to 760 AM, WJR Detroit. Veteran announcer Ernie Harwell broadcasted the game live from Tiger Stadium, coloring the airwaves with his unique play-by-play, "Well, Ti-gah fans, that one is long gone!"

Driving along with twilight approaching, Grandpa signaled, turning right, the car pointed in the direction of a one-lane dirt track at the end of Kalmbach Road. Dark shadows of approaching dusk and tall stands of deep green with shady mixed forests of trees surrounded us. Grandpa would toot the horn before taking the blind curves along the way to warn oncoming cars and deer. Grandma's warm, soft hand holding mine, we drove past a galvanized gate holding a small hand-painted tin sign: "Welcome to Clear Lake Shores." Smiling, Grandma caught my eye as I sighted the lake, listening for the mournful call from a loon or the distinctive *whip-poor-will, whip-poor-will*. All of us, birds of a feather, waited, watching for sunset.

Snapping back to reality and the urgencies of the here and now, I stood with Jeff and Yankee Gentleman in the inn's kitchen and listened as the guys wrapped up their chat and we got down to the business of hanging draperies. I was flying high on cottage memories, to say nothing of the inn's décor installation being two weeks ahead of schedule.

I swung open the heavy kitchen door and held it for the guys, skipping ahead of them to turn on the lights in Room 1. Cutting left at the doorway, I reached out with my arm, stretching, searching with my fingertips for the light switch, set deep in the darkened corner near the front windows.

In an instant, my left foot stepped lightly into the void of an air shaft, a small door-sized chute to the basement. I collapsed violently forward and plummeted through the open heating grate as I tried to grab onto the windowsill. I missed. My left leg went straight through, and I crash landed on my pubic bone. I was dangling, suspended between the basement and Room 1. Stunned, breathless, and hanging in the darkened room, with my left leg dangling, my body was submerged into the floor, caught up by my hip. My right leg was jackknifed into my abdomen, an awkward and painful crouch, my shoulders and arms posed akimbo.

Yankee Gentleman and his assistant hauled me out of the floor. I caught my breath, gulping air to avoid a hysterical crying fit in front of the guys—I didn't want to be labeled as someone who needed special treatment. Instead, I called a time out. "I need to take a break."

They half carried me as I limped back to the Inn's kitchen. We took seats at the round white wooden table and chairs we had set up for breaks. "How are you feeling? Are you all right?" Yankee asked.

It took me a minute to register his question. "I think so," I said, still slightly shocked and in the early stages of denial. I gamely asked if they wanted a cold one. The guys drank their beer and then respectfully left. Jeff had already returned home to take care of Archie, our dog.

Finally, I was alone. I was in a cold sweat as I hobbled to the public restroom, a space that was still a roughed-out work in progress. I fumbled as I tried to remove my coveralls, my hands shaking as I unsnapped and lowered my pants. Then the shock of a deadly black-and-blue to sickly-green bruise already forming from hip to knee. *It's only a flesh wound*, I thought. I don't remember how I got home. I do remember falling asleep that night and rising the next morning. I could barely move my arms, legs, or head.

I rolled out of bed, firmly in denial, moving through to anger. I began bargaining with myself that my injuries wouldn't compromise opening the inn on time. I had work to do, managing the décor installation and helping Jeff paint guest rooms. I stumbled around while getting dressed, my neck radiating pain from the base of my skull to my eye sockets. Lightning bolts of nerve spasms roiled down my left arm and hand. I silently prayed, *Dear God, please, please, please, no drop shipments today.* I managed to put on a shirt and pull on my coveralls. Jeff helped me put on my socks, and I slid into my work boots; he tied them for me and helped me to the van.

Driving to the inn was a silent torture, each bump and swerve struck raw nerves in my neck. Beads of sweat were dotted on my forehead, and droplets trickled down my back. We stopped off for coffee, and I popped four Advil. We pulled into the roundabout, the gravel crunching under the wheels. I was greeted by the morning deliveries, a drop shipment of twenty cartons of dishes, glassware, and cutlery. Boxes were stacked outside the inn, blocking the stairs, on the sunporch and in the entry hall. The painters were stepping around the cardboard obstacles while trying to work. I remembered my mantra: "Hey, guys, remember, we're on a deadline—no SPF."

Jeff moved boxes. I bent over to slice open a carton, and a spasm took my breath away. "Take me to the emergency room!" I cried.

By that morning, the post-injury adrenaline had been wrung out and was replaced by searing pain. I could barely walk by myself into the ER waiting room, but I felt lucky. It was pre-season, before the torrent of tourists arrived, and there were no injured hikers. I was the only one there. The attending PA examined me and ordered X-rays. I lay on the hospital bed waiting for my results while thinking, *Please don't ask me to sit up.* The PA returned and gave me the full story. Severe whiplash, over-rotation of the lower trunk, left leg with contusions. Basically, extremely fucked-up and in too much pain to brush my hair. I was handed a padded neck collar. "You'll have to wear this for the next month, or you may never regain the ability to bend or turn your neck and head."

"Neck! What about my blackened, swollen, and severely painful left leg? I have an inn that's opening in one month. What should I do?"

He seemed to misunderstand my plight; he said, "It's only a flesh wound; you can wear long pants." I shelved any plans to wear a skirt or shorts for the next six months.

Innkeepers say wellness is hard to achieve during the work season. We had less than 30 days until opening day, and I was beyond sick and tired. *Generalissima*'s plans called for no single points of failure. But the next day, looking in my mirror, mirror, on the wall, fastening on my neck collar, I realized I was the biggest SPF of all.

Countdown

Weeks before opening day, we decided to recruit an assistant innkeeper. The objective was to hire someone with innkeeping experience who could help us get a leg up for our first operating season.

After running a help-wanted ad in the local paper, job applicants called, and résumés were coming in. Our lead candidate came out of nowhere with a rock star résumé, leaving a message on the inn's answering machine. "Hello, my name is Betty. I was an innkeeper at the Inn at Canoe Point." Our once-favorite inn! A classically designed Tudor cottage that reminded us of our former home. It was a stunner, mere steps from the granite shoreline and crashing waves of the Atlantic Ocean.

I couldn't believe our good fortune, and called her right away to schedule a meeting. "Hi, Betty. Jeff and I would love to meet you; can you stop by the inn?" But I wasn't in the driver's seat. Wisely, she played her cards close to the vest.

"Can you tell me a little about yourselves, and the inn? Do you have any experience running an inn? How many guest rooms are there?" It was clear she would be interviewing us, rather than the other way around.

Betty and I scheduled a time to meet. She asked for the grand tour—the kitchen, common areas, and the guest rooms. She arrived early and I invited her in. As we walked around, I motioned to the wicker sitting area on the sunporch and pointed out the sunny dining room with Nantucket red chairs and white tables. We strolled into the main entry hall. I noticed Betty glancing up at the Venetian glass pendants and the Eastlake mirror, smiling, admiring the refreshing, clean décor.

We passed by the oak-paneled lounge, which was flanked by artisan-made glass panels of amber and topaz, and we made our way to the former butler's pantry. The old servant area was now restored, from the tall oak glass-fronted cabinets to the original soapstone counters and copper sink. It was our retro take on homespun antiquity, punctuated with a large black-and-white photograph of my grandfather Henry taken at our family diner, circa 1934. We had converted the room into a self-serve Guest Pantry for snacks and drinks, day and night. "What a good idea—the guests can help themselves!" Betty's enthusiastic words were music to my ears.

We slipped past the pantry's swinging door on our way to the new commercial kitchen, outfitted with double-capacity stainless refrigerators, a full-size freezer, beverage stations, and twin dishwashers. "You could run a restaurant out of this place," Betty said.

"Jeff and I talked about a restaurant option at some point, but the inn will be breakfast only." Both of us were relieved.

We exited through the kitchen's service door out to the oversized living room and the library, the grand rooms reunited and sitting pretty outside of the dining room's French doors. The maple floors had been freshly sanded, refinished, and gleaming, large areas covered with vintage rugs. My antique Weber grand piano had survived the move, as well as two button-tufted sage-green leather loveseats with rolled arms, accented with claret-colored velvet armchairs. Our furniture, artwork, and soft furnishings were evocative of Maine, but had a modern sensibility.

As we strolled around the first floor, Betty said, "This place is beautiful and enormous, Do you have an elevator?"

I sadly shook my head. "We wanted to, but it wasn't required under code, and we were on a tight budget. It didn't make the cut." I noticed a slight shrug of her shoulders as we started our climb up the staircase to the second floor. The stair runner felt soft underfoot. The stained-glass windows cast sunbeams of brilliant color across the carpet's pattern, which held our attention until we turned right to tour Room 2.

The door to the room was closed, the room number still wrapped in its package, labeled, and taped to the door. As I nudged the door open, I revealed an unmade wrought-iron bed with the oyster-shell-colored linens and shams laid out on the mattress. The wall and ceiling behind and over the bed were draped with a silky sage tone-on-tone canopy. The fabric was repeated in the Roman shades on the windows. Hand-colored photographs of starfish and seashells adorned the walls. The small sitting area was large enough for two ecru linen slipcovered chairs and a leather settee, next to an Eastlake marble-topped bureau from the inn's founding family. Betty went quiet for a moment, then looked at me as we stood in the doorway.

"You got it just right," she said.

Tears sprang to my eyes, sticking to my eyelashes, obscuring my view, as her kind words sank in. Then she asked, "What are you doing for guest room amenities?"

I had no idea what she was talking about.

At the end of the tour, Jeff met up with us on the sunporch. The three of us took a seat and chatted for a few minutes. Jeff deftly led the conversation with the usual interview questions. "Betty, we never met you at Canoe Point. What was going well? Why did you leave?" Her responses offered truths about innkeeping, innkeepers, inn owners, and inn investors, along with the pros and cons of running a luxury inn business. We were all ears.

Betty gave us firsthand stories of wonderful guests and innkeepers. She told us a few inside accounts of the demands of running an inn from 6:00 a.m. to 10:00 p.m. with little to no staff seven days a week. Resort areas like Bar Harbor, Kennebunkport, and Cape Cod had perennial shortages of seasonal workers.

Still listening eagerly, Jeff and I hoped to hear more about how great being an innkeeper was going to be down the road. Instead, more war stories of burned-out innkeepers-for-hire, salving their wounds at midnight with leftover guest wine, stale muffins, and cheese. Horror stories of making middle-of-the-night phone calls to inn owners telling them to "take this inn and shove it!"—a peril we wanted to avoid. We agreed there would be no requirement to live on-site. Our plans were to rent out the small cottage we had bought mid-island, so we could live and work at the inn during our operating season, May to October.

We eagerly offered Betty the Assistant Innkeeper position, and she accepted the job. We were elated, sent to heaven, landing in the Garden of Eden. Jeff and I were convinced we'd met our guardian angel. Thinking to ourselves, *Hallelujah!*, the three of us leapt into Eden the following morning.

Paradise was quickly turned into Betty's demanding and delightful hospitality boot camp. She arrived on the first day dressed in a lavender LL Bean fleece, jeans, and sneakers, carrying a tote bag with inventory checklists, tour scripts, and guest room inspection worksheets. After a quick coffee break, we broke out into staircase sprint medleys and guest room high-intensity drills running supplies up and down the stairs. In the afternoon before taps was blown, she supervised exercises to ensure the inn was properly spit-shined. Betty's boot camp convinced us we had an imperfect notion of what we were doing, and that caused us to further fret our prospects. Jeff and I remain convinced that if we had spent even one weekend as an innkeeper-sitter, we would have run away, never to return.

Betty's stoic personality was accompanied by a no-nonsense/businesslike tone with no unnecessary flourishes demeanor. She asked again, "What are you doing for room amenities?"

Once again, Jeff and I stood in the hallway, deer staring into oncoming headlights. "What exactly do you mean?" Jeff said.

She offered a wry smile while shaking her head. "Amenities are shampoo, soap, flowers in guest rooms, special touches to delight and engage your guests."

Jeff asked for a room-by-room audit so we could better understand what was lacking. He said to me, "She'll probably come up with a few nits for us to deal with."

Not hardly.

Betty presented us with her gap analysis, review notes, and a detailed inventory that filled eight legal-size pages. Proof positive we were woefully deficient in our understanding and preparation of the finer points of operating a luxury inn. But we were quick studies, and time was running out. We had three weeks until opening just a few days after Mother's Day weekend, the date our innkeeper marathon event would begin.

We spent days pouring over catalogs of soaps. Sniffing and bathing ourselves in products until we settled on the right stuff. Almond-scented soaps, honey-and-milk shampoo, conditioners and lotions to silken the guests' skin, lubricate their stay, enliven their senses. We set up new vendor relationships and accounts, placing massive orders for immediate drop shipment. Preferably overnight, FOB, ASAP.

As for the rest of the guest room amenities, Betty's proclamations between what the rooms needed and where we were was dizzying. Her guest room punch list specified: 3-way lamps and light bulbs for bedside reading, full-length mirrors, privacy pillows, water glasses and carafes, remote-control devices, padded hangers, wooden hangers, luggage racks, laundry bags, and tissue box cozies, each item multiplied by ten. The clock was ticking, and the cash register was ringing.

Jeff and I sprinted to the big white van, tanked it up with gas and our business credit cards, and headed to the closest Bed Bath & Beyond and Curtainshop more than an hour's drive away. We made thrice-weekly buying trips, loading up the van with comfort products, maxing every credit card to the hilt. Returning to the inn, we drove through the roundabout, van still idling, to unload our purchases at the front door. Betty ran circuits to the guest rooms, deploying lamps, light bulbs, and amenities, and checking off the punch lists. At midday, we'd grab lunch in the kitchen and take a deep breath. We kept moving.

Betty transitioned from guest room readiness to the next movement of the inn symphony: inn operations. "Next time you're out, you need to buy two large whiteboards. We'll hang one in the office and the other in the kitchen."

"What are the whiteboards for?" I asked.

"To record guest names and their breakfast beverage preferences. All the staff should know."

This was a surprise. "You mean we actually have to remember everyone's name?"

"Yes, we do!"

Betty's advice and expertise was indispensable, but it also grated on us, shining a hot 1000-megawatt klieg light on the fact that we had no business being in the innkeeping business, at least not yet. But she was only getting started. She thought, *Hmm, now would be a good time to discuss housekeeping.*

Betty was the queen of housekeeping details and a steel-toed stickler. She reigned supreme in the realm of guest bed and bathroom cleanliness and agreed to train us and the student housekeepers who would be arriving in time for Memorial Weekend. In the meantime, she offered to work housekeeping with me until the new staff was up to speed. This meant getting up at 5:45 a.m., prepping and serving breakfast, chatting with guests. Then a quick pivot, rotating to the housekeeping detail, lunch (hopefully), turn-down service during wine hour, dinner, dishes, closing the inn for the night, and bedtime.

After climbing down, fresh off my paint ladder, the thought of the upcoming iron-woman event kept me up late every night. I imagined a horrid stretch of fifteen hours a day, seven days a week for several grueling weeks. I chafed under the padded neck collar I was wearing. It felt like an iron shackle to the inn's chain. It was then I realized I was a prisoner—an Inn Mate.

Running on Empty

With opening day approaching, the inn was cleaning up nicely, as were The Builder, the contractors, painters, bankers, and suppliers; but it all had a cost. We were concerned about funds, and working capital in particular.

By the time the crews were packing up and the guest rooms were readied, Jeff and I realized there was no turning back. We'd drained our savings, maxed-out our credit, and punctured our retirement accounts. Marketing was challenging, construction wasn't completed, and the website had no room photos, only hand-drawn renderings. Yet reservation activity was strengthening, and we had bookings with names and deposits.

As days ticked past, the gas tank of our account was perilously close to empty. We had to pump more gas into the tank and began looking around for other assets to assist the refueling effort.

Jeff was feeling twitchy about his baby, the Aventurine Green Porsche 911. He had bought the car nearly a decade after surviving a near-death car collision while skiing at Mad River in Vermont, back in 1984. Yet despite his four-wheel brush with mortality, Jeff still loved cars, and even went so far as to attend a defensive driving course at Skip Barber Racing School at Lime Rock Park in Salisbury, Connecticut. He went to learn performance driving skills professional drivers use to navigate the last fifteen seconds before a collision. Now, he and I had to learn how to navigate the last few weeks before a financial crash. Jeff's beloved car was languishing in storage in a boatyard over in Southwest Harbor. Selling the car seemed a desperate and sad move; we decided to take a joyride in Acadia National Park to talk it over.

We climbed into the bucket seats, and Jeff turned the key. She turned over willingly, and Jeff patiently waited for her to warm up. Porsche emitted her signature growl as he pulled out onto Main Street. Her engine burbled, complaining loudly, as we cruised along to the entrance of Park Loop Road, a 26-mile circuit with a maximum speed of 25 mph. Porsche would remain in low gears for the entire trip. "I remember how I felt when I bought his car. It was the most extravagant purchase I'd ever made, until we bought the inn," Jeff said.

I felt sad, too. "Hon, you don't have to sell your baby. We'll figure something out."

"Teri, the numbers don't work. And I'll never be able to enjoy Porsche on a 108-square-mile island with a top speed of fifty miles an hour."

Jeff handed me a round leather case of CDs and asked me to play one of his favorites. "Can you find *The Last Record Album* by Little Feat?" I popped it into the player, and he queued up a well-worn track, "All That You Dream." Jeff sang along in his rich baritone a song he knew by heart, both of us feeling down and out. Finally, the new math made sense:

Idle European Sports Car / Dwindling Funds x Uncertainty = Sell Car to the Highest Bidder

After the drive, Jeff bucked up and contacted a used Porsche dealer who snapped her up. Coincidentally, the dealer had a driver traveling in Maine and gave the green light for him to pick up the car. He arrived at the inn with a certified check and a flatbed truck. But the driver made Jeff load it onto the truck. If it went off the rails, let Jeff take the hit.

Jeff climbed into the driver's seat and revved her up for his final turn at the wheel, guiding her up the ramp to the truck bed. The funds and paperwork were then exchanged with a handshake as the bittersweet event was consummated in the neighboring bank parking lot. As the flatbed truck drove away, Jeff looked down at the check in his hand as he stood in front of the inn still in pieces, waiting to be completed with opening day looming. Convinced that his former life in the fast lane, as an executive, a mover and shaker, was over. There are few examples of marital downsizing more poignant than watching your husband wave goodbye to his beautiful, expensive, European girlfriend.

Breaking Glass

We tried to not sweat the small stuff, and we didn't think twice before contacting someone to clean a stained-glass skylight panel. We had contacted a local woman who made and sold stained glass and she grandly informed us that she was a stained-glass "artist." We explained the nature of the project and asked her to stop by to take a look.

She swept through the front entry like she owned the place, twirling in circles, swathed in shawls tossed over a kimono, draped in layers of beaded necklaces, wearing enormous red glasses.

"I've never noticed this place before! What's going on here?" she said.

"We bought the inn last year," Jeff replied, "and we're running as fast as we can to reopen. We have a glass ceiling panel that needs cleaning—do you think you can help us out?"

She paused thoughtfully, taking a look around, following us to the lounge. We stood together and looked up at the stained-glass panel that was set in the ceiling ten feet over our heads. A substantial work of art glass, the panel was nearly seven feet long by four feet wide, swimming in blues, deep yellow, and rose-colored glass. "It doesn't seem like a big deal," she said. We hammered out the logistics to have the panel removed and cleaned; we'd handle reinstallation to avoid future leaks. "I'll have this done for you in a flash!" she said. "But you have to get it to my studio quickly."

The next morning, Jeff had three guys on the crew remove the panel from the ceiling. They cut it loose and hoisted it down with strapping. It was laid out in a wood-framed crate made especially for transport and was promptly delivered to the artist's studio.

There was no communication for several weeks, not a peep, so we dropped by her studio in Southwest Harbor to get a progress report. We parked in front of the shop and walked into an empty room. Looking around, we wandered further and found her in the back workroom surrounded by a gang of people. We spotted the stained-glass panel completely disassembled on a huge table, laid out like a jigsaw puzzle and covered with tracing paper, the group hovering over it.

"Well, hello! I've been meaning to get in touch with you two," she said. "This is turning out to be much more work than I thought."

Jeff glanced at me sideways, a signal: *I'll handle this.*

"It's such a unique panel, and it's very old. I decided it would be a wonderful project for my students. We'll work on it together to save time."

It sounded plausible, and Jeff paused for effect. "I guess so, but call us the minute it's ready."

She waved him off. "OK, OK, I know—I'll see you in a few weeks."

Back at the inn, the absence of the panel left a gaping hole in the ceiling. The work crew fashioned a plexiglass bubble (yep, another change order!) to keep the rain out, and we waited.

Three weeks later, a few days before the inn's opening reception, we went back to the glass studio. We parked in front of the shop and read a large sign that was posted on the front door: CLOSED FOR THE SEASON, while at the same time catching sight of the words FOR SALE, painted in large letters across one of the plate-glass windows. Jeff and I looked at one another slack-jawed. Our efforts to locate her were fruitless. Phone numbers were changed, snail mail was returned to our post office box. Sometime later, we received a written invoice for $10,000, no explanation, no forwarding information. Finally, Jeff was able to reach her by phone.

"I'm shocked by the price; we're not paying."

"Well, the inn restoration was such a big deal, I figured somebody would pay me, so I could do what I wanted," she said.

Now we were stuck with a plexiglass dome in the middle of the ceiling, without a written bid or a contract. We had engaged her services with a verbal agreement and a handshake. Too bad, since it was crystal-clear we were being taken to the cleaner's. Only then did we realize we'd been wearing rose-colored glasses.

We offered to split the $10,000 fee 50/50, but she refused. Instead, she placed a mechanic's lien on the inn, which did not play well with The Bank. We contacted our lawyer, threatening suit; the matter went to mediation. Two years later, we settled for a 50/50 split, exactly what we had originally offered. Shortly afterward, the panel was finally reinstalled.

Inn Quest

An innkeeper friend suggested we become members of the Bar Harbor B&B Association, a community of innkeepers who met periodically to discuss hospitality trends, review the shockingly large numbers of cruise ship visits, and vent about wacky guests. We plunged into the pool of like-minded people, finding the temperature both warm and, at times, chilly.

The local business community was supportive of our efforts to restore a historic landmark in the center of the village. A few naysayers let us know we were way over our head. As if we didn't already know, yet we found it comforting to connect with folks who knew what was in store for us.

Our first meeting was held at an inn owned by a former schoolteacher. She was elfin in stature with a feisty disposition. She opened the meeting: "Good Morning! Nice to see all of you." Her manner was cordial while addressing the group. The agenda was informal; everyone took turns introducing themselves, despite most of the innkeepers already knowing one another. The introductions were for our benefit. Her tone became frisky as she spoke her first words after Jeff's introduction.

"Ohhhh, you're the dreamers," she sniffed. Glancing over her shoulder to the recording secretary, she whispered loudly, "Let's see if they make it."

I looked over at Jeff as he slowly chewed her words along with his oatmeal raisin cookie. I took a sip of my water and had trouble stomaching her sentiments myself. It was Jeff's turn to address the group.

"Teri and I are happy to report we're going to open on time!" The sound of light applause was mildly gratifying. "The Bar Harbor Chamber of Commerce asked us to host the season's opening event, Business After Hours, at the inn. We hope to see you there!" And we hoped they'd come out in large numbers.

Bar Harbor is a small village, but local business referrals were welcome—and crucial to our early success. We wanted the business community to visit the inn to get good vibes flowing. Later in the week, the meeting minutes were sent to the membership by email, along with an invitation to the Chamber gathering.

A few days later, the Chamber of Commerce called and left a voice message. "Teri and Jeff, you better wear your roller skates tonight. You're going to have a lot of people at your inn."

By 5:00, groups of people were strolling down the lane on foot, and those who drove were jammed into every space in our and the neighboring parking lots. I timidly asked a few of our new innkeeper colleagues and friends to help out as ushers, welcoming guests and checking on the buffet we'd set up. Platters of shrimp cocktail, assortments of cheese, crackers, fresh fruit, beer, wine, iced tea, and other refreshments were offered.

Soon visitors were streaming past the front door, heads turning as they made their way down the entry hall into the lounge and the library, commercial kitchen, guest pantry, then into the dining room, hovering over the refreshments. Other visitors took the stairs to explore the ten newly designed and decorated guest rooms. A few folks were knocked off their feet and took a rest, rocking-out on the wicker chairs on the porch.

At 6:00 p.m., the inn was packed, standing room only. I scanned the room in disbelief at the commotion. Looking past the front door, I noticed a line of people waiting to come in. I recognized the elder sister of the former innkeeper standing at the foot of the steps. We had heard she was a tough cookie. After all, the inn was her former home—the hospitality business was started by her mother. She stood a few moments, then took the granite steps up to the front porch. I felt a chill in the air as I opened the door to greet her.

"Hi, it's nice of you to visit."

She looked at me with a blank face. "I'm only here because someone said it's nice," she sniffed.

"Would you like a glass of iced tea?" I asked.

"Noooo, de-yah," she replied, brushing past me. My attempts to be friendly drifted silently in her wake.

I quietly followed her at a distance as she walked slowly through the entry hall and glanced at her reflection in the hallway mirror. I'd overheard one of the guests say it had been an anniversary gift given to her mother. She stood at the foot of the staircase and looked up at the massive rainbow-colored fleur-de-lis stained-glass panel situated above the landing. It was shining in its glory after being covered with plywood for years. A full spectrum of purples, blues, and green rained down upon the carpet and warmed the oak balustrades and wainscoting.

She stepped into the formal dining room, which we'd converted to the guest lounge. It was now comfortably furnished with an antique empire sofa and clubby leather chairs. Turning to her companion, she said, "They didn't want our dining room furniture," and she sadly shook her head. The mild criticism was hard to hear, but I tried to imagine her feelings and fond memories of the dining table as the gathering place for family Thanksgiving and Christmas celebrations, her mother serving lamb chops with frilly bows, presented on a silver platter.

She gazed up to the coffered ceiling and was taken aback by the plexiglass bubble now covering the hole where the missing stained-glass skylight belonged. Her eyes quickly darted to the carved fireplace mantel, which we'd decorated with vases of flowers and bracken. Her gaze returned to the place where the dining furniture once stood. She must have been thinking, *No dining room furniture. A hole in the ceiling. The inn has new owners.*

I said to myself, *Let it go*, and made my way out of the room. It was the "golden hour," sometime before sunset. Suddenly, I felt a tap-tap-tapping on the back of my arm. I looked over my shoulder and she gave me a Mona Lisa smile, lukewarm and enigmatic. I turned around to face her, not knowing what to expect. This was the closest I'd been to her. She was slender and petite, wearing a pastel twinset and pearls. Her head was crowned with lively white hair. She tilted her head up, as if to whisper in my ear, and quietly said, "Honey, I think I'm ready for that glass of iced tea, now." My heart was bursting with happiness. We had done it!

She followed me into the Guest Pantry. We smiled as we stood under the portrait of my grandfather Henry, and I poured the tea into her chilled glass. She walked back into the lounge and took a seat on the sofa. I stood at a distance and watched as she drank it all in. The iced tea, her family memories, and thoughts of her deceased sister and mother, the former innkeepers. She finished her tea, placed the empty glass on a wooden serving tray, and left without saying goodbye. I never saw her again.

Jeff and I bumped into The Builder and his wife as the evening was wrapping up. They were basking in the accolades and praise from members of the Bar Harbor Historic Society, Chamber members, and community leaders. "It irritates me to see the self-satisfied look on his face while we still have unfinished business." Jeff said. It was a fair point. But we would deal with repairs later. It was time for us to switch gears. To transform ourselves from inn restorers to innkeepers.

We tossed off our party hats. We stowed our hard hats, work boots, and paint coveralls, and changed into street clothes. We crossed the finish line, just in the nick of time. Opening weekend was here, and check-in time was 3:00 p.m.

PART TWO

CHAPTER THREE

Everything born in spring, dies in fall. But love is not seasonal.
—Rumi

Family Affair

In 1982, I moved to Boston for love, and for practical reasons. Detroit, the Motor City, was in the midst of an economic downswing. After the Big Three automobile gold rush of the fifties and sixties, factories were shut and jobs were exported or eliminated by the 1970s.

But for me and millions of others, it was Berry Gordy's genius, the music of Motown, that put Detroit on the map. Dad was a gadget and hi-fi guy, an audiophile and music buff. Motown was the soundtrack of my youth—Marvin Gaye, Stevie Wonder, Aretha Franklin, Smokey Robinson and the Miracles. The hit tune "Going to a Go-Go" playing on a Garrard turntable, Sony reel-to-reel tape deck, and portable record players. We danced our way through the '60s and '70s.

One Christmas, Mom, Dad, my brother Paul, and I traveled "downtown" to the tune of Petula Clark on the car radio, on our way see Santa at the J.L. Hudson department store. Paul and I held on tight riding up an escalator to Santa's Village. Later strolling along Woodward Avenue under Christmas lights. Future trips to see Santa rarely included my three other siblings, Robb, Alexandra, and Michael. We weren't often able to celebrate together. The stars in our eyes were dimmed by our Mom's bouts with mental illness and frequent hospitalizations.

One weekend, Jeff and I bumped into my cousin at Tiger Stadium, where we enjoyed a family-friendly rivalry between the Detroit Tigers and the Boston Red Sox, Jeff's hometown team. After the game, we went to Greek Town for plates of flaming saganaki, spanakopita, and gyros. The next day, we took a field trip to the Detroit Institute of Art for a curated view of the art collections of the automobile titans, two of whom were also cunning geniuses: Ransom E. Olds, for his invention of the first automobile assembly line, and Henry Ford, for the introduction of the Model T and mass production. He later became the richest man in America.

But I knew from firsthand experience that there was more to the Motor City legend than cars, music, and interchangeable component parts; workers were interchangeable, too. Folks like my mom, who worked the midnight shift at a Ford factory, were out of work, down and out. The revolving door of factory work wiped out the livelihoods and aspirations of many families and small family businesses that grew up alongside America's craze for the automobile.

Joe, my dad, and his family started a diner chain called Joe's Snappy Service in the late 1930s; it was later called Snappy Joe's. From a single location in Owosso, Michigan, the diners stretched to other family-owned locations close to the University of Michigan, Eastern Michigan University, and the auto manufacturing communities.

Snappy Joe's diners were open six days a week. The chow was simple home-style fare, made daily from scratch. Blue-plate specials, chili, hamburgers, cinnamon rolls, pies, donuts, and coffee were served all day long. Baking prep began at 3:00 a.m., followed by breakfast, lunch, and dinner service, closing by 7:00 p.m. The diners were closed on Sunday. It was family day. A time to rest up for the coming week. Dad's clan relaxed together in modest cottages they all built around Clear Lake Shores, a half-hour drive from Ann Arbor.

After swinging on rope swings, sitting on porches, or bobbing around on a Chris-Craft or buoyant Sunfish, we'd gather around an outdoor fire while Dad cooked breakfast. Platters of bacon, blueberry pancakes, and scrambled eggs. The aroma of coffee percolated up and down the shoreline, enticing cousins, aunts, and uncles to wander along the dirt road for casual family visits and a bite to eat. Tempted by the aromas of wood smoke, coffee, cigarettes, and conversation. But memories of our family's idyllic diner and cottage life are limited, and most of them belong to my dad. He called those times "the good old days." Yes, Dad, I bet they were.

The Snappy Joe era left a deep impression on me. I taught myself rudimentary cooking and baking skills in a play kitchen. I was too young to cook with Dad and Grandma. Eventually, I enrolled in culinary school to fill in the gaps from my days standing in front of a toy stove, earning my chef diploma and learning the classic traditions of American, French, and Italian cooking. Skills that served me well when I switched careers at midlife and became an innkeeper.

My recipes for scones, muffins, and breakfast were a hit with inn guests, friends, and family. My dad's favorite was pineapple pie, a new favorite we never ate when I was growing up. Most often, it would be blueberry, apple, cherry, or the occasional coconut cream, and, of course, mincemeat pie, which none of us liked. So I created a recipe for him.

Years later, Jeff and I cared for Dad after his health had taken a turn. Serving his favorites—fresh cinnamon rolls and pineapple pie—both at home and later in the hospital. On our last visit, my siblings, Jeff, and I gathered with Dad for pineapple pie. A special version this time. It was a deep-dish pie with twice the pineapple filling and a sugar lattice crust, served with coconut ice cream. We could tell Dad enjoyed it—his smile said it all. Jeff asked, "Joe, why do you love pineapple pie so much?"

Dad sat quietly and thought for a long minute. He said, "I don't know, Jeff. One night, I had a dream Grandma made it, and I wanted to know how it tasted." We smiled and nodded our heads. I imagined the pie tasted like heaven.

Meet Your Innkeeper

My earliest memory is being pinched in church. I was instructed to keep quiet and act like a big girl. As the eldest of five kids, I earned my Big Sister merit badge early. Making peanut butter sandwich lunches, walking my brothers, then a sister, to school. I was a babysitter at eight, an unsupervised "adult" by 14.

My mother was a brilliant, temperamental beauty, and impulsive. We moved seven times between kindergarten and high school. I was a flowering plant attempting to bloom where I could until the trowel dug down and heaved me up out of my snug bed. Here we go again, transported to another garden: Michigan to Pennsylvania, California to Florida. Miraculously, Paul, Robb, Alex, Michael, and I emerged as healthy adults despite the upheaval.

At 17, I graduated high school and left home, returning to my family for short visits and to take my sister to her first day of kindergarten. But I was adrift, no plan for a career, a family, or a way forward. I returned to Ann Arbor to be close to my godmother Tusa (Romanian for *aunt*). A former professional dancer, she was stunning, petite, and hardworking. Her dance company toured in Las Vegas, Chicago, and Cleveland, and she dated Liberace (it's true!). After marrying Uncle Bob, she became a successful businesswoman and trustee at a local college. Her obituary in the local paper read:

Business Owner Was Glamorous and Ethical. "She was one of the most ethical persons I ever met," said the owner of a local restaurant. "She had a ministry in her store," helping Romanian immigrants learn English, and volunteering as an interpreter in the court system. "She never failed to help homeless people, reformed alcoholics, immigrants, and relatives with problems of their own." After my parents divorced, my mom was one of her hires.

At Tusa's funeral, I stood in a packed room of people watching a video of her in her prime. But years earlier, she memorialized our lives together. Five photo medallions, me, Tusa, Uncle Bob, and my two cousins, hung from five branches on a bronze Tree of Life. One of the few keepsakes of my youth. It was given to me after she died.

I recalled Sunday afternoons dancing in hair ribbons, wearing my parents' wedding crowns. Swanning in circles, chewing gum, and blowing bubbles. Tusa suggested ballet as a creative outlet for my energy. I pirouetted into dance, and music became the sunshine for my growth, emotional support, and enjoyment. Unfortunately, our close-knit extended family affair didn't last long. With a fresh wind under our wings, we took off. A family of homing pigeons in flight, destination unknown.

Inn Mates

Some say I'm sensitive, that I have a jaded view due to my upbringing; it's probably true. I have a penchant for following the rules, for fresh starts, hard work, and second chances, traits that continue to serve me well, after brushes with life's hurricanes. Then, after college, marriage, my stock market and culinary careers, I became an innkeeper. Or rather *it* became *me*.

Internal Affairs

When we moved to Boston, I was an unemployed college student. Jeff covered some of my expenses for a while, and I had savings, but I needed to get back to the work of finding my way in the world.

In Ann Arbor, I worked retail, and I was an auditor, second shift. I landed that job due to my math skills and a connection who gave me a reference. Now in Boston, I didn't know a soul. I contacted a temp agency and started interviewing.

After several hot and cold leads, the recruiter asked, "What do you know about the stock market?"

I knew as much as any college kid without a trust fund. "Not much," I replied. But Tusa was a saver and a savvy investor. She discussed companies like Sun Oil, Coca-Cola, Ford, and Chrysler. I knew just enough to know I knew nothing. But I was eager to learn about this road to better financial horizons.

An interview was scheduled with a Boston-based start-up, a discount brokerage company eager to hire women to round out the trading desk. It sounded intriguing. An interview with the firm's Vice President was scheduled. I was warmly greeted by Maura, a smart, hip, and personable woman on a mission to introduce women to the closeted world of white male financial success.

"The auditing experience on your résumé stood out. But you haven't finished college. What happened?"

"It's complicated, a family thing." It didn't feel like the right time to talk about my gap year caring for Mom and my baby brother. So

I punted. "I've been accepted at Boston College; I'm a full-time night student."

"What are your career plans?" she asked. It was a good question.

"I've tried retail and auditing, but I want a challenging career with room for advancement."

She nodded her head. "I worked on the trading desk after grad school. The other brokerage firms wouldn't hire me. They're a bunch of boys' clubs. I think you'll like it here."

She made me an offer, and the salary would cover tuition and my share of living expenses. I accepted it eagerly, and gratefully. We smiled and shook hands. Maura gave me a tour of the back office, the trading room, and then out to the lobby. I took the revolving door out to the redbrick sidewalks and concrete colossus of Boston's Government Center. My head was spinning as I walked vaguely along the pedestrian boulevard in the direction of the subway. I took the steps up and into the T station and grabbed onto the old escalator's warm, sticky handrail, carefully landing on the moving stairway down to the train platform. The heady aromas of popcorn and coffee wafted up from the concessions, mingling with the acrid, smoky stench from hydraulic brakes, with tangy undertones of urine. Trolley cars screeched and shuddered, then shook to a halt. I dashed onto the C-line trolley headed outbound.

I took a seat and gazed through the darkened window. The trolley moved slowly underground, and I closed my eyes. Having accepted the job offer, I felt I was on the brink of a new reality. An old mind loop played: my life growing up in a family of modest means; memories of my caregiving role with my siblings and with Dad, both of us knowing I couldn't stay home forever, and the time would come for me to fledge the nest. Luckily, I'd dodged the obvious young adult threats: dropping out of school, substance abuse, and teen pregnancy. Still, the conversation with Dad had been difficult.

"I'm going to leave home after high school," I said. He nodded; despite the challenges he'd face. "Dad, I don't know what to do with my life," I said, wiping away tears.

"Honey, you can do whatever you want." His voice was gentle, consoling, but without useful specifics. I didn't have a life or a plan. No career or guidance counselor other than my swim coaches, who always rooted for me. They knew I could go the distance, but where was I going?

After a merry-go-round of school, jobs, and boyfriends, my destiny changed when I met Jeff. He was my soul mate; he knew my story, and I knew his. Never ones to veer too far from our orbits, gravity always tilted us back on track, both of us spinning in the same universe. We were two imperfect celestial bodies who came together and were made whole. Both of us knew our emotional common ground was exquisitely uncommon and unknown to most of our friends. Some of whom thoughtlessly called us "strivers."

The passenger bell rang for my stop on St. Mary's Street. The trolley scraped along and crawled out of the tunnel, thrusting me into daylight. I walked along Beacon Street, contemplating the enormous balloon of opportunity that was floating above me. I convinced myself it was high time to close my eyes and jump, trusting for once that I wouldn't worry about hitting the ground. So, on that cloudy November afternoon, a day that had started out angst-filled, a middling sort of day, turned out to be one of the luckiest days of my life.

On my first day at work, I was fingerprinted, the ink staining my skirt as I brushed against the desk. Maura introduced me to the folks in the trading room. One of the guys hollered out, "Hey, Mo, I'm glad you hired somebody easy on the eyes." He shook my hand. "I'm only jokin'. It's nice to meet you." He flashed a smile, a twinkle in his eye. "My name's Miles—Miles Long."

He'd whipped out his cocky joke within earshot of the Trading Room Manager, Herbert, a punctilious, well-scrubbed Harvard grad, and former altar boy. He tugged at his bowtie and straightened his seersucker jacket as he stood to shake my hand. "The moral tenor in this office has struck a new low."

The trading room rang out in whoops of laughter. Thus began my OTJ training in friendly female-taunting banter, '80s style. The close camaraderie had begun. Soon I was answering phones, talking with brokers and clients. Running breakfast orders around the corner to the Steaming Kettle coffee shop for coffee, tea, and banana walnut muffins; it was a wild, wacky family. I fit right in.

I memorized stock symbols, gave quotations, learning trading-desk lingo coding trade tickets. I was a quick study and was offered a promotion to trader—if I could study, sit, and pass three NASD qualification exams while taking my full course load at Boston College.

Studying on the subway, during lunch, after class, a break for dinner, most every night before bed, and all weekend. Jeff and I had to squeeze in moments of fun and relaxation when we could. I was determined, and I passed the exams. I was nestled into the semicircle of the trading desk, equipped with a headset, a market monitor, and a phone bank with speed-dial to brokers on trading floors in Boston, New York, and Chicago.

My new vocabulary consisted of market orders, limit orders, fill or kill and stop orders. Options lingo was my specialty. A sexy universe of long puts, naked and covered calls, butterfly spreads, and straddles. Calling orders to the floor of CBOE in Chicago, I hit speed dial, and the runner picked up on the first ring.

"Yeah, go ahead." He was straining to hear me above the crowd shouting in the pit. "This is STX. I'm a buyer of 100 calls I-BEAM, Christmas, double-nickels at a teeny," I said.

"Does this guy know he's way out-of-the money? These calls are expiring today!"

"Yeah, we're buying to close!" I replied.

"Nice." He hung up.

I had a knack for financial markets. I loved the pace: boredom, punctuated by panic. Good practice for innkeeping, years later, when unexpected events like fire alarms, earthquakes, and midnight phone calls from guests could yield drama or pandemonium.

Three years later, I graduated from Boston College, the first in my family to earn a college degree, but not the last. My siblings and I boot-strapped our way to careers in finance, law, academia, medicine, and theology. Each of us hardworking and grateful, believing that a minute portion of our mother's unconventional genius was lightly sprinkled on us all.

After graduation, the ambition bug bit me. I sought the advice of Jeff and our friend Rich. A friendly journalist from Chicago, he'd moved to Boston from New York for a gig with *Inc.* magazine. We shared our midwestern sense of humor and opinions about our new lives in Boston. As well Rich's fondness for pretzels and fizzy soda. He encouraged me to interview for jobs with two firms on the rise. One a trading gig with a boutique broker-dealer, the other, a regulatory role with Boston's leading investment company (which would become a household name).

The boutique firm interview was scheduled after the stock market close. I walked a short distance to a new glass office tower with million-dollar views out into the blue horizon of Boston Harbor. The Head of Office kept me waiting for thirty minutes. I sat outside his office. Then he showed up, a mid-forties guy, well-dressed in a charcoal pinstriped suit, a white shirt with French cuffs, and a big watch. He wasn't smiling, and he didn't greet me. "Hello," I said. He didn't reply. He raised his arm, as if aiming a pistol, and pointed it straight ahead. I walked, and he followed behind me, while I imagined a large bull's-eye on my back. A target for his bad attitude. Reflexively, I took a seat across from his enormous desk, which was littered with family photos. It made me wonder if I'd misjudged him; *Maybe he's a regular guy*. Still, I could feel a pulse beating in my ears; my blood pressure was rising.

The unnerving silence in the room and my roiling gut told me we were off to a bad start. My mind was crazily racing to find calm. Instead, it bumped into my worst enemy, my inner critic, who loudly whispered, *What are you doing here?* He abruptly broke the silence.

"Give me one good reason why I should hire a *woman* for this job?"

His question tripped me up, and I searched for a polite response. "A mix of men and women is good for business. Gender doesn't matter."

He didn't reply, but instead he looked down at his watch and glanced at his reflection in the window. "I find women join the firm, get pregnant, and leave. It's a waste of time to on-board people who don't put the company first." I sat quietly and waited for my opening. He leaned back and shook his head. "Women always want special treatment."

"By the way, how old are you?" he asked.

I took a moment.

"I don't think it's legal for you to ask me that question." His raised eyebrows told me it wasn't the answer he expected.

He eyed my résumé. "How did you get this experience? Do you use your charms, your appearance? Maybe it's the way you dress."

I looked down at my navy skirted suit and burgundy mid-heeled shoes, and primly folded my hands. I was losing my balance and my patience. I feigned a smile, while I searched for words.

He reached across his desk and toyed with a pen. *Click!* He sat back, and with a sly gaze fixed on the wall behind me, *click-click-click-click,* "Do-you-use-sex-to-get-ahead?" *Click-click-click-click-click.*

I was knocked on my back foot. The staccato from the pen was more obscene than the gesture. I was speechless, and I had no time to reply. He had a killer instinct and kept coming.

"Are you married?"

I looked down at my wedding ring to avoid making eye contact with him. "Yes, I'm married." I leaned back in my chair, rapidly blinking my eyes to avoid tears; *Act like a big girl.*

"Well, what are your plans for children?"

Finally, I found my voice. "IT'S NONE OF YOUR BUSINESS!" I was bubbling with rage, amid miserable reminders of my past ectopic pregnancy. The late-night pain in my abdomen. The midmorning trip with Jeff to the ER. The exams, palpations, and urgent looks on the faces of the doctors and nurses. My woeful surprise waking up in recovery, after a deeply invasive surgery saved my life.

I shook off my anger and stood up.

"This meeting was a huge mistake. I'm done answering your horrible questions."

He looked relieved; my outburst was exactly what he'd hoped for.

I walked out of the office and found my way back to the glass-enclosed elevator. Avoiding my sad reflection, I descended to the glitzy, garish lobby; *I hate this place. I'm outta here.* Pushing my way out of the revolving doors, I was furious and shaking as I walked back to my office to pack up for the day. On the way, I took a last-minute detour to the ladies' restroom, and I cloistered myself in a stall, sobbing. *What did I do to deserve such treatment?*

I calmed down on the bus and wrote up a transcript of the interview, and had it notarized the next morning, asking a lawyer friend to read it. He and one of his law partners gave me valuable free advice: "Teri, you have a case. But if you win, you'll get the job." It took a nanosecond to realize working there would be a losing bet. And traders know there are three ways to cut your losses. Sell your position. Hedge your bet. Or buy more, put more on the bet. More-on. Moron.

Mr. Head of Office was a fucking moron. "Thanks for the advice, guys—forget it!"

My second interview was with a firm at the opposite end of the spectrum, in both style and substance. I had a couple of days to recover from the stick fight, but I was wary. I thought about canceling the meeting.

On the morning of the interview, I knew exactly where I was going. I'd been walking by the building for years. It was modest, with a small bronze plaque hanging outside the entrance. Arriving early, I entered the building and advanced to the security kiosk. I was struck by the understated elegance of Carrera marble, antique bronze elevator doors, and the friendly security guard. He signed me in and gave me a pass to the fifth floor.

Stepping off the elevator, I glimpsed an atrium and a towering bamboo forest. I was transported by the greenery, the branches, the leaves swaying in the sunlight. It felt good, and I was tempted to strike a goddess pose. Balancing an image of the sun in my right hand, the moon in my left. An impromptu meditation to find strength to firm my balance, a few cooling breaths to calm my nerves: *Ommmm*. I took a seat, waiting for my appointment in the high temple of Boston's investment world. An antique grandfather clock quietly ticked away. Soft, low spotlights focused on the rare beauty of a statuesque Ming vase. All my senses were engaged by the elegant, hushed tones of cultivated good taste and opportunity. The aroma of old Boston money: modern artwork, tender orchids, an innovative spirit. The company was rocketing through space like a meteor. My new career would require diligence and patience, in hopes of auspicious good fortune.

My interview with the CFO was perfunctory, professional, no personal information or interests were discussed. No indelicate questions about my age, marital status, reproductive health, or comments on my sartorial point of view. Instead, "How would you describe your management style?"

I wasn't expecting the question. I blurted out, "Caring, compassionate."

He quickly looked up. "Nice; it's in short supply in this business."

A few days later I was offered the position of Compliance Director. I accepted it, banking on my trading experience, regulatory knowledge, and years-long work as an industry arbitrator resolving disputes after a major market meltdown. It was all about following the rules. I had this.

Several years and promotions later, I had major responsibilities and a large staff. My reproductive health was declining due to a large mass that was growing in my pelvis. My physician ordered me to bank blood for an upcoming surgery. Just in case of an emergency.

Discreetly and on a monthly basis, I slipped out of work to have my blood drawn. I squeezed a round stress ball and sipped orange juice. Afraid to confide in anyone at work about my covert maneuver, I concealed it from others, and to some degree from myself. The moron's words were still ringing in my ears: *Women always want special treatment.*

My doctor's precautionary directive was sound, but it didn't help on the day I needed it. I was away on business, presenting to a group of portfolio managers, who, by the way, generally didn't look forward to visits from the Compliance Director.

My flight to Dallas left late afternoon. The company put me up at the Four Seasons Hotel, so serene and comfortable after my long flight. Beautiful white orchids, luxe flowing draperies, a fluffy king-sized bed floating like a cumulous cloud. Exhausted, I fell into bed. Early the next morning, I woke with a start. I was freezing cold and saturated, lying in a pool of blood. The luxurious bedding was soaked, from the pristine white bedsheets and linen duvet to the layers underneath, all ruined. I resorted to using the fluffy white towels to staunch my bleeding. How will I get through my meetings? I was panicking. I should have called 9-1-1, but I didn't want to be "that woman."

Women always want special treatment.

I showered and patted myself off, carefully putting on my suit. I stuffed the last of the clean washcloths and hand towels into my briefcase and crossed my fingers. I was a former Girl Scout, and I usually traveled with a hygiene kit in my luggage. Still, despite my planning, I hadn't thought it necessary to pack an extra change of clothes.

Wandering around the room in shock, I thought it would be a good idea to get to the office before anyone else. To make sure I would be the first person in the conference room, and the last to leave. I took a taxi and arrived early, waiting for the portfolio managers to assemble. Once we had a quorum, I quickly opened the meeting, passing around the SEC guidance for mutual funds on the use of liquidity buffers in times of stress. Ironically, I too was stressed, and obsessed with remaining hydrated to avoid passing out during the meeting. Then there was the flight back to Boston…

Before checking out of the hotel, I frantically tried to tidy my room, but the exertion was complicating my situation. My room looked like a murder scene. I was mortified, and left a note of apology, plus a large tip for housekeeping. I gathered my things and went to speak with the hotel manager.

I stepped into the elevator and hit the down button. The floor was shiny, reflective, I gazed at it nervously, and exited the sliding doors. Approaching the front desk, a dark-haired, willowy, friendly front desk associate smiled at me. "Good morning!" she said. I was shivering, my temperature had plummeted, and I'd had no breakfast.

"Good morning," I stammered. "I'm checking out, but I had a problem in my room. I ruined it." Her kind smile and polite silence urged me to continue. "I have a medical condition and almost bled out in my room. I had to go to work, so I took some of the towels. I'm so sorry." She nodded her head as I continued. "I'm worried about the cost of the ruined sheets and towels appearing on my company credit card."

My mind was swirling over concerns about hotel damage charges, my meeting, my flight back to Boston, my expense report, and my need for secrecy. Especially my need for secrecy, since I rarely confided to friends, colleagues, or family about my health worries, past surgeries, and infertility. I was still living to disprove the motto; *Women always want special treatment.* Yet here I was, crying in a hotel lobby, tears streaming down my face, sharing personal information with kind strangers. The caring compassion of the hotel staff and management made a lasting impression on me. A lesson I never forgot as an innkeeper.

My flight landed at Logan Airport, and I flagged a taxi home. Jeff was in Malaysia on business. Earlier, I'd sent him an email to call me, but with the time zone difference it would take time to hear from him. I walked past the front door, ditched my luggage, and crawled into bed.

The next morning, I woke up with barely enough energy to get dressed for work. I drove to the parking garage diagonally across from my building and took a detour to the bamboo garden. I took a few deep breaths. I needed a friend, so I reached out to my soul brother Rich for advice—equal parts big brother, rabbi, and career counselor. He had time to meet me for lunch near his office on Chauncey Street. We met outside a deli, and he wrapped me in a rib-crushing bear hug. I clung to him; I didn't want to let go. After ordering turkey on rye, apple juice, and pretzels, we found a table.

"Hey, Richie, how are you?" I asked, but Rich had a knack for getting right to the heart of things.

"Listen, we can talk about me later. How are *you* doing?"

Tears were spilling all over my sandwich. "Richie, this week has been the worst. I'm a wreck. I'm stressed at work, my health is shot, Jeff's traveling, and I need to do something."

"Teri, you're doing too much for other people. You're always trying to fix things, employee problems, old houses. Have you thought about helping yourself?" I knew what he meant, but I didn't want to hear it. "Have you thought about going to counseling?" I hung my head at this notion. My experience with mental health was filtered through the lens of my mother's illness. A combo of heavy meds and electroshock therapy. I had trouble swallowing my pretzel.

"You and Jeff are living like crazy people. It's like the left hand doesn't know what the right hand is doing." His heartfelt assessment fell like an anvil on my head. I realized I was at a crossroads. My life plan, using work as a solution to distract myself from myself, was not working. I started counseling.

"Do you have any hobbies?" my therapist asked.

I shook my head. "My weekends are rest time at home, cleaning up, cooking, getting ready for the week ahead."

"What do you do for fun and relaxation?"

"Not much. I enjoy cooking, and taking long walks with our dogs. I used to dance and play the piano, but I don't have hobbies anymore."

We started meeting twice a week. But the time away from work was a luxury I couldn't afford.

After a while, she said, "Have you thought about taking a leave of absence from your job to take care of yourself?"

All I heard was a broken record: Women always want special treatment.

"No, no, no! I'd have to share my problems with everyone. That option is definitely out."

"Do you like poetry?" she asked.

I wasn't sure I'd heard the question, and it seemed beside the point. "Sure, I like poetry, and creative writing, I studied it in college." She recommended a few books, and I started reading poetry. Later, I began practicing yoga. She encouraged me to think about my life outside of work, a new path with an emphasis on living with purpose.

Still, I didn't have the courage to discuss my personal needs with the company. It was easier to resign with four weeks' notice. I loved my job, but I couldn't confide in anyone at work. The executive team was understanding but brutally honest, calling my decision to place out "a career-ending move." I was worried they were right, but I was stuck in the weeds on my path through the bamboo garden. And I failed to trust my colleagues would be understanding about my health challenges.

The announcement of my departure circulated. "Teri has been an exceptional manager. She will be sorely missed." My heart sank. The company held a going-away party, honoring me with a plaque with everyone's signature, a beautifully framed souvenir to mark the end of my brilliant career.

On the way home from the party, Jeff reassured me it would be OK to call it quits for a while. He encouraged me to do something completely different, to dive into a hobby. We talked about my going to culinary school. A fresh start.

The first few weeks at home were rough. I was anxious, and wanted to call the office, catch up on work chat, talk with my peeps. I resisted the urge, but it was difficult. I had to ready myself for surgery in May.

I submitted an application to attend a culinary school in Cambridge and forgot all about it. But through the application process, I was gently urged to think about why I was interested in a culinary career. Given my age, almost 40, my employment and earnings history, I learned the cost for the year-long chef program would not be the best financial investment. But it could offer me a fresh start, possibly a basis for a new career. Maybe innkeeping or writing books for cooks?

A few months earlier, Jan, my mother-in-law, informed us she would visit in early June. Despite our experience with her erratic, sometimes inebriated behavior, we agreed to host her visit. Two years prior, Jeff had spent weeks researching and booking a once-in-a-lifetime, nine-day trip to Ireland for her 65th birthday. He and I were pilot and co-pilot, merely on board to serve as chaperone and concierge. After an uneventful flight to Shannon, we rented a car and toured the magnificent environs of Adare, Ballylickey, heading south to Kinsale. The brown bread, scones, and fresh butter were wonderful.

One morning, our stay at a lovely guest house in County Cork was marred by Jan loudly referring to Irish locals as "Micks." Jeff was ashen—he'd written his college thesis on James Joyce. "Hey, Mom, it isn't polite to call Irish people Micks." His antennae started working overtime.

"What do you know, Jeff. I'm Irish too—we don't mind it." We couldn't wait to put her on a plane. Now she was planning a return visit to our home.

Jan arrived for a three-week stay with us while I was recuperating from surgery. The six-hour stint on the operating table had left me weak and hollowed-out. Dad had recently left, after staying for two weeks of sleeping in the guest room across from mine, helping me get out of bed, and meeting with the nurse and physical therapist when they visited while Jeff was at work.

Jan quickly made herself at home. She waltzed into the kitchen with her usual fanfare, sporting a red dye-job, a fresh manicure, and a lit cigarette.

"Hi, Jan, I'm in here," I said. I was propped up in the sunroom, resting and recuperating.

She spotted a coffee cup to deploy as an ashtray, and took a few steps to close the distance between us, her gaze fixed on me. She stood a few feet in front of me, pursed her lips, and took a long drag on her cigarette, blowing wisps of smoke in my direction. Cigarette ashes were tapped into the cup. "Tsk, tsk, tsk," she muttered, the cigarette bouncing on her lips. "Well!" She sighed. "I guess I won't be getting any grandkids out of you."

My mother-in-law's words cut like a knife, and even though I was thoroughly medicated, I was now hurting inside *and* out. Jan was true to form, plain old mean. Still, she'd outdone herself. My pain taught me a valuable lesson about hurtful, despicable people: *Let them go.*

Jan was never invited to visit again, and she earned a special distinction on this, her last visit. Jeff and I unanimously approved her admission to the DNB Club. A small, select group we later created for very special inn guests:

DNB—DO NOT BOOK.

CHAPTER FOUR

*Don't be satisfied with stories, how things have gone with others.
Unfold your own myth, so everyone will understand the passage.*
—Rumi

Opening Day

On May 12, 2004, the Boston Red Sox played the Cleveland Indians at home at Fenway Park. Although the team was fresh and healthy after a warm spring-training season in Fort Myers, the Red Sox lost the game 6 to 4. Still it was early season, the team getting back to business, while perennial rumors circulated this could be the year for the Red Sox to reverse the "Curse of the Bambino."

The superstition was a bad omen placed on the Sox after trading Babe Ruth to the New York Yankees in 1919. Red Sox fans blamed the curse as the reason the team hadn't won a World Series championship in 86 years. But in 2004, the Red Sox were hoping for a strong season and a championship playoff. And so were we.

Jeff and I had placed the largest wager of our life, betting everything we had on our prospects at the inn.

But we were far from fresh on opening day. We were worn out and exhausted from our grueling pre-season training with more than 150 days ahead of us until closing for the season.

Despite our fatigue, our early morning was playful. We slept in, knowing it would be our last morning to lounge in bed for many, many months. Our joyful romp was unexpected, given the relentless nonstop stress roller-coaster ride up, down, and around the "Inn from Hades." Dizzy with vertigo from the restoration, we were trying to calm down and relax, to act mellow and become the calm hosts we wanted to embody for our guests. But we were unsteady as we stepped off the crazy ride and needed to regain our balance to walk a straight line from the front office to the kitchen, to the dining room.

Mired in our expectations, we were hoping that the first season would start strong with an opening day of twenty guests, a full house, an audience of people to entertain one another. It didn't happen. We had a single booking for a seven-day stay.

Jeff and I wandered around the inn, up and down the staircases, pacing the first floor. Keeping watch on the front door, waiting for our opening day's only check-in.

Check-in is generally after 3:00 p.m., most guests arriving on time, or shortly thereafter. Jeff and I wanted to make a good first impression, so precisely at 2:45, all of the inn's lights were blazing, I removed my neck collar, and we were standing by. Sometime around 5:00, a silver Toyota rental car drove through the roundabout, then pulled out. "Where are they going?" Jeff asked. We watched as the car slowly came to a stop right in front of the walkway to the wheelchair ramp, instead of one of the many empty parking spaces along the privet hedge. Their car parked in the wrong direction. We didn't have proper signage in the lot.

The guests popped open the car trunk and began unloading luggage. We rushed to help them up the three granite steps to the inn. No sooner had they stepped to the front porch—"Hi! Welcome to the inn"—than Jeff and I eagerly raced them through the tour, the history of the inn, explaining breakfast was served from 8 to 9:30 a.m., wine hour at 6:00 p.m. Without allowing time for them to catch their breath.

In our haste, we didn't stop to realize they had traveled a long way, and we forgot to ask, "How was your journey?" A little caring and compassion at check-in would have been a good idea. It also might have given us notice that they had reservations for dinner at 5:30 at a local restaurant.

Jeff checked them in and showed them to their room. He and I looked at one another. "Now what do we do?"

I put my neck collar back on, and I started prepping for 6:00 wine hour, slicing and plating enough cheese and baguette for a small army, decanting wine into two carafes. While busy with my prep, I glimpsed out the window as our solo booking stepped out the front door and headed off to Main Street. "Jeff, where are they going?" I cried. "What did we do wrong?"

With our single booking out the door, there was no need for wine or snacks. One of us remembered it was turn-down time. Turn-down is a service amenity for evening housekeeping. Turning on room lights, changing towels, ice delivery, remaking the bed, removing dirty dishes. But it's also the innkeeper's opportunity to put the room in order.

Even though we knew they were out to dinner, we knocked on the door and announced ourselves: "Housekeeping." Jeff opened the door with the innkeeper's master key, and the two of us stepped in, feeling a little paranoid. We'd entered the tabernacle of their private chapel. And we were also curious to check on the condition of the room. EVERYTHING was new: walls, bathroom, mattresses, pillows, coverlets, sheets and towels, all in pristine condition. Fortunately, our guests were neat, the room unsullied. I picked up a wet washcloth and threw it in a bag, thinking, *How did we get here?* We remade the bed, turned on the bedside lights, locked the door, and left.

We spent the next several hours keeping an eagle eye out for the return of the guests. Finally, they returned. We quietly hovered from a distance, like raptors watching prey as they moved from the front porch, to the library, to the lounge. Lighting from room to room, taking turns sitting in each chair, in every room. We stayed just out of sight.

"Now what do we do?" I asked Jeff. Betty would have said, "It's time for you to do a little breakfast prep for tomorrow, and leave these poor people alone." Jeff had a better idea. "Let's eat dinner!"

Prior to innkeeping, our evening routine was leisurely, a home-cooked meal, a glass of wine, listening to music and chatting. We were not accustomed to the front desk bell ringing, along with the front door chiming "Hail, Hail, the Gang's All Here."

"Who the hell can that be?" Jeff said, while taking dinner out of the oven.

"I'll check." I poked my head out of the kitchen. "We have a couple of looky-loos on the porch. Should I offer them a discount?"

"Only if they ask." Jeff said.

Established inns in Bar Harbor rarely have vacancies in season. Most inns are booked from May to October, and the No Vacancy signs keep looky-loos at bay. Since we had few bookings, the vacancy sign was a beacon.

"Hi, I'm Teri, the innkeeper, can I help you?"

"We were out to dinner and asked the waiter for ideas where we could get a room tonight. You folks look like you might have something."

They were right about that—with one car in the parking lot, it was a good bet.

"How much do you charge for a room?"

"$225 per night."

"Huh, forget it! No way—I'd never pay that much to stay anywhere."

The exchange was discouraging. So, instead of fielding more guest prospects that night, we hung the No Vacancy sign with only two guests in the house. A white flag of surrender, signaling our defeat. As opening day wrapped up, we forgot to celebrate. We felt like the walking dead, and crept to our crypt for the night.

Breakfast Is Served

The next morning, our two guests took a window table, sitting quietly, hoping someone would say "Good morning" and serve breakfast. DJ Jeff queued the "morning muffins" playlist, but we were missing in action. No menu. No muffins.

Hospitality 101 had taught us it's a good idea to plan breakfast and set the tables the night before service. Our dining tables looked beautiful, with white table linens and flowers for twenty guests. But we'd prepped nothing for breakfast—nada. We were scurrying around the kitchen, appalled at our lack of preparation. Still in shock and confused after the Restoration Vortex, I hadn't cracked open my recipe files. And, after falling through the floor, I was wearing a padded neck collar and had trouble looking down. We decided Jeff would become the pinch-hitter breakfast chef, and I would serve in the dining room, sans collar.

While making coffee, I printed a menu card with breakfast ideas we'd cobbled together.

"Good morning! Would you like coffee or tea this morning?" I placed the card on the table.

WELCOME!
GRAND OPENING MENU
Blueberry corn griddlecakes,
applewood smoked bacon, Maine maple syrup
First-of-the-season asparagus, shiitake mushroom frittata (GF)
House-made granola, Greek yogurt, berries

One of the guests said, "You don't need to go through this for the two of us."

"Yeah, we don't eat that much." They smiled as I poured the coffee. "Why don't we tell you the night before what we would like so it will be easier." A good idea that had never occurred to me.

They are so sweet, I thought, trying not to look down to spare my injured neck.

I was worried my chin-up expression came off as aloof, so I overexplained that we were in start-up mode, it wasn't any bother, any day we would be far busier. Yep…any day. They read the menu card and ordered breakfast.

I slowly walked to the kitchen, careful not to look down, hoping there were no more obstacles in my path. Passing down the hall, I caught a glimpse of my exhausted self in the tall mirror. *How did I get here?* Shaking my head (slowly), I swung the kitchen door open with my hip, and the chaos in the kitchen smacked me between the eyes.

Heaps of flour, sugar, and eggshells flew everywhere. Mixing bowls, spoons, and spatulas were strewn across every surface. Juice carafes, containers of yogurt, mounds of blueberries, sat on the counter, with several berries rolling across the floor.

"What's wrong with us? I was so nervous out there!" I cried. "We can't even handle a two-top for breakfast!"

Jeff was doing his best, but the neck collar had strangled my judgment. The frittatas and griddlecakes looked beautiful. "Thank God we don't have twenty guests!" Jeff said. Breakfast was supposed to be as easy as ABC. Instead, we gave our performance a D+. We didn't study, didn't prep, and it took us all day to complete the exam.

Fortunately, we remembered one of our lessons from Hospitality 101: The guests are always right—so we took their suggestion, offering a simpler menu during their stay, rather than a multiple-choice quiz, and asked that they give us the answers the night before. Learn as you go; we were quick studies, and with a little bit of practice, our breakfast stats improved quickly.

Help Wanted

As the early days were wearing away at us, guest occupancy started to grow, and we were counting the minutes until our student workers arrived. They would need a ride from Boston. We later learned this was their first trip outside of their home country and the first time they'd flown in a jet. It was doubly important that we pick them up and greet them with a welcoming face.

With Jeff remaining at the inn, I drove to the airport and arrived with a handwritten sign. Our meeting in the Arrivals Hall was awkward; language issues and jet lag made our encounters difficult at first, but after we loaded their bags into the rental van and got back on the highway for the five-hour return trip to the inn, the students relaxed. Exhausted, they slept most of the way.

The students started work on the third day after their arrival. Since there weren't many bookings until high season in mid-June, we found projects to keep them motivated and compensated. We organized painting of the new fence and outdoor Adirondack chairs. The young women were team players; they donned work shirts and aprons and got busy. One of the students, detecting something not quite right, insouciantly asked, "So…what do you think you are trying to accomplish?" But business started to pick up, and the students began their housekeeping training. Their work experience in small European hotels had prepared them well for our aspirations. Betty, our Assistant Innkeeper, marveled at their job performance, attitude and cheerfulness. "These young ladies are amazing," she said. We grinned with relief. "Don't get used to it."

Happily, that year we were fortunate. And we did get used to it.

Doctor in the House

Jeff received a reservation request described as a "doctor and a colleague on a research writing retreat." We Googled the Doc's credentials: ivy-league, first-rate hospital affiliation, and his sizable deposit was processed without a hitch. An excellent booking.

- Two one-week bookings, full rack rate
- Two expensive rooms
- Two guests at breakfast instead of four

We assumed the Doc and patient were conducting business at a world-renowned scientific institution located in Bar Harbor. "Nice to have a doctor in the house." We couldn't wait to meet him. Later, we wondered if we were off our meds accepting the two-room, seven-night booking when a wacky doctor and teenaged patient arrived at the inn's front door.

Surprisingly, he arrived disheveled and a little smelly, his lumbering, sullen teenaged protégé shuffling along behind him. I welcomed them with, "How was the drive from New York?" I wasn't sure if they heard me. There was no reply. I figured…he's probably tired.

We checked them into two of our best king rooms. The luggage was standard, unexceptional except for two large Samurai swords in leather cases, blades sheathed, silver handles protruding. They took the keys and headed up the staircase to the rooms. Doc said, "I'd prefer no housekeeping during our stay. We'll be working." Uh-oh, not a good omen. Housekeeping is not only a service to please the guest. It's also the way innkeepers keep tabs on the condition of the room. And the swords!

At breakfast the next morning, Doc arrived alone; the other guy was nowhere in sight. Since no housekeeping was requested, we didn't have a clue regarding the condition of our rooms, or the status of his traveling companion. Was he still sleeping? dead or alive? was he breathing?

Over a period of days, Doc arrived alone for breakfast. He then invited a stream of unregistered guests to join him. While we were rookies, this struck us as odd. Where was his companion? Was he eating? Was he alive?

Jeff and I were concerned, as Doc didn't appear to care about his no-show friend. We offered to freshen the room towels, and he agreed. The housekeeper entered the room and found the patient—dead asleep—on the bed. Pill bottles were strewn across the bureau. The combo of heavy meds and occupied, unmade bed, was a sorry sight. "Thank goodness only one more night," we said.

That afternoon, Doc and his tranquilized companion repaired to the garden, Samurai swords tucked into waistbands. Doc's sweatshirt was covered in food stains and tied around his waist. He stretched out in the grass, then rose to his feet, swinging his sword high overhead, a few slow turns, slicing the air in wide arcs, chanting. Was this some type of counseling ritual?

Guests from the inn watched bemused, if not alarmed, from the library. We tried to look on the bright side. Maybe he was practicing alternative therapies. Nah—he might have been incompetent. That night, all was quiet. A good sign, no screaming.

Early the next morning they ate breakfast together—a first! Doc was in a hurry and asked to settle his room charges ASAP. He paid the substantial bill for the week's long stay with a credit card. They left.

Jeff gave a signal to the housekeeping team to turn over the guest rooms. Not knowing the condition, we figured there was plenty of time to get the rooms ready for 3:00 p.m. check-in.

Within minutes, housekeeper Martina raced to the front desk. She was hysterical, in tears. "I cannot believe what happened to Room 2. They were animals." She motioned for us to see the damage for ourselves.

Jeff and I went first to the Doc's suite, Room 4. As I approached the door, I suddenly flashed back to the details of the breaking and entering that had taken place at our first apartment in Boston. Late one afternoon, we returned home to find the door ajar. A stiff breeze wafted into the apartment from a window next to the fire escape. As I stepped in, I saw the contents of our dressers, desk, and closets strewn on the floor. Apparently, someone was keeping an eye on the new kids in town. The same feeling of violation reared its head again.

Jeff turned the key in the lock, opening the door. The shades were drawn, the room dank, dark, unhygienic. The bedding was an unholy mess of sheets, blankets, and pillowcases soiled with food stains, crumbs, and smears. The room's mirrors, décor, and artwork were placed on the floor, turned backward. Filthy towels were thrown over chairs and sink and stashed in the tub. The room was sullied, but the condition was not terminal.

We moved on to the other room. Stepping on feathers strewn at our feet, the patient making a pointed statement about his stay, stabbing and slashing the bedding, pillows, and leather settee with a Samurai sword. Pillowy guts spilled over the floor; the chairs were inscribed Zorro-fashion. Hardbound book covers were torn and defaced. The damage was so extreme there was not enough time to remediate the room by 3:00. Jeff tallied up the damages and the lost room revenue and charged the Doc's Amex card preemptively to cover large repair bills and lost business. At last, taking room photos in case of a challenge, we locked the door.

Jeff called Doc's office: "The doctor isn't accepting phone calls." Instead, Doc later called to complain that his credit card had been hit with the damage charges. Doc argued with Jeff, shouted F-bombs. "I'm going to sue you!" he said.

"Good luck finding an attorney in Manhattan to take a $1,500 case. If you don't like it, challenge the charges." Jeff was livid but unfazed. We had the photos.

Doc did challenge the charges, but he lost. The credit card company sided with us. Like a good loser, Doc was sanguine. "I'll just pass along the damage charges to the kid's Dr. Daddy." Then he apologized.

Jeff and I promised each other: The next time a doctor brought sharp instruments to the inn, we'd cut him off first. Or ask for a couple of aspirin. We'll call *you* in the morning.

Family Matters

After moving to Boston, Jeff and I threw our lot in with the corporate world. Sometimes I felt like a fish out of water, but I became an expert swimmer in a pool of sharks. But my family mantra, "Be Your Own Boss," was often repeated as our pledge of the American Dream. But Jeff and I had no idea what the phrase actually meant until the inn was open for business. Then we quickly learned.

Being Your Own Boss required a different set of life skills than we'd mastered in the deep end of the corporate pool, offering few to no lifelines if you became too weak to swim. It meant gaining the stamina and discipline to provide a caring, high-quality guest experience each and every day. Plus, meeting the challenge of finding friendly, like-minded people who wanted to work with us, leaving us with extra time to fret our sleepless nights together, tossing and turning over who, what, or when something might go wrong.

So, when Jeff and I had drifted down from corporate life and came to the fork in the road, we took the one less traveled. And it got lonely out there. To stay connected with friends and family, we sometimes offered them free guest nights if we could. This was often fun for everyone: They would enjoy the inn free of charge, and we would get feedback while being able to spend time with them. A good trade.

We missed our close friend Rich, my "big brother," rabbi, and career counselor, who by then had moved from Boston to San Francisco. He was one of our first Friend and Family guests, arriving in late September of our first season. He was a discriminating, very fussy traveler, and we valued his opinion. When his car arrived in the roundabout, I nearly cartwheeled to greet him. We swept him off the front porch and escorted him to his guest room. His first reaction was, "Wow, you guys did it."

"Yes, we certainly did it," Jeff replied. We were still figuring out the *why* part of that response, but we were getting good at running the inn.

"Does my room have blackout curtains?" Rich asked. Yes! We remembered Rich was a night owl, staying up until one or two a.m. And Maine sunrise arrives early during the summer, sometimes as early as 4:30 a.m.

"Is there an iron in my room?" Yes! We patted ourselves on the back. Remembering to buy irons and ironing boards during the amenity circuit/training event during boot camp.

"Do you have a pillow menu?" Uhhhhh…we hadn't thought of that. Apparently, pillow menus were the rage in California; who knew?

"Do you stock condoms in the butler's bureau?" Nope. It was getting a little too personal for us at that point. We figured the guests would arrive primed for foreplay. This line of questioning reminded Jeff of his favorite innkeeper joke.

"Rich, two ducks meet for a date. They become intimate and book a room at an inn. The duck calls down to the front desk to ask about a condom. The innkeeper asks if he can put it on his bill. The duck says, 'What kind of a duck do you think I am?'" Rich rolled his eyes in my direction.

Early autumn is a wonderful time to visit Acadia National Park—warm sunny days and cool, crisp evenings. And during Rich's visit we took time off to hike up Acadia Mountain. It felt good to be away from the inn, enjoying a change of scenery, nature, and fresh air. So much was finally making sense.

At seminars we were told, "First priority, buy a solid, going concern. Second priority, you need to love your inn. You'll be spending most of your life there." The instructors were right. Jeff and I infrequently left the inn. We were too worried something might go wrong if we weren't around.

Dad booked the next Friend and Family visit, arriving after his birthday in mid-October. He was impressed with the inn's commercial kitchen. "This reminds me of mornings at Snappy Joe's. Grandma was at work by three a.m.; Grandpa and I followed later. God, it was hard work," he said. Thanks, Dad, *now* you tell me.

"Teri, would it be OK for me to have breakfast in my room tomorrow? I don't like to eat early."

"Sure, I'll bring it up. What'll you have?"

"You know what I like—a couple of cinnamon rolls, coffee, and scrambled eggs."

The next morning, after serving the last of the guests, I prepared Dad's breakfast tray, picking up extra cinnamon buns for us to share before heading to his room.

Standing outside his door, "Knock-knock," I said, and he sang out, "Who goes there?"

"It's the Ice Man," I said.

"Well, Ice Man, cometh!" he chuckled. It was one of Dad's favorite jokes. He enjoyed stints in community theater, and had performed one of the leads in the play *The Ice Man Cometh*, written by Eugene O'Neill. Another story of dreams, illusions, and grandiose plans. Dad was usually cast in the role of Harry Hope, a bartender who hasn't left his bar in twenty years. I now felt I was cast as his understudy, rehearsing the lines of the same script.

I walked into the room, setting the breakfast tray on the bedside table. After giving me a hug, Dad took a few sips of coffee and a bite of the pastry. "Teri, these cinnamon buns are out of this world! Where did you learn to bake like this?"

"From you and Grandma," I said, choking on my emotions. I turned my head to hide my sad and bitter feelings from the Restoration Vortex. I wiped a few tears on my sleeve and opened a window for some fresh air. Dad could read my mind.

"What's the matter, honey?" he asked.

"It's nothing Dad, we're doing OK."

"You don't look OK."

"I'm just tired."

Yes, I was tired. But the truth hurt so much more. I wanted to say, "Dad, we've made a huge mistake. What are we going to do? I'm scared. What do you think we should do?"

I was desperate to share my feelings with him because Jeff, the other inn mate serving time with me, didn't need or want to hear it. Still, as much as I wanted to put my head on Dad's shoulder and cry my eyes out, I held back. I knew the truth would frighten him. Instead, we drank our coffee and he took my hand.

"I miss you, Dad. Can you visit us here every year?"

"I'm not sure I can, Teri. I don't like to see you working this hard, and I don't want to see you get hurt."

Thank goodness I didn't share my worries with him. And it was a good thing I'd left my neck collar in the kitchen.

Double Vision

By late October, the first operating season was thankfully winding down. The dwindling light and cooler temperatures seemed a harbinger of fall, yet the sun was still warm.

In the garden and along Shore Path, the beach roses were replaced by beach plums that hung heavily on the branches. Chickadees were flitting in the birch trees. The last of the flowering summersweet played host to bees bouncing on the branches. Hummingbirds flew in circles, seemingly weightless. Despite the delights of the late fall garden, Bar Harbor's parking lots and attractions were still buzzing, the *beep, beep, beep* of tour buses counting down the days, hours, and minutes until the village would close for the season.

Most inns in Bar Harbor close sometime around Columbus Day. We hoped to remain open until Halloween to capture the last dwindling dregs of late-season bookings to help us make our numbers. It didn't help much.

We planned to stay open through the Thanksgiving and Christmas holidays. But now we were hanging around a vacant property, and the faucet of guest bookings had shut off. Not a trickle of reservations. Remaining open was simply not a profitable option. Our quaint beautiful village, and the inn, would be closed until May.

The last guest of the season had a question before checking out. "I took a few photos of the inn last night. Do you see the rainbow-colored auras?"

"Yes," I said, but her question had fallen on dead, tired ears.

"The auras carry energy from people who passed away," she said.

Paranormal ideas, auras, or spirit anomalies had never crossed our minds. But in theory they seemed to explain the occasional thump, or the mysterious opening of doors that occasionally caused us to do a double take. We associated objects going bump in the night with late-returning guests. But the auras did seem to explain a few things.

One night, midseason, well after 3:00 a.m., a webcam in the foyer was tripped. An ethereal dancer, an elderly guest, had tiptoed away from her room. She slowly descended the center hall staircase and stopped in front of the imposing hall mirror. The sconce and overhead lighting were low, in soft focus, the Exit signs loomed overhead in blood-red. She closely examined her face in the wavering light and smiled at herself. Then she curtsied in her nightie and began waltzing in circles. Head tilted back, arms extended like a ballerina Baby Jane, spinning a web of dreams.

While we waited for the arrival of the plumbers to drain the pipes, we too courted visions of shadows climbing up and down the staircases and wondered if someone or something was lurking around corners. As the night music of the inn ruffled the fabric shrouds covering the furniture, they cast a ghostly appearance beneath the red emergency lights glowing in the dark. Closing time was way overdue.

It took the plumbers only a few hours to shut the mechanicals down for the cold winter to come. The system was engineered to a single shut-off valve in the basement. An apt metaphor for our first season performance: draining.

First season bookings were encouraging, but any earnings from operations were washed away by four five-figure seasonal loan payments. The Bank was unquestionably our most valuable cheerleader and business partner, who secured a loan with a government guarantee to cover the $500,000 funding gap from the Restoration

Vortex. We calculated it would take at least a season or two for us to reach break-even. The Bank gave us a heads-up to expect an official visitor.

Just in time for Halloween, we met a pleasant middle-aged dude dressed in a snug three-piece suit and sporting a mullet haircut. While touring the inn, he was complimentary about the property. He quizzed us about the inn's bookings, ADR, and operating ratios. Jeff had all of the answers. "I'm happy to see you've done your homework," he commented, further requesting financial reporting on a quarterly basis. He made it clear we didn't own the inn, the draperies and curtains, the furniture, or the appliances. And the presence of another financial overseer tempered the encouragement we garnered from fellow innkeepers, 5-star reviews, and reservations for the next year.

"So, what are you planning to do until next May?" he asked.

Jeff and I looked at each other, wondering, *What is he trying to tell us?* We knew we needed money to clean up our act, but we were up to our elbows with remedial punch-list items from the inn's restoration. The construction contract stipulated a six-month window for reporting defects. And despite our best efforts, some simple basic functions were not working as expected. Some of the defects required remedial action when we were open for business.

Hospitality 101 requires an inn's front door to open and shut properly. But our front door was improperly installed; visitors couldn't operate it easily. We'd had guests knocking at the door after midnight if they couldn't open it. Or the door wouldn't close. Swinging open without warning, the door beckoned to Archie—the inn's lovable Airedale terrier—to head to Albert Meadow for solo midday antique-store dog-crawls.

During rainstorms there was water, water everywhere. The living room ceiling still had a mysterious leak, and rainwater coursed down the outside walls, breaching seals on the fire escapes and the new basement windows, which were not weathertight, necessitating blue tarps, buckets, and fish tubs to collect rainwater. Very unsightly for guests, and unacceptable to us. As were the poor placements of

HVAC temperature controls, which made it difficult for us to heat and cool the inn to guest satisfaction.

Jeff hired a second contractor to trouble-shoot the problems and contacted former construction crew members for information they might have to assist us.

"Yeah, the wrong people were assigned to work on key aspects of the job."

"Some of the guys didn't know what they were doing."

"One guy said he wanted to just get paid and not show up."

We built a fact set of the construction defects and employee statements in support of "failure to perform" clauses in the contract. But after partial remediation, we gave up. We were cross-eyed with exhaustion, and tired of the renovation rodeo, so we resolved to walk away. We later learned The Builder went bankrupt, and any and all warranties were null and void. On Halloween night, we finally closed for the season. And decided one of us had to go back to Boston and get a job.

Trick or Treat!

Holiday Letter

Dear Family and Friends,

So here we sit writing a holiday letter as Archie the inn dog gnaws a chair leg. A lot has happened over the past two years, and we're here to answer the tough questions:

"Where did Jeff and Teri go?"

"What are they doing?"

"Have they lost their minds?"

Jeff and Teri spent May to November running our hospitality business in scenic Bar Harbor. The inn enjoyed its first season. We welcomed hundreds of wonderful guests from around the world.

The life of an innkeeper is busy and unpredictable. There were days we looked back wistfully at those all-day corporate meetings and business trips. But we're very proud of the inn and how it has been received. Onward.

Some of you may know that Teri, the other erstwhile innkeeper, took a sabbatical from her career and went to cooking school, followed by a stint in the kitchen of a top-rated restaurant. Teri did an amazing job decorating the inn and setting the menu, but her old financial services career came calling. Well, she's proven you *can* go back again! Just when we thought she was out, she was pulled back in!

Teri will be returning to Boston as a vice president in a new job. On most weekends she'll be heading to Bar Harbor, where Jeff will be doing the innkeeping thing by himself. Since he'll be the sole helmsman on deck, Jeff hired a new Assistant Innkeeper, Susan. She's an avid hiker, a nature lover who loves yoga, music, and books. With her dark curly hair, she could pass as Teri's sister!

We wonder if the guests will notice?

Jeff had an idea to improve communications called Front Desk Notes, an attempt to keep the crew on course 24/7. Once a product guy, always a product guy! So don't be surprised if amusing anecdotes start showing up in future holiday letters!

Finally, in addition to the inn, and our cottage in Downeast Maine, we've moved into an outpost in Boston. Sounds relaxing? No.

So we hope we've answered some of your questions. You now know where we are. What we're doing. And we're convinced you must think we are indeed nuts.

Please accept our best wishes for the holidays, a prosperous new year, and peace on earth. Stay in touch—or better yet, come visit us at the inn in Bar Harbor!

Check-in time is 3:00 p.m.

PART THREE

CHAPTER FIVE

If you are irritated by every rub, how will your mirror be polished?
—Rumi

Front Desk Notes

Susan,

Today's arrivals checked in without incident; sweet guests traveling from Switzerland and a family of four from Asheville, North Carolina. The Campbells arrived without a reservation the night before last. We had an unexpected two-night vacancy in Room 2. The scheduled guests had canceled their stay due to the heavy rain. I put out the Vacancy sign.

A camper van drove into the gravel parking lot. Rain splashed against the fender wells, sending small waves into the bushes. Once parked, they fought to get into rain ponchos and ran into the inn, seeking cover on the front porch. Soaked, and dripping with rain, they were happy to learn the room was available. Price seemed to be the least of their concerns. I helped with their backpacks and showed them to the room. "This beats sleeping on wet ground," Mr. Campbell said. "We've spent the last four days huddled under a leaky tent. I'm dying to take a hot shower."

Later, they joined the other guests for Wine O'clock and snacks in the lounge. This morning, they were delightful at breakfast, and seemed happy. "We loved spending two warm, dry nights here at the inn. Everything has been perfect!" They were all smiles at check-out, and so were we. They gave us some news when they returned the key at check-out.

Mr. Campbell said quietly, leaning over the desk, "We had a great stay, but we had a small problem in our room." I was all ears.

"I had a small mishap opening a bottle of red wine. It splashed a little, but we fixed it. We didn't have the heart to mention it until now."

I sent Vera up to take a look, fearing the red wine stains had set. She immediately scampered back down the stairs.

"Jeff, the campers sprayed red wine all over the room! It's on the bed, the carpet, and curtains. What are we going to do?"

Vera laundered the coverlets and drapes, but the stains didn't budge. The fabric was stained and ruined. I shampooed the carpet, and it's soaked. We're taking Room 2 out of service tomorrow. No good deed goes unpunished.

Naturally, we've added the Campbells to the DO NOT BOOK list.

FYI—Teri just called. Traffic out of Boston is still heavy, and she's running late. Don't wait up.

Meet Your Innkeeper

Jeff's summers spent on the coast of Maine count as some of the best days of his life. Waking up to views of the rocky coastline, sometimes fog lurking on the horizon. He kept busy sailing and working two jobs to save money for college—a day job at the Sundial Inn on Kennebunk Beach and an evening job waiting and bussing tables at a local restaurant in nearby Kennebunkport. Good on-the-job training to learn skills to navigate the high-tension wire between adolescence and independence.

One night, a group of guys with flat-tops and loud sport coats made fun of Jeff's long hair. "Geezum, looky here, Jesus is pouring water."

Jeff raised his voice. "Stop bothering me. I'm making minimum wage. I'm not paid to take your abuse." The dining room broke out in applause.

Growing up in Connecticut, Jeff was the eldest of three siblings, and a friend to a sometimes incontinent dachshund named Heidi.

Jeff's father's dignified cool collided with his Mom's feisty heat, creating squalls of hostility and chaos. The angst was often ignited by alcohol. Grandmother Edie, known to family as Nan, was the firm yet gentle guiding hand during times the temperature or tempers at home flared up. Jeff sought refuge in music and books.

One fraught summer, Jeff moved out of the house. He couldn't wait to graduate from high school and claim his life. Fortunately, his great-grandmother had left funds for his education. Now living the underage bachelor life, he buckled down at work and play, gaining an insider's view of the hospitality lifestyle, hanging out with college-aged waiters and chefs. Most of the jobs were seasonal, June to September, the friendships short-lived, many of them forged in the camaraderie of hot kitchens and dining rooms, and they quickly cooled off by Columbus Weekend.

Jeff was devoted to his college studies and took a gig as a DJ. He loved the one-way communication of broadcasting, creating a mood, telling a story, without criticism or interruptions. Working college and commercial AM/FM radio gigs, he was on the air most days, spinning music at parties, exploring his new musical favorites. He entertained thoughts of a broadcasting career, but only briefly. Most radio DJs didn't make much money. Jeff graduated from Middlebury College with a BA in English Literature. Tucked his passport into his backpack and bought a Eurail Pass for a grand tour of Europe. Returning to the US, he landed in Ann Arbor, where his parents had lived and finally divorced. He was surrounded by the Great Lakes, far from his New England roots.

Jeff and I met at work, both of us working retail jobs. We went to lunch a few times and got to know each other better at his girlfriend's birthday party. She was older than Jeff and wanted to get married. He wasn't ready. He asked me to write my phone number on a piece of paper, and he secretly tucked it into his wallet. Three months later we moved in together. The following year, we decided to make plans to find our way in the world. Jeff decided to work toward a professional career in high tech and took a job as a technical writer, hoping to one day get a marketing job in Boston or New York. My work and college plans were vague. So together we hit the highway to Boston.

Two years later, a warm February day of skiing in Vermont turned freezing cold after dark. Jeff was alone driving home to Marblehead, where we lived. His ski trip to Mad River with a few friends was, in part, a celebration of his new job at Lotus Development Corporation in Cambridge, Massachusetts. He'd given notice at his then current job. Meanwhile, I remained home prepping for spring midterms. Jeff had a few good days skiing, and called to say he was coming home early. He missed me.

According to the police report, his car slid on black ice, crossing the center line. The driver's side of the car buckled around a utility pole, sending the vehicle ricocheting, spinning, zigzagging across the icy pavement and finally plunging headfirst into the Waitsfield River. Fortunately, it was partially frozen—an ice floe prevented him from drowning.

The impact tore the driver's seat off track and left Jeff's feet jammed under the gas pedal and brake, pinning his legs under the dash. The rest of his body was thrown, laid out supine, slumped in the backseat. Barely conscious, he was found by a Vermont state trooper who climbed into the car next to him, yelling in his face to bring him around. "What's your name? Do you know your social security number? What's your telephone number?"

Jeff gave the officer our home telephone number, then passed out. The EMTs put him on a body board, rushing him to a small local hospital in Barre, then immediately on to UVM medical center in Burlington—STAT. I got the call sometime before midnight.

"Hello, this is the Barre, Vermont, police department. Can we speak with Jeff Anderholm's parents?"

"Jeff's parents? They don't live here. Can I help you, what's going on?"

"There's been a car accident. We're trying to reach Jeff Anderholm's next of kin."

"Is Jeff all right? What happened?"

"Who are you to Jeff?"

"Well, I'm his girlfriend; actually we live together, sort of like a fiancée."

"Jeff was in his car, caught up on an ice floe in the Waitsfield River. Somebody coming home from work at Blue Cross/Blue Shield was five minutes behind him and called it in. He was rescued and is being transported to University of Vermont Medical Center in Burlington. He's one lucky guy."

"What's his condition?"

"He has lacerations, that's all we know."

I was flustered, not knowing what to do. "Should I drive to Burlington now?"

"No, don't come tonight, it's late. Besides, only immediate family members will be permitted at the hospital."

His comment took me aback; after all, Jeff and I *were* family. Still, after living with him for four years, I'd never met his father.

"Can you help us out and notify his parents?"

I said, "I would, if I knew how to reach them. I'll call his sister." I called Liz and gave her the news. That was Thursday night.

The next morning, my girlfriend Karen and I drove to Burlington. During the four-hour car ride, my thoughts drifted to my brother Paul's accident. He was struck by a car one morning when we were walking to school. He was eight, I was ten. It was snowing heavily when we left the house for the eight-block walk to St. Joseph's Elementary School. We were running a little late, and the nuns frowned on tardiness. We paused at the corner and waited for the light to change from red to green. The light turned yellow, and Paul dropped my hand and shot into the street. The impact of the passing car tossed him into the air, and he landed on the pavement next to the rear wheel of a truck. The driver looked down at me from the window and shouted, "Go get your mother!" I raced home in the slushy snow, my footfalls heavy, like running in quicksand. I was worried the accident was my fault…a feeling that crept up on me as Karen slowed the car at a traffic light. I roused myself out of my accidental memories. But by the time we got to the hospital, visitors' hours were over. Jeff was still unconscious in the ICU. I wouldn't be permitted to see him until the next day.

On Saturday morning, I checked in with the head nurse. "I'm here to see my boyfriend Jeff."

"You're not a family member."

"No, but we live together. Has anyone from his family been here?"

"No, not yet," she said.

His sister Liz and I had been in contact. She caught a flight from Florida and told me to expect visits from Jeff's divorced parents, who hadn't seen each other in five years.

"Would it be OK for me to see him?"

"Sure, go ahead."

I walked slowly into the dark, beeping, tenuous calm of the ICU, and found his room. I paused outside the door, afraid to enter, then I stood next to his bed. Jeff was naked, a light drape covering his loins and pelvis. He drowsed under warm overhead lights. Pressure was swelling his brain, he had dislocated his hip, broken many ribs, his pelvis and his face had been crushed. His lower jaw was split in two. His prognosis was uncertain. The doctors thought it was better to wait a few days before tending to his injuries so that he could stabilize and gain strength. I brought photographs of him, so the doctors would know what his face looked like before the accident.

My fingertips lightly touched his hand, and he woke up. "Hi, Jeff, it's me. Do you know where you are?"

"Hospital," he managed with his broken jaw.

"Do you know what happened?"

"Car accident."

"Jeff, your mom and dad are on their way to see you." He didn't respond, only nodding his head slightly, his eyes moving rapidly from side to side. I was concerned he might be in shock and wanted to comfort him. "I love you, Jeff. You're going to be OK."

"I love you, too," he said. Then he fell back to sleep.

When he woke up again, he seemed unaware of his traumatized condition, but he did notice there was a phone in his hospital room. "Teri, call Lotus. Tell them I'll be at work Monday." Still in shock, his brain swollen, broken jaw not set.

I said, "Hon, you won't be able to start your new job Monday."

He became agitated, eyes darting rapidly, worrying someone else would get his dream job.

Inn Mates

A little later, I spoke with the recruiter, and Lotus HR hatched a plan and held his job until he could make it in to start it. Offered to extend health insurance and short-term disability payments if the old company wouldn't cover him, despite the fact he hadn't worked a single day.

His parents arrived and stayed the weekend. They soon left, and they didn't visit again. Jeff was on his own and remained in the hospital for more than a month. I was able to take off two weeks from my college studies and work, finding a Good Samaritan who offered me housing in Vermont, then I visited weekends. Jeff spent most of his time alone.

A month later, Jeff was checked out of the hospital on a cold, crisp morning in mid-March. Bright sunlight was glancing across the snowbanks, making him squint as he walked along on crutches to the taxi. It was a short drive to the airport. I'd made plans to fly him home on a small commuter airline, knowing the four-hour drive would be too uncomfortable. He folded himself gingerly into the taxi, then into a seat at the front of the airplane. Rough turbulence caused excruciating pain due to his pelvic injury. Thankfully, it was short flight.

When we landed in Boston, friends picked us up in a balloon-filled station wagon. Jeff was able to stretch out and rest in the backseat. They helped him up the three flights of stairs to our apartment. It was time to celebrate! Jeff sipped juice through a straw. It would be four more weeks before he'd be able to eat solid food.

Jeff's grandmother Nan was scheduled to stay for a few weeks to help out. I was worried about leaving Jeff alone during the day. With his broken jaw wired closed, the hospital issued a pair of wire cutters, to be kept on his bedside table. Just in case of emergency. Fortunately, they were never needed. A few weeks later, Jeff started his new job walking with a cane, and his jaws still wired shut.

At Lotus, becoming one of the top software companies in the world was as easy as 1-2-3. Good Karma. And Jeff never forgot the kindness he experienced. He was determined to do well after recovering from his accident. How could he ever repay the generosity he had received? Thus, his career pursuits became central to his life. His confidence and self-image derived from work. His career was more than a job; it was an identity, a family. My career helped me to manage the financial anxiety I'd grown up with and was a form of self-expression. But our careers pulled us in opposite directions, and there were times we were isolated and lonely.

At Christmas, many years later, Jeff sifted through old photos sent from a friend. He sat quietly, staring at the images of his younger self with work friends and colleagues, basking in the limelight, standing in the shadow of genius. Flooded by memories of presenting with Steve Jobs in front of thousands in San Francisco. Hoping to reinvent the business world one desktop at a time. After twelve years, these once-in-a-lifetime moments came to an end. The Lotus era ended. It was time for Jeff to move on.

Jeff cycled through a few tech start-ups, discovering that most corporate cultures did not resemble the new normal he had gotten used to at Lotus. He became discouraged by corporate politics, infighting, and posturing. Although he was dismayed, he kept plugging along. He turned his head when the young CEO showed up at an all-hands meeting wearing a cape and flaunting the company logo painted on his toenails.

In 2001, Jeff was a senior vice president of marketing for a Boston-area software firm when he had an epiphany. He was in London, at a conference making a speech after long red-eye flight. When he looked up from his text he noticed a crowd of sleepy attendees wearing raincoats. He thought, *What am I doing with my life?* I found him back in the hotel sitting in the dark, nursing a drink from the mini-bar. He was contemplating his next move.

Jeff's company was acquiring another small company. He had an opportunity to leave with a golden parachute. But in reality, he was pushed out the door after he helped close the acquisition he identified. Assembled on stage, the new executive team was introduced as he sat in the audience as a spectator. The CEO mentioned Jeff as an embarrassing afterthought, and invited him onstage. The investment bankers gave the new executive team bottles of Dom Perignon. Jeff, whose merger and acquisition strategy was relabeled with the investment bank's logo, didn't get the gift of champagne. One of the other execs regretted the oversight and gave Jeff his Dom. At that point, Jeff had had enough. It was time to wave goodbye to his former job and career. Then he contacted an attorney, and a severance deal was hammered out.

Ultimately, Jeff and I each realized that a job is only a job. It's not a family, nor an identity. And we learned important lessons. Hope for the best, prepare for the worst. Keep your options open. Don't forget to have both Plan A and Plan B. Because, in the wisdom of one former heavyweight boxing champ, "Everyone has a plan, until they get punched in the face."

Two years later, we christened the inn with the Dom Perignon.

Inn Mates

In 2005, the inn was still in start-up mode. Jeff and I needed to take extreme measures to keep it afloat until it became profitable. We organized two work details. Jeff agreed to run the inn alone. I would return to Boston and work until I could afford to come home. We were handcuffed to unshakable financial commitments at the inn. All of our energy, hopes, and dreams had been swept away in the Restoration Vortex. We'd committed our life savings to buy and restart the inn, *and* we were on the hook for the terms of a million-plus commercial loan. Twenty years of hard time, and no parole. The contract felt like a life sentence, plain and simple, the agreement inked in black and white, the collateral held by The Bank. Failure wasn't an option.

Before opening for the second season, I took a week's vacation from my Boston gig to help Jeff get up to speed running the inn by himself. His first few weeks were like sailing singlehandedly over the Atlantic during hurricane season. All senses set to high alert, eyes and ears primed for unusual events, sounds or utterances indicative of doom—like staff no-shows.

As a solo innkeeper, Jeff needed an experienced and dedicated crew to help him run the inn. So with reservations piling up, the recruiting season started early, continued through the operating season, and extended into the off-season. And in Maine, where the tourist business is seasonal by nature (many inns are only open May–October), it's doubly difficult to staff. And most innkeepers can't offer year-round employment, so workers look elsewhere. To add to the difficulty, affordable year-round housing in most resort destinations is next to impossible to find. It was a vexing and continual business problem to solve. And no two seasons are alike.

To head off hiring problems, we joined up with an organization that offered study-abroad programs for international students. The company played matchmaker between employers and students relying on the timely issuance of work and travel visas to permit their employment and temporary residency. A lot of moving parts—the recruiter, the student, the government, and the innkeeper. The hiring need was the only constant; all of the other factors needed to be managed, influenced, and cajoled by the inn owner.

Imagine you're the owner of a ten-room inn, striving to book every room, every day. A happy problem, an extended house party for six hundred invitees monthly. All invited guests plan to stay overnight, expecting breakfast, noontime snacks, and a wine tasting event every single day, May through October. And you have only one permanent, full-time staff. Jeff, working alone at the inn. Teri, the other innkeeper, was working a desk job in Boston.

Jeff promoted our summer jobs as industry training for students in hospitality and travel programs. We treated the inn like a business and sought to treat our staff as respected professionals. This meant orientation for the incoming students, written policies and procedures, and early-season kickoff meetings, plus periodic pizza parties and guaranteed housing. Fortunately, we had many candidates.

Shortly thereafter, three students contacted Jeff by email: two sisters, Vera and Mariana from Bulgaria, and another young woman from Romania. Typically, the student emails read:

> Good Afternoon, we are looking forward to coming to work in Bar Harbor for the summer. Then we want to go to California and Miami.

Jeff sent the students copies of the job descriptions, and an offer letter, which outlined wages, tips, and a rent-free living situation for the summer. They were responsible for their airfare to Boston. Jeff and I breathed a sigh of relief. This portion of our staffing equation was solved. He then hired a full-time Assistant Innkeeper, and a part-time back-up to act as our proxy, who would work afternoons and evenings—locals, who were able to provide guests reliable information about Bar Harbor and Acadia National Park.

Jeff left me a voice mail at work. "Teri, the students are arriving at the airport in Boston on Friday, Can you pick them up?"

"No problem. I'll get them on my way to Bar Harbor."

Three women were traveling together on a flight from Paris. I had a small compact car and rented a minivan for the trip. I fashioned a sign out of cardboard—"Bar Harbor"—parked the van, and headed for the Arrivals gate. Soon, three sleepy-looking young women dressed in youthful Euro-fashion (tight skinny jeans, T-shirts, and black leather jackets) waved to me. I waved back, and they walked in my direction, rearranging their cross-body bags over their shoulders, smoothing their hair, and dragging their suitcases with them.

I was worried whether we'd be able to communicate. I knew they spoke some English, but I didn't speak Bulgarian or Romanian. I decided to try out my cobbled greeting with Katia.

"Buona sera, Katia. Mi chiamo Teri." Good evening; my name is Teri.

"Hi, it's nice to meet you, too. I'm Katia."

"And I'm Vera; this my sister Mariana."

All spoke perfect English. I sighed a breath of relief. "Is it OK if we all speak English?" I said.

"Da," said Katia, nodding her head.

"Si," said the sisters, shaking their heads. All of us laughing about our new nonverbal vocabulary. Vera said, "It's OK; we shake our heads when we say yes. She nods her head when she says yes. It means same."

We walked to the parking lot, loaded the luggage into the van, and they climbed in, exhausted from their flights. "Ladies, it's a five-hour drive to Bar Harbor. Are you hungry?"

"No, voda," Mariana mumbled sleepily.

Vera translated. "She wants water."

I passed out the Poland Spring bottles I'd brought for the trip. "We'll leave the airport and I'll stop for a rest in Kennebunk on the turnpike." They were already asleep.

My weekly trips between Boston and Bar Harbor were already a well-worn rut, the route etched indelibly on my mind. Usually, I'd tank up on gas and water in Kennebunk, often not stopping until I reached Bar Harbor. Tonight's weekend traffic was moving along well. I pulled off the main highway to the rest stop.

"Ladies, wake up—time for a break."

They jolted awake, yawning, crawling out of the car toward the front doors. Amid the aroma of coffee and cookies, I turned to find them among the many in a long line of customers at McDonald's. Suddenly, they were famished. Vera took a spot at the rear of the line to the counter. I stood by closely to listen in, in case she needed assistance. She placed her order.

"Did they get your order right?"

"Oh yes, I always eat four cheeseburgers."

Katia and Mariana ordered burgers and French fries. I had a large coffee to make sure I'd be alert for the long drive ahead.

As we drove past the outskirts of a former mill town, Katia asked, "Why are there so many American flags at that house?"

Some of the flags were accompanied by spray-painted scrawl about no government, more guns, and live free or die. I said I'd explain it all later. They quickly figured it out for themselves. They asked questions about Miami, Las Vegas, and New York City, but were happy to be working in Bar Harbor, a quaint, small, New England village. A safe first step in the United States. They fell back to sleep.

We got to the inn at 10:30 p.m. Jeff greeted us at the back door and showed them to their bedrooms. They shared a kitchen, a separate bathroom and shower, and a laundry area. Jeff said, "Have a good night's sleep. We'll have a team meeting tomorrow afternoon."

The next morning, we kept our ears open for our new staff members, remaining available to serve them breakfast, but they were late sleepers. Later in the afternoon, Jeff gathered everyone into the lounge to introduce the three newcomers to the inn's regular staff: a breakfast cook, a standby Assistant Innkeeper who covered Susan's day off, and a part-time housekeeper who was filling in from a large hotel. The regulars would train the students for their jobs.

Everyone was excited, a little nervous as Jeff introduced everyone. He passed around pages from the guest information booklet with background about the inn. Then he handed out the L.L. Bean polo shirts embroidered with the inn's name and logo, which they would wear while working so guests would recognize employees if they needed assistance.

Jeff kicked off the meeting:

"Welcome to the inn. Teri and I are happy you're here! We're going to talk about what you can expect, and then we'll answer your questions." Our new arrivals were giggling, nodding and shaking their heads.

"Our motto at the inn is to be friendly, clean, and complete. 'Complete' means to exceed our guests' expectations. It's our most important goal."

All heads were nodding and shaking. "Yes, Si, Da!" Everyone was speaking the same language.

Jeff continued, "Guests who visit the inn are important. While we are working, doing housekeeping, resetting the dining room, or washing dishes, the guests always come first. If a guest rings the bell at the front desk, or the doorbell, or asks for help, remember the guest is not an interruption of our work, he or she is the purpose of our work."

"Yes, Si, Da!"

"All guests deserve the most courteous and attentive treatment we can provide. Smiling is important!" Smiles all around, more laughing.

I piped up, "We will all make mistakes from time to time, we know it, even when we try to do our best. So we'll spend ninety-eight percent of our time trying to improve the two percent which needs to be better."

Jeff and I were on a roll, drinking in the positive energy from the smiling crew. We felt we were the luckiest innkeepers in Bar Harbor.

"And remember, everyone's job at the inn is important, we're a team. If something doesn't seem right to you, it's probably not right. Let's work together to fix it, tell somebody about it, or ask for help."

"OK, Boss!" they said in unison.

Amazed by their enthusiasm, Jeff was ready to wrap it up. "I have an important question for all of you to think about." He paused for dramatic effect. The crew waited quietly. Soon they were on the edge of their seats. Jeff was holding out for the punchline. "Does everyone here like pizza?"

The team broke out in hysterics, rolling around, nearly falling out of their seats.

Jeff ended on a high note. "We're happy you're members of our team this year! Any questions?"

None were offered, meeting adjourned.

The team was fired up and gave Jeff a standing ovation. They couldn't wait to start working. But their first workday was the next day, and we encouraged them to take a stroll around the village to get some fresh air and relax.

The next day, the motivation from Jeff's all-hands meeting was still palpable. However, we heard commotion in the kitchen and ducked in to check it out. There was trouble brewing between the housekeeper and the standby Assistant Innkeeper, Chas. He was a slightly nervous, buttoned-down perfectionist. One of his responsibilities was to check each guest room before afternoon arrivals.

"Chas is an OCD jerk, he's driving me crazy! Look at the fucking list of complaints he gave me!"

Assistant Innkeeper Check List Before Guest Arrivals:

Room One:	Clip the threads on the right pillowcase.
Room Two:	Replace the bathmat, it's not fluffy.
Room Three:	Replace the water glasses, they all have spots.
Room Four:	The toilet paper is rolled in the wrong direction.
Room Five:	The remote control had a smudge.
Room Six:	The picture frame is tilted too much to the right.

Room Seven:	There was a strand of hair on the floor of the bathroom. IT'S DISGUSTING!
Room Eight:	The shampoo and conditioner bottles in the shower have the labels facing in the wrong direction.
Room Nine:	The water carafes all need more ice.
Room Ten:	Perfect! Nice Job!

Our part-time OCD Assistant Innkeeper was in many ways a blessing, more than a curse, although his fussiness did cause occasional cursing by members of the team. We valued Chas, but occasionally we had to remind him that even he was not perfect, Jeff coaching him on his phobia about shaking hands with guests and mistakenly serving spaghetti sauce to the inn guests during wine hour. Jeff's attempts to moderate the dispute failed. The housekeeper quit on the spot.

The next day, Sunday afternoon, I got back on the highway to return the van at the airport, get my car, and return to my Boston apartment. Jeff and I chatted several times during the day and that night. Both of us were tired and lonely. We would bide our time during the workweek until we could be together for the weekend. I'd usually arrive late Friday night, crawling into bed to give Jeff a hug while he slept. Jeff's alarm was set for 5:45 a.m.

Late mornings, as the inn hummed along, Riley, the inn dog, and I took field trips to Long Pond, where we sat along the banks of Jordan Stream under a cobblestone bridge. Riley would scramble down the steep banks of the hillside and lie on a flat rock in the water. Lapping up his free time, running the banks chasing sticks. The music of water rushing over the rocks was a balm for our spirits.

Afterward, I drove to the inn to visit with staff and guests. Jeff's shift ended midafternoon. We'd return to our cottage and take a long nap together, make dinner, relax, hoping there were no inn problems to resolve, then early bedtime. On Sunday morning at 5:45 a.m., our conjugal visit was over. Both of us had to get back to work. I'd climb aboard a bus or a train, or drive to Boston, listening to Garrison Keillor spin tales of a simpler time in lovely Lake Woebegone on

Prairie Home Companion. Dad called them the "good old days." Yes, Dad, I'm sure they were.

At the end of the season, we celebrated, hosting a goodbye party with pizza and cookies. We asked the staff if they liked working at the inn. One of them said with Eastern European zest, "It wasn't too horrible." Well, that's one way of putting it.

After the long work season, they hit the road, looking for adventure in the US and South America. We received postcards. They traveled to Miami, flew to Peru, climbed Machu Pichu, and feasted on guinea pig. One of the postcards read, "It wasn't too horrible. See you next year!"

Same time.

Same place.

Same routine.

Pray for no calamities.

Five years passed in the blink of an eye.

Work Release

It was 6:45 p.m. when I rolled out of Boston. My weekly commute to Bar Harbor was getting old. The roads were rain-slicked, and traffic on Route 1 was stop-and-go. I opened a water bottle, took a bite out of a turkey sandwich left over from a lunch meeting. I leaned my head on the car window, *How did I get here?* It was a good question, and not new.

I had to remind myself I was lucky to have a job. I was a legacy player who thought the heavy bronze doors of my career had clanged shut. Permanently. Then a former colleague called. "Are you up for a consulting gig at twice your old salary?" That was an easy question. An interview was scheduled, and I bought a ticket on a train to Boston.

A few nights before the interview, I laundered my innkeeping duds while digging out a few business outfits. I found an old Max Mara suit I had bought at Filene's Basement. The charcoal-gray pencil skirt, matching jacket, three blouses, and pants, were hanging off of me after my rigorous eighteen-month innkeeping marathon. Packing all of it into a large overnight bag, I was traveling light and would be staying with friends in South Boston.

Jeff gave me a lift to Portland. We spent the night before my departure at an inn. A busman's holiday. Early the next morning, I caught the Amtrack Downeaster train to North Station. We kissed goodbye and I waved to him as he drove off.

I stepped onto the train and took a seat by the window. The conductor punched my ticket as I glanced at my reflection in the window. I closed my eyes, drifting back to an earlier time. Recalling my former career. The fear I had about sharing my medical worries, and my fear of being judged.

Women always want special treatment.

I was deep in my reverie, half asleep, as the Downeaster chugged into Boston and slowed to a stop. I stepped out into the hubbub of the city, miles away from the pine forests and granite shores of Bar Harbor. The walk along Canal Street to the financial district, a few blocks from my old office, snapped me to attention. Soon, I'd be only a few steps away from the whispering bamboo garden.

I entered the building and checked in with security. I was given a generic security badge. The guard pointed to the elevator. The elevator doors opened and I got in, but it didn't move. The technology to operate the doors had changed, like so much else. Then the elevator went up, but the doors didn't open. Now I was hanging between floors, watching CNBC on the monitor. Someone called for the elevator, again. This time the door opened, and a man got on. He looked at me askance. I watched as he swiped his badge. He was going to the same floor, and I tailgated him to get to my appointment. I pushed open the frosted glass doors to the room for my meeting. Suddenly I was in a cerulean dream. Cool blue walls, warm sand carpeting, tart citrus-colored furnishings, suffused tones of lime green, orange, and turquoise. Gone were the former soldier tones of dingy gray, navy blue, and drab beige.

I took a deep breath and tried to relax. *Maybe today will be my day in the sun.* But I knew better, I'd been here before and knew what to expect. Hopefully, a fresh start in a new job, and probably a few disappointments along the way.

I waited for my interview, glancing down at my suit. Did I still look the part, or was I a relic from another era? I fretted about the questions that might come up. How would I explain my gap in employment? My home address is Bar Harbor. Where was I living in Boston? *Details, details, details,* but after all Jeff and I had been through, we were desperate to right our financial ship. There was nothing I couldn't or wouldn't do.

The interview was easy. I was eligible for rehire, the company reissued my old ID number, and gave me a badge. I read and signed an engagement letter, and my contract started immediately. I quietly walked through the corridors, catching glimpses of a few familiar faces.

"Where have YOU been?"

"It's great to see you!"

"You were the best manager I ever had!"

I decided my elevator pitch was not:

"Jeff and I have been throwing thousand-dollar bills into a hole the ground."

"I've been pouring coffee while wearing a padded neck collar."

All of which were true. Instead my new elevator pitch went like this:

"I went to culinary school."

"Jeff and I started a business."

"Who knows, maybe I'll get my old job back."

The conventional wisdom says never burn your bridges, and I didn't think I had. But it did occur to me that I may have left a few smoldering embers in my wake. I mentally prepared for a run-in with a few troublemakers.

Among my old group, word soon spread of my return. Some thought I was dead; a few wished I had died; one or two hoped I'd stay around for a while. It was awkward working for people who previously would have been working for me. I decided to keep a low profile, and strove to not call attention to myself. And it was tough being away from Jeff. I slept on a friend's sofa for four weeks.

Despite my discomfort flying in a corporate boomerang, I hunkered down at work, and found an apartment in South Boston. A place where Jeff and I and our dog Riley could live together while the inn was closed for the season. The first six months of consulting salved our financial wounds considerably. Ahhh, the benefits of corporate life. A healthy, regular paycheck, a generous benefits plan, and weekends off.

Jeff worked remotely, responding to guest phone calls, emails, and reservations, gathering bookings and processing deposits for the upcoming second season. And sadly, we agreed it would be necessary for me to score a full-time job for several more years. The inn hadn't reached break-even, and we were deeply underwater. It just wasn't possible to recoup our seven-figure investment and pay back the seven-figure commercial loan we had. We couldn't walk away. Jeff and I were inn mates, on separate work details, in different states. I was in Massachusetts, and he was in Maine.

I started interviewing for a permanent role in my company and explored positions graded lower than my former job. The reality of my career downsizing was soul-crushing. So it was timely when a competing firm offered me a job with a VP title and a window office. I gave my manager, a woman who thrived on making employees cry, two weeks' notice. "How can you do this after all I have done for you?" I was ashamed, embarrassed to tell the truth, again. Back in the day, my fragile physical health was my guarded secret. This time, my financial health was code blue.

Within eighteen months I cleared a path from VP to Chief Compliance Officer at a new firm, which offered me a hefty signing bonus. It was a godsend for us. I accepted the job and wondered why the firm had courted me so actively. It turned out that some members of this boys' club were rude and impolite. "Your job is to talk less and listen more." Except my job was corporate cheerleader, leading cheers and pep rallies to educate employees about the ethical rules of the investment game. A few of the team players intended to have field day with me. "We understand you report to the Board, plus you're a woman. Too bad you can't be fired." I tunneled into myself and cringed as the needle skipped across the same sad, old record:

> Women always want special treatment.

So, after slogging through corporate life while owning the inn and commuting thousands of miles each year to alleviate our family separation, I was discouraged to face another market downturn in 2010. The big soap bubble I'd been clinging to was likely going to burst. "Teri, times are tough; we're cutting your department budget and eliminating their bonuses. You need to lay off a few staff."

But my team was like family. In fact, very young families with two working parents and small children at home. I confided in Jeff. After five years, we were doing well enough to allow me to come home, return to the inn, and unscramble our life. So I made the decision to fire myself, handing my letter of resignation to the Board. Jeff and I would double down to make the inn even more successful. And two innkeepers would definitely be better than one.

Goodbye corporate life, fancy perks, all-expense-paid business trips to Bermuda, Dublin, London, and Milan. *Arrivederci* profit-sharing, health and life insurance. I packed my boxes and called security for an escort. The guys brought a hand truck and wheeled the contents into the elevator and down to the lobby.

Out in the street, Jeff waited in the inn's pickup truck, exhausting relief from the tailpipe. I shed a tear as I had the last time I stood in the street like this. *Here I go again. Another self-inflicted gunshot wound to the career.* Thank goodness I had my MA in innkeeping and PhD in edifice complex to fall back on.

PART FOUR

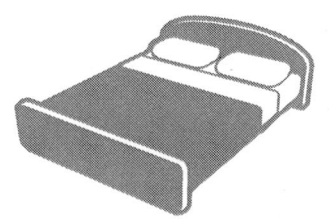

CHAPTER SIX

*Out beyond ideas of wrong-doing and right-doing, there is a field.
I will meet you there.*
—Rumi

Front Desk Notes

Susan,

Thanks for your help preparing for opening day. Teri and I finished painting the entry hall, library, and lounge late last night. We think the results are spectacular! Please be on the lookout for paint drips we might have missed.

The guest folios are all ready for today's check-ins. We're only one room short of a full house. We've left flowers and personal notes for the returning guests. I'll be around tonight if you need assistance. Teri's going to try to get the paint out of her hair before tomorrow morning.

Have fun.

Early Riser

When I returned to the inn full-time, my job description was "early riser." The first on deck to get the party started.

My alarm rang at 5:45. I got dressed, putting on the clothing I'd picked out the night before. My innkeeper uniform: jeans, boat-neck three-quarter-sleeve T-shirt, sneakers. During my corporate days, I showered before work. Now I took my shower after work, to wash off the powdered sugar, chocolate, and other remnants of the workday. Fortunately, I was able to remove the last traces of paint from my hair and hands. I climbed the back staircase to the kitchen.

The brass knob on the kitchen door was cold. May in Maine, the weather is still chilly. The gas ovens needed twenty minutes to get up to temp. I switched on the first-floor lights, unlocked the front door, and went back behind the kitchen doors. I loaded coffee into the pots and watched the fragrant steam waft across the kitchen, filling the Guest Pantry. I heard footsteps from guest early risers passing back and forth outside the kitchen doors. Early-morning hikers. Meanwhile, I remained safely backstage, preparing for the breakfast performance. Curtain time is 8:00 a.m.

I strolled through the Guest Pantry, the place where guests helped themselves to beverages, baked goodies, and fruit overnight—the after party.

There can be a wide range of stuff left behind by late-night revelers. High season guests left wine glasses, champagne bottles, restaurant to-go containers. Low season guests preferred to eat in, leaving stacks of empty pizza boxes, packages of lunchmeat, and tallboys in the guest fridge. Empty alcohol "nips" tossed in the trash often missed the target and were later found strewn on the floor. Still, I had plenty of time to get the area shipshape before the guests started dropping in. I hoped. The warm and seductive aroma of hot brewing coffee had lured more guests, who were now wandering the floors. I stayed out of sight.

At 7:00 a.m., I unlocked the back-kitchen door for the kitchen staff. Perfect timing. Our Caribbean-based kitchen team, Lincoln and Janine, sous chef and baker, were in the house. Tossing on chef jackets and aprons, they were experts at turning out warm deliciousness from the oven. The Wolf commercial range was cranked up, the griddle sizzling. The duo took turns flipping hot, crispy bacon. I backstopped, serving iced coffee. Lincoln gave me a fist pump; Janine and I, a hip bump.

The back door was shut hard. Bang!

Vera and Sara, two student workers from Bulgaria, stormed into the kitchen. Last year, they were strangers. This year, they're BFF twins from different mothers, tying back their raven hair, putting on aprons, and high-fiving. Flying high on the after-effects of the after-hours party they'd just left. Their reward for working double shifts all over town for two weeks.

"HELLO!"

"I AM HERE, BOSS!"

"I LOVE YOU, BOSS!"

Their exuberance was infectious. I greeted them. *"Dobro utro—kaki si?"* Good morning—how are you?

They replied, in unison. *"Dobre sum!"* I'm fine!

Vera wrote a few Bulgarian phrases on the kitchen whiteboard. Our attempts to learn a few words in their language was a complement to their excellent English.

"Vera, how was the party last night?" I asked.

"It was fine—we had new drink—it's called Sex on Beach. Have you heard of that?"

"Yes, Vera, I've heard of sex on the beach, but I didn't know you could drink it!"

"Yes, I really liked it. Then we had Grasshoppers," she said as she kicked open the kitchen's swinging door, carrying a heavy bamboo tray loaded with glassware, carafes, and pitchers of coffee cream. The door noisily swung back and forth.

Shush-ing each other, the servers raced to the dining room. I felt like singing "Hail, Hail, the Gang's All Here." And everyone was here on time. The inn's engine was revving up for the day.

A typical morning.

Guest early risers gathered in small groups on the sunporch, in the lounge or the library to enjoy a cup of tea or coffee before breakfast. The mood of these folks and our interactions at this early hour set the tone for the rest of the day. Many were now strolling past the French doors to the dining room, selecting their tables in the dining room. All seats are general admission. A few guests were anxious, hoping to score the prime tables by the windows. All tables for two.

These days, inn guests are independent-minded, traveling with a significant other or their friends. Often, they are resistant to socializing with strangers during the early morning hours. As a result, very social guests want to hang around with the innkeepers. We love the attention, we're flattered! But we need to remind them and ourselves that we'll soon have twenty guests converging in the dining room. If necessary, we may need to "kill with kindness" any impulse to socialize with guests while we're working. And please, stay out of the kitchen.

Much of the inn's work is performed during the early hours. Baking, breakfast prep, cooking, then expediting entrées. Or, if we have downtime, planning afternoon snacks, washing prep dishes, placing food orders, or chilling wine for evening service. Under such busy circumstances, we might say something hasty to a guest, like "Heads-up!" or "Behind you!" Kitchen lingo for "get out of the way."

While the breakfast countdown clock was loudly ticking, the orange poppyseed scones were cooling. Mushrooms were sautéed for omelets, challah bathed in eggs, cream, and cinnamon for Creme Brûlée French Toast. Only a few minutes before 8:00 a.m. The curtain was about to go up.

I bumped into Pauline, our head housekeeper, an impressive, statuesque Jamaican woman. She ruled over the other housekeepers with her wit and casual vibe. Hanging with us in the kitchen, she helped herself to double shots of hot cocoa and a fistful of carrots, her favorite morning snack. A few sips and nibbles before heading to the laundry area on the second floor, which she nicknamed "The Queen's Office." She was truly royal, one of the most vital members of the staff.

She picked up her clipboard and flipped through the pages of the housekeeping report. "We have five check-outs and five stay-overs. Has anyone checked out yet?" she asked.

"No, Pauline, we haven't even served breakfast!"

"I ran into Susan after she locked up last night. She mentioned we'll have two rooms leaving right after breakfast. I came in early to get a head start on the day. This job is more relaxing than yoga!"

At 8:00 a.m.—sharp—I walked out of the kitchen. It wasn't the best time for me to be cornered in the Guest Pantry by a good-looking, goofy guy staying in Room 10.

"Did you think I was mean yesterday when I didn't respond to your good-morning?" he asked.

I shook my head. "No, some guests aren't morning people."

"Well, I was kinda jet-lagged. I didn't mean to be rude. How about a do-over?"

I gave him a nod. *OK, you go first...maybe it's the coffee?*

Now he can't stop talking, and I'm needed in the dining room.

"What do you think about Hillary Clinton?"

"Did you know, the island of St. Croix was once held by the Knights of Malta?"

"I'm a big fan of Pinot Noir, I'm from Napa."

I smiled, nodded, and looked at my watch, hoping my body language would give him a hint. I was trying to be polite.

"How long have you been married?" he said, and I'm thinking, *Here we go again.* "Why don't you and your husband have any kids?"

"Who's going to inherit this place?" he asked.

Where did he get this information? I shrugged it off.

I was searching for the STOP button on a bad memory loop. The one about a moron who didn't know when to stop asking personal questions. The broken record started playing anyway...

Women always want special treatment.

I turned around; it was time to end the conversation and double-check the common areas before breakfast. To make sure the music and props were ready before the innkeepers walked on stage.

Duty Calls

Earlier in the morning, I had removed my shoes and quietly padded around the inn's first floor. Turning on lights, unlocking doors, checking exit ways. Picking up books and magazines left by guests. Gathering up empty teacups and plates, I returned to the kitchen to put my shoes back on for final inspection. Checking the condition of the public restroom—especially before breakfast. It was up to us to ensure guests were not surprised and inconvenienced when entering a common area that has been "uncommonly" occupied.

For some reason, freaky occurrences tend to happen at night under the cover of darkness. Some people leave their private room to enjoy a moving experience in a public space. Like newlyweds, who may be shy about their privacy habits, often running down the stairs in pj's, finding they have to wait outside the door. Occupied.

Who could forget the guest who didn't return to his room after taking his turn in the restroom. Jeff found him fast asleep, shirt and shoes off, sacked out on one of the library's leather sofas. Why did he leave his room? Maybe he lost a bet with his significant other. Or maybe, because the inn's Wi-Fi is excellent, the free-range guest had been surfing a porn site. Or practicing meditation, or making a private phone call.

On one early inspection, I found the restroom stripped. Only the toilet and sink were intact. The window was open, and the mirror, artwork, towels, and toiletry supplies were all missing. If the walls could have spoken, maybe I'd have had a clue to help me figure out what had happened. Instead, I was puzzled; *Where is everything?* But the clock was ticking, mere minutes before breakfast service, and I was working on a deadline—searching the storage areas for a wall mirror, tissues, and towel replacements to get the restroom back in shape by 8:00 a.m. One year later, we stumbled on the answer during spring cleaning, finding the mirror and most of the other items hidden in a tight space between a wall and a tall, heavy bookcase.

So ask yourself: If you were away from home and had an urgent matter. If you visited the public restroom and found an overnight drama, a whodunit, had taken place. And all of the artwork was missing, the mirrors were removed, all of the toilet paper and towels were gone. Wouldn't you want the innkeeper to come along to tidy up the situation? But we ask only one thing: Please remain seated for the entire performance.

Show Time

Breakfast is innkeeper performance art. The cast, audience, and menu change daily. Jeff's our director on front desk, busy with guest registration. He lets us know which guests are entering, which guests are exiting, stage-managing the moments before the curtain slowly rises in the dining room.

My role is to double-check the names of the guests, make sure the lights are set, fireplaces lit, flowers arranged, soft music playing. My co-stars, the servers, are on cue pouring coffee, taking food orders, chatting with guests. I take a few breaths, thinking good thoughts, remaining present, thinking positive, as I step to center stage in front of a full house. All of us have our fingers crossed that the guests are in the mood to be nourished and entertained. Let the show begin.

I approach each table, "Good morning! Welcome to the inn. I'm the innkeeper."

Usually the response is, "Good morning! Nice to meet you. Thank you." Yes—we're off to a good start!

Breakfast is often the time guests ask for the innkeeper's assistance planning details for the upcoming day, "Where should I hike and have lunch?" "Can you book dinner reservations for me? I'm going kayaking and won't have my phone."

Meanwhile, last night's midnight check-in straggles into the dining room. "Can you help me track down my lost luggage?"

It takes finely honed skills to be service-oriented and sincere while serving twenty guests, seven days a week, month after month. So many details, remembering guests' names, where they're from, who has special diets, food allergies. Who's checking out. "Thank you for staying with us."

"You're welcome, we had a great stay. We need to check out right away. Can you give us directions to Quebec City?"

Meanwhile, guests at other tables are discussing the inn, their rooms, the weather, Wi-Fi, and cell service in front of a captive audience. "We stay here every year. The food is amazing! Teri, can I have a copy of this recipe?"

The breakfast juggling act is challenging, and fun, but running an inn isn't all glamour. It takes sure-footedness and balance, which, admittedly, can be tough if there's a wiseguy in the house. "Hey—

what did you used to do before you started pouring coffee for a living?" Let's hear it for the breakfast heckler. Rather than respond, I act like I'm hard of hearing, in support of my mantra, *Let it go*.

I approached table 9. "Good morning, welcome to the inn."

Silence.

No acknowledgment.

No eye contact.

I guess the guests forgot their lines. There was no response, just two blank faces staring at two smartphones.

I had to remind myself to breathe while wondering if a new drama was going to unfold. Still, I'm pretty confident in my acting skills, which are now second nature. I've also learned how to improvise. But I become flustered by guests who identify as harsh critics. People who are grumpy, implacable, and dangerous when seated next to other guests.

One former guest had a sharp axe to grind. "Does this sausage contain caramel color? If it does, get rid of it, I can't eat it." And another guest, who just loved dishing up drama. "I told *you people*, I only drink decaf!"

Wow! If I run into someone like that, don't blame me for going off script. I'm waiting for my smiling survival skills to kick into gear, sending a subtle, nonverbal message: *Don't mess with me.*

All innkeepers recall situations when nothing will satisfy the mean, vicious guest, as in, "This village is not as nice as it used to be, too many tourists *spoiled* it!" And the times we have done our best, and the guest is still ranting. "I *hate* whipped cream! Take this away!"

If this happens, I go silent, smiling, nodding reassuringly, signaling that I understand the guest's need to vent. Unless they attempt to rudely cross a cultural divide. "Where do all of these foreigners come from? Why don't they learn *English!*"

I'll suspend judgment for only a brief second while the guest's inner child loudly explores intense feelings about fellow travelers. I'm simply waiting for the perfect time to teach an ethics lesson. "At this inn, we're global citizens. We happily welcome guests from around the world." I love the stunned silence of their reply.

When an innkeeper has to manage a difficult, imperious guest in the company of others, the companionship of kind guests is a lifesaver.

"I used to love hiking this trail, until *it* was *discovered* by other hikers. Now it's *ruined*."

The dramatic tension can become so fraught it's observed by the other guests, who later write home about it. Best summed up in one of our many 5-star reviews: GRUMPY PEOPLE: DON'T EVEN BOTHER COMING HERE!" Yeah, it's nice when guests have your back, as they often do.

Fortunately, incorrigible guests are far and few between. But if the mood at the inn becomes soured by a miserable, complaining guest, rest assured we'll take care of it. "Our favorite hotel was already booked by a wave of *horrible tourists*! That's why we're staying here!" Few guests will offer sympathy. Meanwhile, your innkeepers remain gracious, polite, and considerate. But we only appear to be smiling, nodding, and listening carefully. Because we're quietly rehearsing the changes to our script. "Welcome to the inn. Please enjoy our hospitality. Please consider tipping the staff. Thank you for paying your bill. Now please get the fuck out of our house."

Heated Encounters

I returned to the kitchen, the hub for the innkeepers and staff. A place where cooking, ordering, and organizing took place day in, day out. The fresh and crisp gray-painted walls, white cabinets, and stainless-steel fitments were punctuated with bulletin boards and whiteboards with staff schedules, shopping lists, guest information, and Trip Advisor reviews. The kitchen was also the usual place for arguments among staff. If there's heat in the kitchen, someone might be having a bad day.

Most morning stress was due to bad chemistry. Like the day the muffins didn't rise because the baking powder was inert. The batter rose a little, but the muffins didn't crown in the baking tin, resulting in a gooey mess oozing onto the floor of a hot convection oven. The sugar quickly caramelized and began to burn, causing blue billows of smoke to drift up and taunt the smoke detectors. Jeff and I raced to open the kitchen's windows and doors, lest we risk activating the earsplitting, strobing, fire alarm system that triggers both at the inn and at the fire department. Once the alarm is triggered, the fire department's response requires full evacuation of the inn, and site inspection.

We knew the drill well. Several times the fire alarms had been triggered by guests taking a piping-hot, steamy shower with the bathroom door closed and the ceiling fan off, rather than on for ventilation. The instant the bathroom door was opened, the pent-up steam would trip the smoke detectors and activate the building-wide alarm system, which was state-of-the-art: strobing lights, glowing exit signs in doorways, and indescribable screeching fire alarms at a frequency so high and loud Riley the inn dog would howl. Meanwhile guests, often half-undressed, reluctantly straggled from their rooms down the stairs of the inn, then out to the street and the parking lot. Or, worse, believing the commotion was a false alarm, some guests, often the ones who'd triggered the alarm, would simply begin styling their hair, as the fire department and inn staff knocked on their door.

At moments like this, can you blame us for thinking, *Why are we living like this?* Because, on a day that starts this way, it would be a miracle if any of the muffins turned out well, since they would have to be removed from the oven, too.

My fire-retardant attitude stems from flashbacks from junior high days that still keep me a little on edge. My brother and I were sitting together in a movie theater, munching on popcorn and watching *The Legend of Boggy Creek*. Suddenly the theater manager was standing in front of the screen, the film still running, while Bigfoot streamed across his chest: "Teri and Paul, your parents called. You need to go home immediately. Your house is on fire."

We jumped up, hearts racing, and ran for home. By the time we got there, our townhouse was surrounded by fire trucks, hoses running through our living room to permit the FD to staunch the blaze in the kitchen next door. A fondue pot had tipped over. Now, I'm hypervigilant about fire safety, and not a fan of fondue at home or, as it turned out, French fries at the inn.

One of the student workers living at the inn had a mad craving for French fries. We were used to students casually cooking foods from various ethnic locales—interesting soups, goulash, and curries. But the ubiquitous French fry held appeal for one student worker from Turkey.

One late afternoon, off shift, she peeled a bowl of spuds and left them in water. As the potatoes were soaking it all in, she heated a pan with olive oil and walked out of the room.

One potato—a few minutes passed.

Two potato—she found something else to do.

Three potato—she forgot her craving for French fries?

Four potato—the oil reached flashpoint.

She threw the waterlogged potatoes into the pan. Splat! Flames rose up, the acrid smoke filled the kitchen, burning a blue streak straight up to the smoke detectors, sending alarms screaming on all four floors of the inn. Right in the middle of evening wine hour.

As the guests were evacuated, the basement smoke rose and threatened to activate the sprinkler system. As we waited for the fire department, Jeff and I remembered saying to one another, "Remind me again: Why are we innkeepers? This is a crazy hell-ride." We did it because the highs were far greater than the lows. Because we thought Being Our Own Boss would be better than corporate life. And because innkeeping is the perfect way to enjoy Life's Rich Pageant.

CHAPTER SEVEN

There's a sun in every person. The you I call companion.
—Rumi

Life's Rich Pageant

Innkeeping provides a lens on human nature in its myriad forms, the good, the great, and the not-so-hot. My philosophy, "Zen and the Art of Innkeeping," involves visualizing ourselves on a bridge, and flowing beneath is a stream of humanity—our guests.

Guests are fluid, in motion, flowing from point A to point B. So wise innkeepers shouldn't grasp too tightly. Observe the flow, don't obstruct. Remember to breathe, and keep in mind you are not in control of them. But otherwise, what could be better than spending time with happy, wonderful people on vacation? Innkeeping certainly filled in the gaps of my personal life experience, observing happy families traveling together, celebrating birthdays, anniversaries, and other important milestones, like running marathons.

Rad Dad

Every year, the Radcliffes booked four of the inn's king guest rooms. Jeff, the crew, and I always looked forward to their annual family visit to run the MDI Marathon in Acadia National Park, a qualifying race for the more famous Boston Marathon.

We waited for the traveling caravan, happily anticipating their arrival. The family felt right at home again the minute they checked in, offering hugs and handshakes after ditching their running shoes at the front door. Mom and Dad Rad looked younger than their years, and their adult children were also super fit. Everyone knew the location of their room so there was no need for the ceremonial tour of the inn. It was their place.

We gave them their room keys, and they proceeded to get comfortable. After settling in, we'd find them after enjoying iced tea and oatmeal raisin cookies, laughing and playing board games on the sunporch. Jeff and I looked at each other. "Pretty incredible family," I said. Tolstoy wrote, "Happy families are all alike"; perhaps it's true. And this family's energy made *us* happy, too.

On race day, the family gathered together at breakfast, saying grace, holding hands, followed by loud whoops and high-fives as they raced out the door. Returning hours later wrapped in Mylar blankets, they lounged in the library refueling on bananas and chocolate chip cookies before bedding down for afternoon naps.

Early the next morning, I was quietly wandering around, picking up a few wine glasses late-night guests had left on top of the piano. I saw Mr. Radcliffe in the library, relaxing by the fire. I gave him a wave. He waved back and gestured for me to come over.

"Good morning!" I said.

"I have a question for you." I nodded. "Why do you and Jeff do this?"

His question stopped me in my tracks. Was he asking why I picked up wine glasses in the morning? Or why do we have guests who leave wine glasses on the piano? I wasn't sure what he meant.

"Do what?" I replied.

"All of this—the inn, the food, the flowers and cards in our rooms. Why do you do it?"

Up to that point, I hadn't thought about it. And I began to fret a bit. Our motto had always been "Less is far better than more" when it came to asking or answering personal questions with guests. My response surprised me.

"At first it was a passion; we wanted guests to be happy. Now it feels like second nature, plus a little improvising," I said.

And come to think of it, I had a few questions of my own. And figured he was giving *me* license to get a bit personal. "I was wondering about all of you. How did you raise such a harmonious family?"

He picked up the thread. "We're very blessed, and we live life one day at a time and give thanks each day. And we're thankful and appreciative of how you and Jeff treat your guests like old friends."

That was nice to hear.

"Next year, when we come back, there's going to be a new addition. Would it be all right if we bring our new grandchild?"

How could we refuse an old friend? "Sure! We'll give you the family discount."

Springtime in Maine

Spring is short and chilly in Maine. The giddy excitement starts before the first flowers bloom, bringing a wicked dose of spring fever. It's easy to tell those who've got it—they're the folks wearing shorts, T-shirts, flip-flops, and a down vest when the temperature hits 45 degrees.

Spring is also the time budget-minded tourists hit the road for a holiday. Nothing fills guest rooms more quickly than the first hint of spring blossoms, gourmet breakfasts, and off-season rates. An early-season bacchanal, a rutting season for innkeepers and thrifty-minded guests. Most bookings are made last minute, inviting a parade of eccentric guests to get their groove on.

One unseasonably warm afternoon, Jeff and I watched a red convertible pull into the roundabout with the top down. The color of the car matched the rosy redness of the driver's cheeks, likely the effects of sunburn from the windswept drive from Portland, three hours southwest of Bar Harbor.

The passenger was a surprisingly ample woman, a blond bountiful babe who made her way to the trunk of the car. The driver (we nicknamed him Romeo) was nondescript, his weight approximate to his height, in his case, medium. They arrived without fanfare, but as they approached the front door, it seemed likely the Big Bang was going to take place, and soon.

They walked up the granite steps. Babe was wearing skin-tight leggings, sneakers, and a rhinestoned, fringed tunic. She was petite, a beauty of extreme proportions. Romeo was wearing jeans, a NASCAR shirt, and a cap, nothing exceptional. But from the looks of him, I could tell he was thrilled and finding it difficult to conceal his erection. The incongruity of the couple was notable.

I extended my usual greeting. "Welcome to the inn! How was your journey?"

Babe said they'd spent four days in Boston, with a stay over in Portland. She had always wanted to visit Acadia National Park.

Jeff handed the keys to Babe and offered them a tour of the inn. From the looks of Romeo, he wanted to avoid the formalities and head straight to the guest room. He had trouble concealing his eagerness, and his effusive smile and giddy expression told us they needed a private setting…soon (i.e., "get a room"). And that's exactly what we were intending to do.

After checking in, they now had a room, and we wanted to get them there before someone became too uncomfortable.

Romeo slid his hands around Babe's waist and gave her a squeeze. He gazed around the front hall, his eyes syrupy, glassy, liquid pools of lust. Babe finished up the check-in formalities, and he picked up the luggage. I started for the staircase to Room 2, a beautiful king bedroom with a silk canopy, low lights, and soft surroundings. At the top of the stairs, I invited them to continue ahead of me.

Romeo was a polite escort. He stopped in front of the door, and I opened it with my key. I wondered if I should show them the room, or whether time was of the essence. I switched on the ceiling fan to demonstrate the fan speeds, then the location and operation of the light switches. I opened the closet door and switched on the light, revealing ample luggage racks, an iron and ironing board, then pointed out the well-appointed en suite bathroom. I was just wrapping up when I thought I heard a low growl. It was time for me to make my exit.

I was no sooner out the door before it was shut firmly behind me. The door lock clicked shut from the inside. As I turned, I think I heard the beginning of Act 1. There was a muffled sound of thumping footsteps and bouncing box springs. From the sound of it, Romeo was claiming Juliet while the curtain was still going up.

Hours later, I bumped into them when I was refilling the cookie jar. Babe was enjoying snacks; her fingers were dainty, sausage-like, pinkies up. She was draped in a leopard-spotted caftan. Romeo nuzzled his head into her overflowing cleavage and made an effort at decorum, running his hands up and down his legs as if to iron out the wrinkles in his sweatpants.

One of them asked me for a dinner recommendation, and I stupidly asked, "What are you in the mood for?" It was an honest question, and truthfully, I didn't think about the double meaning until later. So, I handed them a binder with restaurant menus.

The next morning, Romeo arrived for breakfast early, selecting a table by the window. He sat and waited, and we made chitchat. I poured coffee and tended to the other guests. Babe arrived fashionably late. Her man rose at the sight of her, clutching her with both hands as he helped her take a seat.

They ordered a hearty breakfast of blueberry buttermilk waffles and sausage. Romeo said he was starving. I returned to refill their coffee. He was taking Babe's fingers into his mouth. Unnerved, I quickly left to place their order.

When I returned with their breakfast, Romeo was sweating and his mouth was gaping open. He appeared slightly dazed. I wondered, *What the hell is going on out here?* worrying whether the other guests found their public displays of affection as awkward as I did. I put the plates down. Romeo and Babe fell on their breakfast.

After eating, they had questions about Acadia National Park.

"Is this your first visit to Bar Harbor?" I asked. They both said it was. I wondered why they had decided to visit a place whose claim to fame is hiking and pitching a tent. Babe must have read my mind, and she gave Romeo a wink. I'd have thought they'd prefer a place sightly burlesque, with more amusements. Or maybe part of the thrill was flaunting their show in front of small-town innkeepers and anonymous guests. One more night…

The next morning, Babe was crying, sitting with two other guests at breakfast.

She stopped by the front desk and told me Romeo had stepped out on her last night, and it was her birthday. She had big tears in her eyes. "He didn't come back until four a.m. Then he packed up and left."

Not a gentleman. In fact, what a creep! Who ditches a date on her birthday, dumps the rental car and the room charges on her to boot? Babe's new friends consoled her at breakfast, and we felt sorry for her, too.

As she was checking out, she quietly shook her head, not believing what he'd done. "I've been paying for everything," she said. She opened her purse and pulled out a receipt from their stay at the Ritz in Boston. The room charges were more than $10,000 dollars.

Jeff and I helped with her bags and escorted her to the car. She smiled bravely and gave us a wave as she drove away. Neither Jeff nor I can recall her name, but her dignity and graceful acceptance of circumstances made an impression on us. And we hope, one day, good karma will finally come her way.

Privacy Please

The inn's seasonal employees from Eastern Europe and Jamaica were pros. Wonderful, fun, and warm-hearted, we were a hospitality family of work friends, occasionally enjoying team lunches and celebratory birthdays.

We shared breakfast and chitchat every day, and learned that many of our housekeepers had once worked at large hotel chains, often cleaning twenty or more rooms solo. The Jamaican team referred to such properties as "the plantations"—and all that implied. They much preferred working at a small family-owned inn like ours, enjoying friendly guests, generous tip sharing, and a mellow pace. After breakfast service ended, the kitchen tune box was switched on. We all enjoyed music.

Deep into July, the inn was completely booked, so for the staff and the innkeepers, each day blurred into the next one. By this time in the season, the innkeeping routine is second nature, and every minute of every day has been mapped out: early coffee service 6:45 a.m.; breakfast 8:00–9:30 a.m.; guest check-out by 11:00 a.m.; housekeeping detail completed by guest check-in at 3:00 p.m.; afternoon refreshments; evening wine service 6:00 p.m.; and finally, front desk shutdown 10:00 p.m. We had created a streamlined, consistent routine, with a script we all knew by heart, each of us happily performing the roles we played, reciting our lines with earnest enthusiasm. The guests bring the energy; we were on standby to wash—rinse—repeat.

On this warm July day, we had a light housekeeping routine, only two check-outs; the rest were stay-overs. It may sound simple to have only two room turnovers. But cleaning ten rooms, two of which will be stripped and deep-cleaned before the new guests arrive at 3:00 p.m., is serious business. I was clearing and resetting the dining room, as well as covering the front desk. The housekeepers were on track, with everything humming along, but I noticed two of them had been spending a lot of time outside Room 1, chatting animatedly in Jamaican patois.

Faith stopped by for a chat while I was standing by the coffee machines in the kitchen reaching into the cabinets for silverware.

"Teri, Room 1's 'privacy please' pillow been hanging on the doorknob all morning. We're not sure we'll be able to get in there before our shift ends at two o'clock." She was on a tight schedule and was worried the guests would later complain if the room wasn't serviced.

"Oh, I forgot. Jeff said we had late check-ins last night. They told Susan they planned to skip breakfast and sleep in late. Sorry I forgot to mention it on the housekeeping report. I'll slip a note under their door. They can ask for fresh towels at the front desk."

After resetting the dining room, I passed by Room 1 on the way to the kitchen to get fresh flowers. The late arrivals had left for the day after all. The double doors leading to Room 1 were open. Faith was bundling bed linens into the laundry bags. Iris had finished shining up the mirrors in the bathroom. The room looked perfect, beautiful, as usual. We turned out the lights, locked the door, and walked to the kitchen. Lincoln grabbed the heavy laundry bags and hauled them to the back porch for pickup by the laundry service. The day shift was over, time to clock out. After finishing their shifts, the team hung out, snacking on maple-oat scones, bacon, and fresh fruit from breakfast.

"Thank God that's over," Faith said, chewing on a piece of bacon. "Room 1 was a mess." She stifled a laugh with a mile-wide smile. "It was a ramping shop!"

Iris nearly choked on her orange juice and glanced over at Faith, who was bent over in hysterics, tears streaming down her face. I shook my head. "Ramping shop—what's that?"

Quietly, Lincoln, the sous chef, piped up. "Faith, don't be talkin' about stuff like that! Teri don't need to hear more dirt." He was old-school, the strong, silent type, and slowly shook his head.

"Ohhh, it's all right, Lincoln. Jeff told me they were late check-ins who had a long flight."

"Yeah, he was right; they said they had a long flight. I bumped into them after I saw you in the kitchen," Iris said.

"Ohhh, yes—they're British—real nice and proper," Faith smirked. "And they left a good tip. Good thing, too, since the room was a ramping shop."

While they were laughing, they could see the puzzled look on my face, and Iris gave me the scoop. "Teri, *ramping shop* is a Jamaican patois thing; it means sex room."

Faith took it from there. "And let me tell you, girl, they may be older, but they're still doing it!"

"Doing what?" I asked, as if on cue.

Lincoln was blushing and couldn't keep a straight face holding out for the punchline. He left the room and Faith took the floor.

"Well, you tell me. There were little blue pills all over the bedside table, the sheets were all bundled up and left on the floor, and the towels were all used up. They needed new sheets, new towels, but left a big tip."

"OK, OK, I get it!"

"No, no, no, girl! *She* got it!" Faith said, nailing the punchline. The three of us collapsed with laughter.

Lincoln walked back into the kitchen, knowing he'd missed something. "OK, OK, Faith, back up—who got what?" he asked.

"Lincoln, I don't need to tell you because you already know. It was a ramping shop, all kitty-dis, and titty-dat!"

Lincoln blushed and covered his ears with his hands.

I walked over to the whiteboard and picked up a green marker, drawing two smiley faces next to the guests' names. "Hey, Lincoln, tomorrow let's put a few extra sausages on their breakfast plates. They obviously have very healthy appetites."

Frisky Business

The Maine Human Rights Act defines "service animal" as any animal that is necessary to mitigate effects of a physical or mental disability, or to provide comfort and companionship. Inns are required to permit one service animal per guest, almost always a specially trained dog.

Early one morning, Jeff checked a reservation request that had been processed overnight. The online booking from Las Vegas was unexceptional. Four nights at the inn, one of the best rooms, the $1,000 dollar deposit processed without a problem. However, shortly before arrival, the guest called.

"I'm coming with three dogs. I tried to board them at a kennel on the way to the airport, but it was full."

"We can allow one service animal, but three is too many," Jeff said.

She said she'd make other arrangements.

Jeff thought the exchange was strange, so he Googled her. The search revealed photos of a healthy young blond woman, totally nude and shaved, with a link to her website. It also included explicit photos of her anatomy any gynecologist would easily find during an exam. Her more obvious sexual attributes were also explicitly showcased in before-and-after photographs of her breast augmentation, along with info for solicitation of her modeling and escort services. Jeff said, "Nah—this can't be the same person. Why would she be visiting Acadia National Park? It can't be her."

Inn Mates

Naturally, it *was* her. She strolled in the front door dressed in white short-shorts, tennis shoes, and a lime-green tube top two sizes too small. It barely contained her grapefruit-sized breasts. She reached up and rang the buzzer. Pulse quickening, Jeff greeted her at the front desk, thinking, *She looks like she'd give a good wrestle.* Not exactly his type, but he could certainly see the appeal.

"Welcome to the inn; how was your journey?"

"It was OK," she said laconically, fingering her credit cards with her French manicure. Her male traveling companion was a twenty-something kid in a baseball cap. He trailed along carrying her luggage.

Jeff offered up the standard check-in spiel about parking, breakfast service, and housekeeping. She interrupted him. "What time do the bars close around here?" Not the usual question.

"Usually around midnight."

"Harumph. Thanks. By the way, I won't be needing housekeeping."

Uh-oh. As any innkeeper or parent of teenagers knows, "no housekeeping" means "stay out of my room."

By all appearances, the situation was starting to make more sense. Our underdressed guest was on a "business trip." Except she wasn't carrying a laptop, or a lap dog. We made a bet, figuring she was a lap dancer. She took the room key, and her minder followed her up the staircase. Jeff's suspicions were mildly aroused, and he was getting anxious. "Do you think she'll be bringing clients to the inn?" he asked. "That might not be good for business." And we'd heard a few horror stories. In particular, a tricky situation at another large hotel. Rumor had it that a sexual tryst had gone wrong.

Two guys checked into a hotel room and requested no housekeeping. No one saw the pair during their stay, and only one of the guests checked out. That's not a big deal, since plenty of people request privacy while staying at inns. But in this case, the hotel's housekeeper was stunned to find a nude man tied up and hanging from a hook in the closet. He was otherwise unharmed. Dead, no. Kinky, yes. By definition, probably *beyond* kinky.

There was no trace of our X-rated guest for the next two days. No breakfast taken in the dining room, no pop-up appearance for wine in the afternoon. On the third day of her stay, well past check-out time, she made an appearance at the front desk.

"Sir, I'm leaving, I have to check out *right now*." But she wasn't due to check out until the next day.

"OK, but you understand you're still responsible for the rest of your stay." Jeff gave her the invoice; the balance due was more than a thousand dollars.

"Yeah, fine, whatever," she said, shuffling a 52-card deck of credit cards, finally selecting one. She returned the room keys.

Jeff had a few questions. "Is anyone in the room? Is it empty?"

"Yeah. I'm done," she said.

But what about her minder? Where was he?

Jeff hit the stairs to her fourth-floor guest room, worried the kid was tied up in the closet. Or worse! The room was orderly, no service animals left behind, no prisoners taken, no bodies hanging in the closet. Later, one of the housekeepers did find the woman's thong under the bed. "Did you put them in the lost and found?" Jeff asked.

"No, they were too small for me, so I threw them away."

Good thing, although it wasn't the inn's policy to throw away guest property. But it seemed unlikely she would have called the inn asking about her missing underwear. After all, she'd cut her Bar Harbor business trip short, turned tail, and left a day early. Business elsewhere must have been brisk.

Golden Moments

I checked the inn's voice mail. "Hi, this is Claudia. My mom and I are arriving tomorrow. We can't wait to meet you and Jeff! And we will need access to the wheelchair ramp. I hope that's not a problem. If it is, please give me a call."

I called her back. "We're all set for your arrival. We'll see you and your mom tomorrow. Check-in is any time after three p.m. Safe travels!"

Claudia had booked a two-night stay in Room 1, the room with the door in the floor where I fell during the renovation. It was now a safe and accessible room with all the necessary handrails and door openings offering easy access to the library, lounge, and sunporch. We also took extra care to ensure it would be one of our most beautiful rooms, since we wanted to welcome extraordinary people of every ability.

Later on, I was on my way out to walk Riley. Susan was on duty at the front desk. A small van pulled into the roundabout. I gave a wave and meandered to Shore Path, taking in the fragrance of beach roses. Stopping under a flowering apple tree on the edge of a breakwater, Riley and I sat listening to the waves. I relished a few moments of quiet, in private, charging my battery. We strolled up Albert Meadow back to Main Street, dodging tourists with ice cream cones, dogs, and skateboards.

Returning to the inn, I ambled down the hall and noticed a gathering of guests in the library. The late-afternoon sun was shimmering through the windows, bouncing off the brass chandelier, radiating sun around the room. An aura settled on one of the guests: a golden-haired woman who was sitting in the center of the group in her wheelchair. I joined the group. Most of the guests I'd met earlier that day. "Hi, are you Stella?"

"Yes, I am. We saw you walking your terrier. Susan helped us check in. We love our room, it's beautiful! We're so excited to be here!"

"Well, it looks like you've met the rest of the guests."

"I was chatting with the other guests to get ideas for tonight. We're going on a sunset cruise!"

It was a great idea. A beautiful sunset, a cool ocean breeze, maybe a bit of fog, and who knows, maybe a whale or seal sighting.

Hours later, Jeff and I were finishing our dinner. I walked into the kitchen to wash the dinner plates and to make a cup of tea. Ducking my head into the Guest Pantry for a tea bag, I heard roars of laughter and tiptoed around the corner, spotting Stella, who was surrounded by the other guests, drinking wine. She spotted me and waved me over. "The sunset cruise was amazing! We saw seals, the moonrise, and now I'm sitting in front of a roaring fire with new friends!"

I smiled, confident the guest party was in full swing. I didn't think anyone would notice as I found my exit. Claudia, Stella's daughter, passed by me on the way to fill her wine glass. I couldn't help but notice a gold butterfly necklace she was wearing. "Your necklace is beautiful," I said.

"My mother bought it for me. It matches hers." So sweet, I thought. "Butterflies are meaningful for us," she said, blinking back a tear. "This is a special trip." She took a sip from her wine glass as a sob caught in her throat. "She's not well; this trip may be our last."

Her words tore at my heart. There were private moments with guests and discoveries that still took my breath away. We turned and watched her mother. She was shimmering with life, lighting up the room like a golden butterfly, fluttering in the garden of life. Claudia and I stood together, tears welling up.

I said good night to Claudia and waved to Stella, then turned in for the night. I fell asleep savoring a moment of grace that still lives with me.

The next day, we gave Claudia and her mom a token of thanks for staying at the inn. A simple card with the following poem:

A butterfly lights beside us, like a sunbeam. And for a brief moment,
its glory and beauty belong to our world.
But then it flies on again, and although we wish it could have stayed,
we are so thankful to have seen it at all.
—Author Unknown

Last Call

Friday arrivals from points far south tend to be late-nighters. And after a long day at work, the five-hour drive to Bar Harbor is a long slog. We often waited for check-ins to help them get settled. Navigating the halls of the inn late at night can be confusing. We wanted to avoid guests knocking on the wrong door, bumping into walls, or lugging heavy luggage and loudly heaving it up staircases.

Our two guest check-ins, a party of four, were running late. Thankfully, both parties called from the road to let us know they were nearby. Susan clocked out at 10:00 p.m.; Jeff and I decided we'd wait up.

Finally, two cars pulled into the driveway. Jeff and I agreed I'd check in the first party, arriving from Boston. Jeff would handle the second party traveling from Orlando.

A hip, good-looking couple walked in. I offered the usual greeting. "Good evening; how was your trip?"

"We're exhausted. There was a backup on Route 1. When we finally got on the turnpike, I set the cruise control to eighty and cranked up the music. We're starving. Where should we go to eat?"

"Let's get you checked in," I said. "Not many restaurants are serving this late, but a couple of bars are open." I gave them the room keys and a map of town. I'd circled a few places for bar snacks within walking distance of the inn. Easy.

It was after 10:00, time for me to think about going to bed. My alarm was set for 5:45 a.m. Even though I knew I'd be asleep the minute my head hit the pillow, I decided to hover around the kitchen and wait for Jeff.

Jeff's arrival party pulled into the driveway as the Boston couple headed out for dinner. An attractive blonde teetered unsteadily to the front door. She introduced herself. "Hi, I'm Sandy. We flew in earlier to Bangor. We got in late, so we decided to stop in town for dinner and a few drinks before checking in."

Innkeepers dread waiting around for late check-ins, only to later learn they were a block away without their room key.

Looking around, Jeff asked if she was traveling alone. Her companion was nowhere in sight.

"Oh, Jess is outside, parking the car. He's bringing in our luggage. Why don't you give me the keys and show me to our room?"

She was tipsy, and stumbled up the first few steps as she followed Jeff up the staircase. Destination, Room 7 on the third floor. A sweet, cozy guest room, at one time a nursery tucked into the eaves. We had vaulted the ceiling, added cove lighting and a full bathroom, and transformed the small space into a sexy, swanky studio. The perfect love nest for two lovebirds from Florida. We knew they would LOVE the cold efficiency of the air-conditioning, but the room did have a minor flaw, a low doorway.

Sandy stepped into the guest room. Looking around, "I love it!" she said. She flopped onto the bed, her short skirt riding high on her thighs. The effect of the air-conditioning and her excitement were apparent through her light T-shirt. With nipples in full salute, she bounced up and down on the bed then sprang up and wrapped her arms around Jeff, giving him an unexpected hug. Jeff was worried her boyfriend might misinterpret this little scene, so he unwrapped himself from Sandy and headed downstairs to the parking lot to help him with their luggage.

Jess was hard to find at first. The car was nicely parked, but he wasn't around. Jeff caught sight of him heaving into some rose bushes. Staggering around his car, he opened the back hatch and stumbled forward, nearly tumbling into the trunk. Jeff offered to give him a hand. He brushed him off. "I'm OK, I've *got* it."

Jess organized the bags, steadied himself, and followed Jeff into the inn. He went unsteadily up the stairs. His weight shifted left, then leaned right, bumping the walls. Jeff was worried he might wake other guests. Jess picked up speed and staggered straight into his room, headfirst. WHACK! "Goddammit!" Sandy led Jess—who by now was slurring his complaints loudly—to the bed. Jeff quietly closed the door.

I waited for Jeff to meet me in the kitchen, and we took the stairs down to our bedroom. A few minutes later, lying in bed, I asked, "Jeff, what happened up there? What took you so long?"

"The couple from Orlando went out to dinner and got drunk. After I showed Sandy the room, she hugged me and gave me a nipple press. It was getting weird, so I went to help the guy with his bags, and he was throwing up in the bushes. He wouldn't let me help him; then he hit his head on the doorway." Life's Rich Pageant. We had a laugh… and turned in.

At breakfast the next morning, the Boston couple were quiet, wearing mirrored sunglasses and the clothes from the night before. They drank water, ate lightly, then crawled back to their room.

Sometime later, they changed clothes, leaving their room at midday. They requested housekeeping ASAP. Iris had been on standby after breakfast, waiting to service the room. Jeff gave her the green light to head upstairs. Almost immediately, she stormed back to the front desk.

"Jeff, the couple in Room 2…they pissed the bed!" She was livid.

"Are you kidding, Iris?"

"Nuh-uh, it's soaked! Everything. The sheets, mattress pad, the mattress. Everything's ruined. What are we going to do?" she cried.

Jeff and I followed her to the room. She was right, the bed was a sodden mess. Iris flipped on the ceiling fan to get the air moving. Jeff found a floor fan and got it going, then called a local furniture store. "I need a king mattress ASAP." The clerk on the phone put him on hold while checking the store inventory. All eyes were fixed on Jeff. We waited.

"Great, I'll take it!" Jeff gave us the thumbs-up, then he frowned. "You can't deliver until tomorrow? But I need it right away…OK, OK!" He hung up. "The new mattress will be here Monday. Tonight, they'll have to sleep on the wet one. And I'm going to charge them for the new mattress."

Iris tried to dry the bed with towels, kept the fan running, and remade the bed with fresh sheets. But she wasn't happy about it. She was a stickler for keeping the inn perfect, like her own home, but reluctantly agreed. There were no other options.

The next morning at breakfast, the bedwetters were in fine spirits. When they checked out, Jeff asked. "Did you enjoy your visit to Bar Harbor?"

"Yes, we had a blast!" they said.

"Well, how about your time at the inn? Was everything OK?"

"Yeah, it was great—wicked pissah—you guys are awesome."

Jeff continued with the check-out, handing over the invoice. "Well, thanks, and here's your final bill. You'll notice there is a damage charge we added to cover the problem with the bed."

"What problem with the bed?" he asked with a whiff of attitude.

"Ah…the urine-soaked mattress…" Jeff replied discreetly.

"OHHH, yeah—that!" Suddenly he remembered, and his girlfriend did, too. She strolled up to the front desk to have the final word. "Thanks, Kevin."

Some time later, Faith had been working in Room 8 and was anxiously hovering around the front desk to speak with Jeff.

"I think we have a problem," she said.

"What's wrong?"

"Jeff, it's embarrassing, and very personal. It's not about me; Room 8 has a problem." She looked upset and disgusted.

"It's OK, you can tell me. What happened?"

"One of the guests pooped in the bathtub and left soiled towels all over."

"I'm sorry that happened, but maybe the guest has a medical condition. I'm sure it wasn't on purpose."

"Well, OK, but I wanted you to know, and I don't like surprises like that. They didn't even leave a note or a tip."

Later she found liquor bottles in the bureau and cigarettes tamped out on the windowsills, even though the inn had a no-smoking policy. The daily parade of Life's Rich Pageant taught us that some guests thought they could write their own house rules. Unsurprisingly, we had a few rules of our own, and once the rules were breached, unruly or rude guests were unanimously voted into the DNB club.

DNB—DO NOT BOOK

Coffee To-Go

The Devaneys arrived with their teenaged daughter Erica for their thirteenth stay at the inn. This time, the family was staying three to a room. The online reservation read, "Just put an airbed on the floor for Erica, she doesn't need a cot. And don't forget, we are taking the innkeepers to dinner, our treat. We insist!"

Mom and Dad Devaney were always among the inn's early birds, waking up before everyone else and getting a head start on the day, hiking the Ocean Trail before breakfast, coffee cups in hand. Erica slept in. I bumped into them on their return, as they were bounding up the front steps. I was watering flowers. They whispered sweetly to me, in unison, "We'll be down for breakfast in a little while."

A few minutes later, Erica strolled into the dining room, finding a seat at their usual table, set for three. She sat quietly reading on her iPad and watching chickadees flitting back and forth by the window. The morning sun shone on her golden hair, neatly combed.

Her mom arrived smiling, and Dad popped up, chipper as always, coffee in hand. "Hey, what's cookin'?" He sat down, and they bowed their heads, clasped hands.

Mrs. Devaney said, "Blessings to God on this beautiful day and on the breakfast we are about to receive. And blessings on this house, and our friends Teri and Jeff."

My eyes filled with tears upon hearing such beautiful, lovely thoughts directed at us! I was embarrassed by my sudden emotions and had to excuse myself. Such tidings of love and friendship—at first, seemingly unreal and unexpected—had become an annual affair. And their loving cups of kindness and gratitude were overflowing. So much so, they shared them with us.

Jeff and I are indebted to this family, and to the many, many, too-many-to-count, wonderful families and couples we met at the inn. The encounters filled us with gratitude, which helped to smooth over our difficult moments and transformed our beliefs about our personal struggles. They were a guiding light we followed while forging a new path as innkeepers.

Paradise Bound

In 2012, the Atlantic hurricane season was forecast to be above average: nineteen tropical storms, of which ten became named storms. Two of them, Hurricanes Michael and Sandy, were Category 3 or higher. During mid-October, Jeff and I tracked the storms as they moved north, hoping Maine would be spared the aftermath.

On closing day, the last guest shuffled off and Jeff locked the inn's front door. During the following days, the water was drained and the inn's contents were secured and bedded down for the winter. We loaded Riley into the car, took one last look over our shoulders, and waved goodbye, heading south from Bar Harbor to visit family in Florida. When we got to the Sunshine State, the balmy November weather felt like a summer vacation. We found storage for our car and caught a nonstop flight from Miami to St. Croix in the US Virgin Islands.

Jeff had a dreamy look as he gazed out the window of the plane.

"Hon, do you remember what happened last March?" I asked.

"How could I forget," he said, shaking his head.

The date was memorable. We returned to Maine after a family visit to find 18 inches of ice on the roof of our cottage. The living room ceiling nearly collapsed, and water was leaking through the light fixtures. Dripping cold water was collected in bowls and saucepans scattered across the floor. Our house sitter hadn't had the heart to spoil our vacation. Our insurance policy covered the damage; still, we spent the remaining weeks before reopening the inn negotiating with insurance adjusters, roofers, and painters before moving back to the inn for the start of the season.

While sweeping up the debris, we explored the idea of trading our Maine cottage for a winter home and office in a warm-weather destination. A way to enjoy our off-season, rather than hunkered down shoveling snow all winter. We figured we could handle the inn's calls and emails in the tropics. Why not?

My brother had lived on St. Croix at one time. Years later, we visited the island and fell in love with the weather, the diverse, vibrant community, and the easy proximity to Puerto Rico. St. Croix was perfect for us, and it was easy for US citizens to buy and sell property. In mid-June I'd stumbled across a new real estate listing for a West Indian beauty nestled high on a ridge with sweeping views of the Caribbean Sea. We called our realtor, who went to the broker open house to take a look.

"If you want this place, you better get down here tomorrow. It won't last," she said.

Jeff flew to St. Croix the next morning, and we were under contract by dinnertime. We were pinching ourselves at our good fortune and felt somewhat guilty to be embarking on this new adventure. Did we deserve it? We figured, if *we* didn't deserve it, then who did, and we tuned out our imagined critics and counted our blessings. Our Maine cottage was quickly sold to complete the purchase in early September.

In early October, the contents of our home were wrapped, packed into a shipping container, and trucked to the Port of New York for the trip to St. Croix via cargo ship. A six-week ocean voyage.

Now, flying over the Bahamas, I was captivated by the deep, vibrant blues of the Atlantic Ocean melding into lighter turquoise hues of the Caribbean Sea. On the plane, I was surprised so many people knew one another. We soon learned the Miami-to-St. Croix flight is known as the "shuttle." At the departure gate, we bumped into the lawyer who had handled our real estate transaction. He introduced us to fellow travelers, neighbors we'd later meet on-island.

The plane banked over Puerto Rico, leveling off on the approach to the St. Croix airport. Over the west end of the island, I looked down at the Frederiksted Pier, the reds walls of Fort Frederik, and the blue, yellow, and ochre painted buildings along Strand Street. An assortment of tropical bonbons.

After landing, the flight crew opened the cabin doors, giving passengers a thumbs-up farewell. We stepped onto the metal stairway high above the tarmac where I quickly succumbed to the sweet, humid caress of the Caribbean trade winds. Jeff, Riley and I had landed in paradise.

We picked up our bags and a rental car that we'd be driving for a few weeks. Our household goods were still in transit. Jeff drove the fifteen minutes to our new digs. Coconut palms and flowering, flamboyant trees waved, chickens pecked the ground while young men rode on horseback along the airport road. Thoughts of stormy weather up north slipped our minds.

Our new house was unfurnished, but we managed. Jeff and I were happy and excited to read and hang out, lying around on outdoor lounges waiting for our stuff. It felt like a badly needed vacation after the long work season. We fell into patient mode, waiting to be reunited with the contents of our home, slated for arrival in three weeks.

In the meantime, we managed with a mattress on the floor, a few suitcases, a couple of paper plates, plastic cups, two forks, two knives, two spoons, and instant coffee. We kept ourselves busy running the inn's winter office, which took place around a metal table on a shaded porch while we were wearing bathing suits and flip-flops. Heaven on Earth! The perfect spot for taking reservations and writing our holiday letter.

We took lunch breaks for grilled mahi sandwiches, cold beer, and long swims in the deep turquoise blue of the Caribbean Sea. A complete 180 from the winter back in New England. Guests making reservations had no idea whether we were in Maine, St. Croix, or on the moon. This working vacation could actually work!

We enjoyed our bohemian lifestyle for a few weeks, then began counting the days until our container would arrive at the shipping company in Christiansted. The company kept tabs for us as they awaited bills of lading and customs documents. They promised to contact us the day it arrived.

One week passed, then another. Thanksgiving came and went. Brandy from the shipping company called. "I think it would be a good idea if you got in touch with your stateside shipping agent to see if they have more information than we have."

Jeff got on the phone. "I'm calling about our cargo shipment. It was picked up in Maine on October twentieth, heading to New York. Can you tell me when it sailed?" There was a pause, then the call was placed on hold.

Several minutes later: "Yes, the cargo was trucked from Bar Harbor to Bangor on October fifteenth. In Bangor it was loaded into a shipping container and trucked to New York on October twentieth. The final destination for shipment is St. Croix, USVI."

So far, so good.

The shipping clerk continued. "Our records show it shipped."

"When did it leave New York?" Jeff asked.

"I'm not sure; there were delays at the container port. I'll get back to you."

Delays? we thought, as clouds of apprehension were gathering, dampening our expectations for the next few days. Early the following week, Brandy called back.

"Your shipment is arriving in the Port of St. Croix on Thursday. We'll pick it up at the container port and unload it to our truck. We'll see you at your place early Friday morning."

Jeff and I were ecstatic! Our dominoes falling into place one right after the other.

Friday morning, we were up at daybreak, drinking instant coffee, nervously excited to finally settle into our island home. Sometime around 10:00 a.m., we still hadn't heard from Brandy. Jeff and I were wondering if they were having trouble finding the house. It was a plausible explanation for the delay, since the house was hidden from the road, and the entry was not well marked. Jeff called Brandy.

"I'm checking to see if your crew need directions or anything."

There was long silence on the other end. Finally, "Jeff, have you heard from your shipper?"

"No one called, Brandy. Is there a problem?"

"You should come down to the loading dock as soon as possible. We can't unpack your container."

Jeff shot me look and put the phone call on speaker. "I don't understand. What's going on?"

Brandy's long sigh echoed from the phone. "Jeff, you and Teri have been so patient. I hate to tell you this, but everything in the container is soaking wet. The shipper used a container that wasn't waterproof, and according to the bill of lading, it was sitting on the docks in New York when Hurricane Sandy hit."

Jeff and I hung our heads, not believing our worst fears had been realized.

Brandy continued, "They closed the Port of New York for a few days due to the storm surge."

This meant the cargo—our household goods, our lives—had been packed into a leaky box and loaded onto a cargo ship, where it sat for six weeks in the hot sun.

Brandy continued, "Everything is covered in mold. We can't touch it, we can't unpack it, put it the warehouse or in our trucks. It's been classified as hazardous cargo. I'm so sorry."

By now, Jeff was highly agitated. He ended the call and said, "I can't believe this is happening! I knew all of this was too good to be true! Why do we have such bad luck? Let's go down there and see if we can salvage anything." I agreed with every word he said.

We drove along the dirt road past the waving palms, the bougainvillea, and the beautiful yellow, flowering Ginger Thomas, the state flower of the US Virgin Islands. The idyllic surroundings were in stark contrast to our mood. Along the route, we passed our favorite restaurant, the Chicken Shack, our car bumping along the road, thumping to the tune of the reggae music playing in the restaurant bar. "I guess we can pick up dinner on the way back," I said sheepishly. Jeff had no words.

We drove through the security gates, catching sight of two men dressed head-to-toe in white coveralls, wearing white caps and respirators. Brandy gave us N-95 face masks and took us to the loading dock. Jeff and I stood side by side in the hot sun. The crew opened the container doors as water gushed out onto the pavement below. The packing boxes were soddened and discolored, and had collapsed into unrecognizable heaps. The heat and fumes made my eyes water, mixing with the tears I was fighting to avoid. We were bereft, and dizzy from the stress of watching our belongings being pitched into the garbage. Jeff spotted his tool kit, something we'd needed for weeks, but it was full of water and rusted tools.

I recognized a cardboard box I'd packed, labeled with special marking tape "Open ASAP." I knelt in the hot sun and opened it. Sifting through the soggy contents, I found a small parcel wrapped in bubble wrap and sealed in a plastic bag. I opened the packaging and Tusa's bronze Tree of Life crumbled in my hands. The five photo medallions of me, Tusa, Uncle Bob, and my two cousins were soaked and unrecognizable. Hot tears ran down my face. I stuffed the mangled tree back into the wet box and chucked it into the trash. We chucked it all. The contents of our home, our dream of paradise, our precious memories, all were deemed a catastrophic loss by the insurance adjuster. I felt my heart break in two, and I didn't have a tape dispenser to my name.

Luckily, we had taken the optional cargo insurance, which was enough to furnish the house, eventually. And initially, the insurance company stalled to pay out our claim until our lawyer threatened a suit. This got their attention, and the insurance proceeds were finally paid after a six-week delay. While we were grateful for a fresh start, it didn't begin to erase the disappointment and sadness we felt.

Even though our luck had turned sour, we counted ourselves fortunate when we met Pat and Mark, the owners of Sweet Lime Furnishings. More than a retail store, Sweet Lime was a community that came to our aid. Offering us a bed while we waited for the insurance company to pay out. Introducing us to a community of new friends who jumped in to help us, offering us support and encouragement that we badly needed, and teaching us lessons in generosity and gratitude.

From then on, and every November for the next five years, Jeff, Riley, and I would fly to St. Croix for a summer vacation in the middle of a Maine winter. A home away from home, where we could run the office and rest up to hit the ground running each spring, refreshed, relaxed, and reinvigorated. Except during hurricane season, which kept all of us, from the Caribbean basin to Nova Scotia, on edge.

Holiday Letter

Dear Family and Friends,

As the year closes, Teri and I look forward to catching all of you up before things rev up at the inn next May. Our winter plans are to enjoy a sunny working vacation on the Caribbean island of St. Croix. We're grateful for our health, for our family and for our new and old friends.

The inn had a fabulous year! Business was booming, with lots of return guests and a fantastic team. The highlight was winning *Yankee Magazine*'s "Best of New England" award. We love sharing the Maine experience with others. Innkeeping is a people business, and we had wonderful guests from all over the US, Canada, Europe, the Pacific Rim, and elsewhere.

But strange things do happen…

One morning a guest requested an omelet with no eggs. "Uh, OK, what do you mean?"

"I want all the stuff in the omelet. No eggs." Yes, we aim to please!

One day, Jeff was at the post office when two cruise ship couples spotted him and started calling out.

"Hello, young [!] man, can you drive us around Bar Harbor?" At first he thought it was a joke, but they were serious. "There are no cabs here."

"I'm sorry, ma'am, but I'm working," Jeff said as he turned to head back to the inn.

"Don't you wanna earn some extra money?" they asked.

The line of questioning was rubbing him the wrong way. *Do I look like a scruffy teenager?* He politely declined. So, friends, if *you* visit Bar Harbor, we are only a phone call away and will be happy to show you around free of charge! And remember, check-in time is 3:00 p.m.

PART FIVE

CHAPTER EIGHT

May this marriage be full of laughter, our every day in Paradise.
—Rumi

Front Desk Notes

Susan,
Cynthia and Phillip, the bride and groom, checked in last night. They wanted to be here before the rest of the wedding party. The mother of the bride called, asking for flowers in her room, a bottle of Perrier with an ice bucket, and three champagne flutes. She said she is traveling alone. The bride's sister is bringing bridal favors she'd like put in the rooms, along with the weekend schedule of activities.

The housekeepers have had to scramble to turn over the rooms before the wedding guests arrive at 3:00 p.m. There are extra platters of chocolate chip cookies in the kitchen, and iced tea and coffee in the Guest Pantry in case the rooms aren't ready. We're staying in tonight to rest up for the weekend. Don't forget to take your vitamins.

We Do Weddings

Before becoming innkeepers, Jeff and I didn't have much experience planning weddings. Our own ceremony was a modest affair, four people plus the two of us in Marblehead, Massachusetts, a quaint seaside village on Boston's north shore. We moved there in 1983 and lived in the historic Old Town district, finding a small apartment in a third-floor walk-up, a sweet and romantic nest for two lovebirds.

In the summer of 1984, a few months after Jeff's ill-fated skiing trip, he planned a getaway for us in Vermont. We were looking forward to taking long walks in the woods and a side trip to the scene of his car accident. The local utility company had sent us the invoice for damaged power pole #902. Driving along Route 100B, the road winding and curved, we couldn't find the pole. It was just as well. Being so close to the scene of the calamity felt close enough, and we were running late for our dinner reservation at Annabelle's. Jeff was behind the wheel as we sped along. What was the hurry?

Jeff spotted the restaurant and pulled into the driveway, kicking up dust as the car settled to a stop. Once inside, we were warmly welcomed by the hostess and promptly shown to our table, like special guests. Suddenly…POP! In a well-orchestrated flourish, a bottle of champagne was uncorked, and Jeff popped the question. Surprised? Yes. I hadn't a clue. But our life together felt inevitable after living together for four years. And in the aftermath of the car accident, Jeff and I knew we only had each other. We hoped we would be enough.

On March 1st, our wedding day came in like a snowy lamb. A sunny, beautiful day with a mild flurry of lingering regret. We'd hastily planned the event, choosing a date between my college midterms and Jeff's business travel. Jeff had ordered beautiful blossoms for my bouquet, a lovely surprise. The guest list was short, given the distance of our families and the time of year. My relatives couldn't make it, and we had few RSVPs.

Standing together in Abbott Hall, Jeff and I held hands. He sensed my unease as I gazed around the room wearily. *Where's my family? What about the church wedding and the ribboned crowns my parents had worn?* I put the intruding thoughts out of my mind. *You're a big girl now, a modern woman.* Still, I was weighed down by old-fashioned sentimental musings. Jeff hugged me and stroked my hand. We took a few deep breaths and said our vows. For better or for worse, for richer, for poorer, in sickness and in health, to love and to cherish 'til death do us part. We sealed our promises with a kiss: "I do."

We left Abbott Hall and drove along a scenic route of snowfields on our way to Marblehead Light. The beacon from the lantern was indistinguishable by day, a harbinger by night, until sunrise, as tradition has it, when dawn breaks over Marblehead. A mariner's omen for these newlyweds. Beckoning us to take care of each other, to be on the lookout for rocky shoals, and to hold position during stormy weather and fog.

We took a few photos, then returned to Old Town for a small reception at Rosalie's. We gathered in the entry, and Jeff approached the owner, nervously glancing at me over his shoulder. There had been a mix-up. They'd forgotten our luncheon but managed to squeeze us in. Soon we were relaxing, enjoying champagne and a lovely meal. But I subconsciously tucked away the memory of our wedding day snafu. It was our first life lesson after leaving the lighthouse. One I remembered when I became an innkeeper, vowing never to repeat the same mistake.

Our inn's size and location, central to the village of Bar Harbor and the waterfront, was the perfect venue for small weddings. We were grateful to book early-season events in mid-May or late October to drum up additional revenue. Plus, there was the added profit of hosting receptions and dinners. From June through mid-October when the inn was booked, there was no need for the hustle-bustle of special event menus, seating plans, photographers, florists, cake bakers, and musicians. But early-season weddings were a good warmup for us and our business partners after a long winter's rest. We had ample energy to manage the expectations of the bride, the groom, and their families. It was stressful at times, and the biggest wild card was the weather.

A few years earlier, my sister Alexandra had received a surprise marriage proposal from her boyfriend, Chris, while celebrating our birthdays. They asked us to host an autumn wedding at our home in Massachusetts. October is a wonderful month for weddings in New England. The maple and oak trees are colorful with red, gold, and green foliage. Most days are warm and sunny, nights are cool and crisp. But the week of their ceremony, the weather turned foul. Cold and windy, and heavy rains drove most of the leaves off the trees.

Dad arrived a week early to help with flower arrangements, dinner prep, and logistics. Dad, Jeff, and I watched the downpours saturate the lawn and walkways. We arranged for a large tent to be set up within the garden walls, which stood like a fortress surrounded by tall pines, viburnum, and honeysuckle vines. We were wistful: *It will pass.* We hoped.

Dad stood on the back porch and shook his head. "Teri, everything is soaking wet."

The lawn was sodden, with wet leaves floating in puddles of rainwater.

"What are we going to do, Dad? Get a giant blow-dryer?" I said, half-joking.

"Very funny. I'll make a few calls to see what I can do."

Dad rented a propane heater, a miniature blast furnace—and set it up under the tent. It chugged to a start. At dinner, the bride and groom had moved beyond nervous to pre-wedding panic. We tried to cheer them up, belting out my sister's favorite childhood song, "Tomorrow." She tossed her red curls and gave us a dimpled frown. Dad got the message. He rose from the dinner table and set the heater to operate all night.

After dinner, we watched the rain fall as sheets of fog wafted across the landscape. I glanced over at Dad; his lips were moving as he murmured a few words. We strained to hear him over the commotion in the yard. I leaned closer and noticed him laughing with tears in his eyes. "Teri, *never* again!" Jeff and I laughed along with him, as he once again buoyed our spirits.

The next morning, the sun burst on the scene vibrant and warm, mist rising on the lawn. Everyone breathed a sigh of relief. Dad fixed early coffee and passed around cinnamon buns. A few hours later, my lovely sister slipped her dress over her head, looking like an angel. The bride and groom glanced over their shoulders and gave us a smile as they started across the damp grass to the floral arbor. They took their vows: "I do." Dad, Jeff, and I did, too: "*Never again!*" Weddings are best left to professionals.

"Look who's professional now!" Jeff joked when we received an email from Cynthia and Phillip, a couple from Washington, DC. They asked if the inn was available to host a destination wedding the following spring. A small affair of forty guests who would be traveling to Bar Harbor from Germany, Thailand, Washington, DC, and Boston. Both Cynthia and Phillip were lawyers, diligent and exacting, who knew what they wanted in every detail. We were a perfect match for the two perfectionists, applying our business skills to innkeeping, and now to wedding events.

First, weddings required booking the entire inn. We'd learned that guests attending special events did not mix well with regular-season guests. And since every inch of the property was needed for events, uninvited guests felt left out. We asked for a sizable up-front financial commitment and damage deposit, which was refundable. The deposit was intended to weed out halfhearted couples, and to provide compensation in case of damage from vendors, contractors, invited guests, or wedding crashers. And there was a service fee. We wanted to ensure the staff were well tipped.

Second, we catered all dining events in-house. We were sticklers for guest service, kitchen hygiene, and care of the property. We often teamed up with August Moon, a catering company owned by our good friends Michael and Fayelle. They had an exceptional track record, combining wonderful food with expert front-of-house planning and staffing, allowing us to focus on synchronizing events with the planner, the couples, and often the parents who generally were paying the tab.

Once we ironed out Cynthia and Phillip's contract, Sarah, their event planner, contacted us. She was a pro. We were relieved. Sarah scheduled time for an inn walk-through and brought along the couple's menu ideas and a detailed questionnaire we asked them to complete to guide the who, what, where, and when of the two-day event. Guests were scheduled to arrive on Friday afternoon, followed by an excursion and light supper. The wedding ceremony would take place on Saturday afternoon, to be followed by a lively champagne reception with a jazz trio, passed hors d'oeuvres, and a formal dinner for forty people.

The inn's maximum occupancy was for twenty overnight guests, so the overflow of invited family and friends booked rooms at the inns next door. The proximity of the other two inns and our friendship with Roy and Helene were ideal. Guests were free to enjoy all three properties, creating a quaint bridal village in the heart of Bar Harbor.

The calendar rolled around to the wedding weekend in May. The early spring weather had not been cooperating; it had been raining nonstop since opening day the prior week. Jeff was concerned the garden was looking dank and drab for photos. But the forecast suddenly changed, and sunny weather was expected two days before the big event. We hoped a few warm days would bring forth the promise of the blossoms in the gardens, giving us one less thing to worry about.

The wedding couple arrived on Thursday, two days before the ceremony. They booked Room 10, the penthouse loft, at the top of the house. Forty-seven steps from the front desk to heaven. This was the second marriage for both, and they traveled light. Unlike a few other bridal parties we'd seen at the inn, some of whom freighted a lot of emotional baggage.

Cynthia showed me her dress; ivory silk with a simply beautiful, delicate lace train edged in satin ribbon. Lovely, elegant, and refined. Cynthia was a dark-haired beauty with a porcelain complexion. Phillip was shorter than Cynthia, and strikingly handsome. A sports enthusiast, he planned to work off his jitters hiking with a few friends who lived nearby. We hoped the champagne they requested would help, too.

On Friday morning, the inn's phones were briskly ringing. Vendors were calling to confirm details for deliveries of lobster, beef tenderloin, cases of wine and champagne. All of the food and beverage deliveries were scheduled to arrive late Friday and early Saturday. But between the wedding prep and busy guest activity, we needed to minimize pinch points in the schedule. So we pushed all deliveries to Friday afternoon with the exception of the flowers and wedding cake.

Joanie the baker called. "I'm dropping off the cake first thing tomorrow morning," and I thought, *What a relief*. Jeff and I were juggling eighteen guest check-outs, three housekeeping teams, kitchen prep, and guest check-ins. Joanie said, "I'm running out of space at the bakery." She was warming up *her* juggling skills, too. And we couldn't afford to have someone bump into her bringing the wedding cake through the front doors. The couple's carrot cake request was an excellent one. Spicy, moist, studded with nuts, topped with fluffy whipped cream cheese frosting, lightly dusted with cinnamon and orange zest. We hoped there would be a few leftovers for us on Sunday.

At 3:00 p.m., eighteen guests rushed the front desk to register. Jeff and I took turns giving tours, handing out guest room keys, and answering questions. Other invited guests who were staying at the inns next door were streaming back and forth, wandering up and down the stairs to catch a glimpse of the wedding couple. They were also checking out the inn, taking self-guided tours of the lounge and library, plunking a few notes on the piano, and bumping into their friends. The cookies and drinks were going fast in an atmosphere of controlled chaos, and were quickly replenished by the kitchen crew. Soon guests were sprawled out in the garden, relaxing after their long trips, resting up for a late-afternoon excursion.

Cynthia and Phillip had reserved two trolleys for a tour of Acadia's Park Loop Road, with an onboard moveable feast of fresh lobster rolls, whoopee pies (a Maine favorite!), and champagne. The festivities topped off with a bagpipe salute on the summit of Cadillac Mountain. After returning to the inn, the guests were on their own until breakfast the next day.

The Park Loop Road is a beautiful 26-mile scenic byway with iconic views of Otter Cliffs, Eagle Lake, and Cadillac Mountain. All apt metaphors for marriage: dramatic cliffs, a calm, placid lake, and a tall, scenic mountain with dizzying hairpin turns. It's also a one-way trip, like marriage, unless someone finds an attractive detour along the route. Otherwise, U-turns are not permitted.

Jeff and I ate a hasty dinner and decided to turn in early, queueing up the film *Four Weddings and a Funeral*, hoping the movie's high jinks would be a fun distraction and would ward off evil spirits for the weekend. In one of the scenes, a guest wearing a kilt drops dead during the wedding toast. We crossed our fingers. Then the phone rang. It was 10:45 p.m.

"Hi, guys, I'm sorry to call so late, but it's important." It was the wedding planner.

"No need to apologize; the wedding is all we can think about," I said.

Jeff nudged me with his elbow and whispered, "I told you, it would be far easier to NOT DO weddings!"

I nudged him back. "Too late!"

"The florist just called, and they're backed up with noontime deliveries. How early can we come tomorrow with the flowers?" I needed a minute to sort the details and resorted to thinking out loud. "Guest breakfast ends at nine-thirty, and the servers will need an hour to clean, rearrange the tables and chairs according to your floor plan, and reset the dining room. Any time after 10:30 a.m.," I said, already jittery. We had less than twelve hours before wedding chaos would ensue.

"I appreciate how organized you are. Please leave room in the fridge for the cake." She hung up.

Saturday morning, Jeff and I woke early and got dressed. We walked Riley and put him back to bed, and meanwhile the kitchen crew arrived for early coffee service and breakfast. The front desk bell rang in the kitchen, and I stepped into the hall. Cynthia and her sister were clustered near the kitchen door, looking cozy in their pj's and furry slippers. Both of them were carrying small bouquets of fragrant lilacs, pale lavender, white, and deep purple they'd cut from the garden.

"Good morning—what beautiful lilacs!" I said.

"They're for our mother. We'd like to serve her morning tea in her room—it's a family custom. Would it be possible to have a few vases and a tea tray?"

Such a sweet, touching gesture, I thought. And such a sweet, thoughtful bride on her wedding day. "Of course. I'll bring it right out."

I organized two tea trays and put the flowers in small vases. The sisters picked up the trays and padded off to Room 1. I caught a glimpse of their smiling expressions in the reflection in the large hall mirror. They set the trays on a table and knocked on the door. They stood hugging each other, waiting for the door to open. Mrs. Chang answered the door dressed in the inn's white bathrobe. She was a petite, slender woman with delicate gestures. She raised her hands in a prayer as her daughters gently bowed to her. She bowed, too, then with a giggle waved her daughters into the room. Good karma.

After breakfast service, we rearranged the dining room according to the planner's seating plan. The tables were dressed with the inn's white linen tablecloths, and place cards were tucked into napkins folded with a pocket. Each table was decorated with a small crystal vase of carnations. Afterward, the maid of honor brought along baskets of the bridal favors, lovely small white boxes trimmed with red satin ribbons, one for each guest.

At 10:15 a.m. sharp, the wedding planner arrived and parked behind the inn. An army of vendors were scheduled before noon. The florist and two vans arrived, packed with four-foot-tall sprays of lilacs and lilies, bridal bouquets, and ten-foot-long ribboned bowers of carnations. The fragrance of lilies and lilacs perfumed the inn. We took a few photos and closed the four French doors to the dining room, looking forward to the rest of the afternoon. We were ready to roll.

The caterers, Michael and Fayelle, arrived. The four of us took a quick stroll to review our plans. Michael took a detour to the piano, my gift to the inn from our home in Massachusetts. He loved dropping in for an occasional gig and offered to give it a sound check. Shaking off his white kitchen apron, he sat at the piano in his chef jacket and gave the keys a workout playing and singing "Sunny," one of his favorites. Bobby and his musicians walked in whistling, right on time to set up for the reception and dinner. Bobby said, "Oh, man—I'm always surprised how much work goes into one of these gigs!"

Just before 4:00 p.m., two trolleys pulled into the roundabout to pick up the bridal party and guests for the wedding procession to Schooner Head for the ceremony.

From the kitchen we watched the wedding party climb aboard, and the drivers started ringing bells as they rounded back out to Main Street. Passersby took photographs as the parade drove past. All were grateful for the mild afternoon, the faint green of the birch trees, and the tall stands of pine filling in the landscape for a magnificent tour of Acadia National Park.

Back inside, servers were decked out in basic black, swaying to a chill vibe as Bobby and the guys warmed up to the tune of "Satin Doll." Champagne bottles were popped open and placed on ice. All of us were excited in anticipation of the welcome toast for the bride and groom. Two life-size photos of the couple were staged inside the front doors, a surprise wedding gift.

In the kitchen, Fayelle and crew were plating the hors d'oeuvres. Gleaming maki rolls with pickled ginger and soy were delicately placed on sheets of nori and garnished with pale lavender orchid blossoms. Michael stood in front of the French top working on the coconut shrimp, which would soon be sizzling hot and served with sweet chili sauce.

Despite the buzz in the kitchen, we heard the returning trolleys before we saw them. The gang was almost here. Jeff stood ready at the front door to welcome the bride and groom. With the champagne flutes filled, Bobby and the guys had the music swinging. Above all the commotion, those of us in the kitchen could hear the hearty "CHEERS!" ringing out as Cynthia and Phillip walked onto the front porch. They were wowed by the two life-size photos. Cynthia burst into tears. Servers took turns swanning around the guests with the beautiful trays of hors d'oeuvres. Guests were spread out across the sitting rooms, sunporch, and lounges.

At 7:00 p.m., the guests were invited to the dining room, taking seats at the tables marked with their names and a small white box. Soft jazz from the trio continued in the background.

The inn's phone rang in the office. Jeff was just in time to take the call. "Good evening, may I help you?"

"Hello. I believe my daughter is getting married today."

Jeff was caught off guard. The mystery of the bride's father was closer to being solved.

"I was wondering if I might speak with her."

Jeff said, "I'll check."

He returned to the dining room and discreetly approached the head table. Tapping Cynthia's shoulder, he whispered, "Your father is on the phone. He'd like to speak with you."

Her lovely smile turned upside down as she blinked back tears. "Please tell him I'm not available." She turned away slightly dazed, as if the magical spell of the festivities had been broken by the phone call.

Jeff returned to the office. "I'm sorry, sir, she can't come to the phone right now."

"I understand, I guess," he chuckled ruefully. "Please tell her I said 'Good luck.'"

Then he hung up.

Jeff took a moment before he returned to the party. Unbeknownst to him, he had become a silent witness to a rare personal moment. A private revelation that revealed all families and relationships are complex, and uniquely complicated.

The evening went on without a hitch as thoughts of the bride's father and his absence faded away.

The next morning, carloads of flowers were taken away by the departing guests, petals spilling along the walkways and through the parking lot. There were hugs and handshakes all around, thank-you notes and generous tips for the staff.

Faith and Iris stopped by the office.

"The bride and groom left you a present." Iris handed me a white box, just like the ones we'd seen on the tables. I opened it, finding a small raku bowl decorated with a Tree of Life. I was reminded of Tusa's bronze Tree of Life with the photo medallions. The childhood keepsake I'd lost to Hurricane Sandy.

I cradled the bowl in my hand. Something old was now replaced by something new. A beautiful wedding gift symbolizing the cycle of life; a vessel to be filled, seeds to be planted, a reminder to tap into resilience and embrace the seasons of change.

After lunch, I found generous slices of wedding cake in the fridge. Sweet reminders of the wedding weekend, which I shared with the team. Still, the clock was ticking. We had less than two hours before the day's arrivals.

Check-in time was 3:00 p.m.

Teri Anderholm

Here Comes the "Bride"

August and September represent the paragon of summer in Downeast Maine. Sun-filled days and starry nights, picturesque gardens, seascapes, and mountain views.

While we didn't court wedding bookings during peak season, large hotels hosted big-top gatherings of 300 or more guests, replete with horses and carriages, schooner excursions, stretch limousines, chocolate fountains, and Jell-O shots. These chaotic events are designed to fill up guests and guest rooms, and to maximize revenues. Meanwhile, daily cruise ship arrivals brought throngs of day-trippers, all looking to take a walk in Acadia National Park. Or to score a souvenir, at least an ice cream cone.

During breakfast service, the sounding of foghorn blasts from three cruise ships anchored offshore shook the inn, rattling the windows. A calliope of dissonant sousaphones and tubas lacking musical signature, rhythm, or harmony. Still, the soundtrack was romantic, and melancholy for the audience of guests seated in the dining room. But the symphony was just beginning. We'd been listening to the overture.

The inn was so close to the town dock, we could hear the ships' public address systems loudly broadcasting muffled instructions to passengers gathered on the deck. Tenders then ferried the tourists ashore and transferred them to tour buses parked end to end for blocks along West Street. Hours before dawn, the buses maneuvered back and forth, *beep, beep, beeping* into position, an unwelcome alarm ringing in the day for innkeepers and guests. But what we considered noise and commotion rang out as the glorious sound of pennies being tossed into a fountain by vendors selling T-shirts and ice cream cones. An idyllic summer day in Eden. What could possibly go awry in paradise?

I took a moment during the lull in my day to water the herb garden. Setting my coffee cup on a granite step, I bent down and turned on the hose. The flow ran thick and warm across the grass. I picked up the hose, enjoying the sensation of water running down my arms and hands. I shook out the hose, casting it out across the grass, and sprayed the lawn and garden in cascades of watery rainbows, casually directing the flow to water several pots of basil that were threatening to go to seed. The tall stands of lovage, parsley, and chives were starting to complain; tender leaf tips were lightly fringed with yellow, blending nicely with the trumpet-bell-sized nasturtiums crisscrossing the iron trellises.

An innkeeper's moment of Zen.

Afterward, standing amid the glory of the dahlia blooms planted under the inn's sign, I waved goodbye to the departing guests. Back inside, I took a seat in the corner of the sunporch, settling into one of the wicker rocking chairs and running my hands along the chair's woven arms. I took in the view of the garden—our divine creation. For a moment, I was only the guest, and I savored the silence. The breakfast performance was over. The guests were headed for the exits after giving us a standing ovation. The inn was quiet as a church, a peaceful refuge for brides and grooms both before and after their events. We called this time of year "honeymoon season."

Most of the newlyweds or soon-to-be-weds arrived somewhat stressed, often exhausted. They were grateful for a relaxing, quiet place to rest, to get some sleep. Frequently, the brides and grooms were overwhelmed with details after months of planning. They became forgetful, often losing or misplacing their room keys.

It was late summer in Maine. The warm, sun-filled day was quickly chilled by ocean bellows of cold air blowing across Frenchman Bay. Wafting clouds of fog descended like veils covering the paths, flowerbeds, and paving stones along the way to the inn's front walk.

One of our newlywed bookings, a couple who looked like they had stepped off the top tier of their wedding cake, snuck away from their big-top affair, which was being held at the resort hotel next door. They had booked with us to avoid the hullabaloo of the pre- and post-event commotion, they said. After the ceremony and reception, sometime after midnight, they took their first baby steps together as husband and wife. Leaving the party, they held hands while strolling past the valets, fountains, and tents, and made their way back to our lovely inn.

The telephone rang. Our newly minted couple had forgotten their key. Jeff put on his robe, climbed to the office, and quickly headed down the hall to the front door.

He watched the couple walking down the lane. Two dreamlike images shrouded in mist that dampened their hair and formal attire. Nature's atmospheric baptism, like a sacrament. They stood holding hands, frozen apparitions in the front door glass. Jeff was still half asleep. *Is this real? Am I sleepwalking?* He opened the door, congratulated them, and gave them a spare key. All of us returned to dreamland. But occasionally, newlyweds were a nightmare.

One tipsy groom forgot his key. Chagrined, as was his bride, he turned into a human battering ram, slamming himself against the front door glass, triggering the security cam. Frustrated and cursing, he walked to his car and returned with a rubber mallet and hammered on the door. The guests in Room 1 called the front desk. "Someone is vandalizing the inn!" Jeff and I hurried anxiously upstairs from our bed to find both the bride and groom yelling and banging on the windows.

Jeff marched down the hall waving his arms and shouting, "STOP IT ALREADY!" He opened the door and the couple brushed past him on the way to their room, acting as if the lockout was our fault. The groom remembered he still didn't have a key. Jeff handed him a spare, eyeing the damage to the front door, and pointed to the outside doorbell—which was clearly labeled and illuminated. "Wouldn't it have made sense to ring this doorbell?" he said. The groom said it hadn't occurred to him to ring it. We hope their future challenges as a married couple are resolved more peacefully.

My pleasant reminiscing on the porch was abruptly cut short. The front door opened, nearly flying off the hinge. Another "bridal" party was ready to check in. Jeff and I had met them—and others like them—before. Difficult and demanding, these repeat guests were named Chloe and Daniel. To ourselves, we called them the "Brides of F*%kenstein," aka BOF.

The BOF party arrived four hours early for check-in. Driving a large black SUV, they pulled into the roundabout as the last of the departing guests were walking out the side door. They stepped out of their car with the swagger of two movie actors onto the red carpet at the Oscars. Looking around, as if for the paparazzi, they stood in the entry hall, gazing about, unaware of the housekeepers and vacuums zooming around them.

Chloe and Daniel were outfitted in black. An unexpected color choice given the balmy weather; was it a harbinger of a threat of rain? Chloe seemed to have taken the forecast to heart. She wore a full-length black trench with fur collar, and carried herself with the puma-like attitude of a maneater. Her hair was highlighted with blond tips, styled in a loose bob. Ropes of pearls were strewn around her neck, her arms clad with silver and gold bangles. Daniel appeared much the same as his last visit to the inn. He still had both of his arms and legs.

Chloe and Daniel were high-maintenance guests who had preferences never, ever, requested in advance. They enjoyed creating an air of tension for staff and innkeepers as we danced on a knife's edge in hopes of heading off lofty, urgent demands usually made in the presence of others.

Often BOF guests have highly contrived appearances, are overly made up. Lots of eye makeup, which is the scourge of every innkeeper, ruining hand towels and pillowcases. Some BOFs are so obviously surgically enhanced it becomes a topic of conversation among the staff. "Did you see the lady in Room 3? I saw her walk down the stairs and her boobs don't move." Others have decent haircuts and clothes, but tacky shoes. Details that smart, stylish, European student workers notice. "She's not Jackie O, she's Jackie *OH NO!*" But not Chloe and Daniel. They stood out from the crowd.

Jeff had finished checking out the last guest. Glancing up, he saw the BOF arrivals as they approached the desk. "Oh, hi, Chloe. Welcome back! How was your trip?" he said.

"We're a little early; I thought we'd drop by," she sniffed, looking around as if expecting a footman. "Can I have my room key right now?"

Her tone telegraphed that she was in a foul mood. Jeff thought it might be a good idea to offer a helpful suggestion, to keep the mood light. A well-worn strategy found in the Innkeeper's Difficult Guest Toolbox, which is labeled "Kill with Kindness," a tactic that usually works wonders, but occasionally backfires.

"I'm sorry, Chloe, but it's several hours before check-in, and your room's not ready yet." It was 11:30 a.m., and it was obvious that the inn's housekeepers were hard at work, dusting the furniture, hauling laundry, and vacuuming the carpets. "In fact, the departing guests just checked out," he said.

Walking past them, my ears perked up as I overheard the opening salvos. Jeff served up, "You can park your car and leave your bags with us at the front desk. We'll have the housekeepers put your bags in your room when it's ready. Check-in is any time after 3:00 p.m." His amiable volley missed. Chloe swung through with a back-handed wave, tossing her hair and rattling her bracelets. Her eye-rolling clearly communicated she was put out. Jeff took another shot. "It's a beautiful day; how about lunch at the Terrace Grill?"

I smiled to myself, *What a great idea!* We were leading this match. The score was now one/love. After all, what's not to like? Oceanfront dining just steps from the inn. A beautiful setting with outdoor tables decked out with sunny yellow umbrellas. A cheery spot for a cool sea breeze and steamed lobster.

"Have lunch in Bar Harbor, with all of the cruise ship tourists? Not hardly!" she snapped. She spun around and walked past me on her way to the library.

"Hi, Chloe, how are you?" I asked.

She took off her fur-trimmed coat and flopped down on one of the leather settees. Silence. Daniel was trailing a few steps behind her, and she muttered, "What are you going to do about this?"

"Do about what?" he asked.

Even he wasn't sure how to placate her. Jeff and I decided to leave her alone. She wanted to be placed on a pedestal—RIGHT NOW. Meanwhile, the inn's housekeeping team was sanitizing the pedestal sink in her room.

Being a repeat guest, Chloe knew the Guest Pantry was stocked with coffee, tea, fruit, and snacks, but she appeared to conveniently forget her past history of pleasant visits. Our acquaintance and past graciousness meant nothing to her. She sat in the library as if waiting for the undertaker.

Jeff bumped into them again on his way to get a few light bulbs from the housekeeping closet. "Oh, hi," he said. I was out of earshot, having finished arranging the flowers. Chloe thought this would be the perfect time for a smackdown tactic from the BOF playbook.

"Jeff, the least you could do is offer me a cup of tea, like Teri would."

Her new game, pitting the innkeepers against each other, backfired.

"She's not here at the moment, so help yourself to tea in the Guest Pantry. Susan will be on duty this afternoon to help you check in later—at 3:00 p.m."

Chloe frowned as she picked and smoothed the fur of her coat. She was clearly put out, wracking her brain over what hurtful thing she should say to gin-up tension and bad vibes.

"We'd planned on booking our stay in Southwest Harbor instead of Bar Harbor. But Daniel didn't reserve soon enough. I don't know what he was thinking." She stood up and rearranged her leather backpack and wore it like a shield. The heels of her leather rain booties click-clacked on the wood floor as she set off for the front door.

Susan came on shift at 2:00. Jeff had informed her about the grumpy twins in the Front Desk Notes. Later, I stopped by the front desk for a quick chat with her.

"Oh, hello!" she said. "Check-in went well, except for the early arrivals. Chloe was in a bad mood, and I think they may be a problem later."

"Yes, I saw them," I said. "They looked like they were going to a funeral."

Susan had a knack for disarming moody guests. "I'll chat with them if I see them before I leave tonight. Some women need special treatment."

I thought to myself, *I've heard that phrase before.*

I was having trouble relaxing and needed an energy reset. I called Helene.

"Let's take a short walk before yoga."

We strolled along Main Street and climbed the stairs to the yoga studio on the second floor. The sun was setting, filling the room with a golden glow. I stretched out on my mat and closed my eyes as thoughts of the day passed back and forth.

David, our yogi, played a few soothing notes on a wooden flute and invited the group to begin the practice with "Ommmm," followed by a chant invoking the image of Ganesh, a one-tusked, powerful elephant-headed god, the mighty one who overcomes all obstacles. After the meditation, I was refreshed, and walked quietly back to the inn.

Instead of checking in with Susan for an update on the grumpy twins, I got ready for bed, setting my alarm for 5:30 a.m., early enough to rise gently and get dressed, with plenty of time to take a quiet morning walk with Riley. My goals for the next day were to avoid stressing, resisting, or rushing.

The east-facing windows were filled with light; nature's alarm went off despite the room-darkening shades. I got up, dressed, and enjoyed my walk with Riley. He was a lazy pup who loved to sleep. After I had settled him back in his bed, I climbed the stairs to the kitchen, then out to the front desk. Jeff was already in the office, checking email and processing new reservations and check-out invoices. Both of us were working away superstitions about how the day could go off course with difficult guests in residence. I gave him a kiss. "Any sign of our fussy friends?" I asked.

"Nothing is in the Front Desk Notes."

So far, so good.

The morning baking was under way. The lemon poppyseed scones smelled delicious. I was confident the scones would be a glorious feast for the eyes after a light dusting of powdered sugar, presented on plates with marmalade and whipped butter. They would be the perfect accompaniment to luscious lobster quiche baked in fluffy puff pastry crusts, served with savory rosemary and thyme–flecked potatoes and fruit kabobs.

Walking out of the kitchen, I was filled with hopeful anticipation for a lovely day. Cheered by the warmth of the sunlight streaming into the dining room, I opened a few windows, double-checked the menu cards on the tables, and straightened the bud vases filled with small herb-and-pansy bouquets. Chloe and Daniel were the first guests to show up. I took a deep breath and put on a smile.

"Good morning!" I said.

"Hi," she said as she slowly strolled catlike around the room. Circling to find a table, she chose a seat in front of the east-facing windows, which were flooded with sunlight. I watched the bees buzzing on the oak leaf hydrangea blossoms outside the window. She pulled out her sunglasses. "Can you lower the shades, please." From her tone, it wasn't a question.

"Sure, no problem," I said. I reached behind her for the pull cord of the matchstick blinds. I lowered them, filtering out the sunlight on the table. I pointed to the menu with the day's breakfast specials. "Would you like coffee or tea this morning?" I asked.

"We'll have coffee with cream. You Americans have no idea how to make proper tea. None of you make a decent cuppa."

Her snarky remark hung in the air as I walked away to the sideboard to get the coffee. I hadn't realized breakfast tea was made so differently in the Canadian Maritimes.

Vera was serving breakfast with me and overheard Chloe order cream for her coffee. She returned to their table with a small white pitcher with cream and the beautifully plated scones, marmalade, and butter. Chloe pushed the scones out of her way while I poured the coffee. She ripped open two sugar packets and stirred up the mixture. She moped. Daniel hadn't spoken a word, just waved me off when I asked for his breakfast order.

From the corner of my eye, I could see four new guests wandering outside of the dining room. I wanted to welcome them. But just then Daniel gave me a signal—he wanted to order their breakfast. "We'll both have the Creme Brûlée French Toast *and* the lobster quiche, half-orders on each plate, with the strawberries. I hope the fruit is fresh."

I took a breath and wanted distance between the BOF and me. I asked Vera to place their orders for me in the kitchen, and to wait their table.

Just then the two couples entered the room from the sunporch. Sara, another server from Bulgaria, greeted them and showed them to a table near Chloe. I looked over my shoulder and glimpsed the sour look on Chloe's face as the four-top sat down.

My sixth sense kicked in as I imagined her thinking, *WTF, I'm going to be surrounded by tourists?* The strange vibe wasn't my imagination playing tricks with me. Innkeepers know you need to keep your radar switched on when difficult guests are seated near new guests. I wanted to provide blocking cover between the tables. I offered my usual friendly greeting.

"Good morning! Welcome to the inn. I'm the innkeeper." The new guests were all smiles.

"We're the Dudleys! And we're the O'Connors!" they sang out. "We're having a wonderful vacation, so far."

Mrs. O'Connor pointed to the small table vase. "I love the herb bouquets. Such a nice detail."

"We're all from Toronto," Mr. Dudley said. "Susan was marvelous at check-in. Everyone has been so pleasant!"

BOF harrumphed audibly in the background.

Back in the kitchen, I spoke with Sara. "What hot beverages did the four-top order?"

"They're having Earl Grey tea," she said.

"I guess we *do* know how to make tea, after all!" I joked.

Sara carefully poured boiling water into two large white teapots. "They seem nice," she said, moving past me, swinging open the kitchen door on her way to the dining room.

Vera picked up the breakfast plates for the BOF table. The food looked beautiful, picture-perfect. I followed her to the dining room and watched Chloe take a photo of her plate, then a selfie. *So far, so good*, I thought. I decided I would kill them with kindness if I found a conversational opening. I walked past their table. My timing was perfect.

"So what's new on Mount Desert Island this year? Any good places for dinner?" Daniel asked.

"Yes, there's a new restaurant at the large hotel in Southwest Harbor. It's beautiful, and guests love it. I recall you enjoyed spending time on 'the quiet side' of the island." I'd forgotten the testy exchange of the day before.

Chloe bristled, "See, I told you. Why didn't we book there instead? It's a much nicer hotel."

I ignored the jab and continued. "I'm told the hotel's restaurant is lovely for a special night out. There's also a café at the hotel, which has a casual menu and vibe." The pleasant look on Daniel's face and his nodding expression encouraged me to go on. "Let us know if we can help out with reservations."

Chloe flipped her sunglasses onto the top of her head for dramatic effect. "I'll think about it and let you know."

I retreated to the front desk to give Jeff a heads-up in case they might ask him for assistance with dinner plans.

After breakfast, Chloe wandered to the front desk to talk to Jeff. He was speaking with another guest. I stepped up. "Hi, can I help you?"

"I have a question about the restaurant in Southwest Harbor. We'd like a nice meal after our carriage ride, but I'm not sure what to wear." In the midst of this civil exchange, I started to ease into the nice back-and-forth volley of the conversation, thinking, *Thank you, Ganesh!*

Chloe continued, "I packed a dress, but I don't think I can wear it on the ride. I'm going in this." She pointed to the beautiful ivory linen slacks, pale-blue wraparound linen blouse, and navy espadrilles she was wearing.

I reassured her, "It's causal here on the island. You could wear the dress, or what you're wearing now. Both would be fine. Do you want a reservation in the hotel dining room, or the café? And what time?" I said, writing her request down on a slip of paper.

"Make it the dining room at 8:00 p.m.," she said, looking me up and down. I was dressed in my work clothes: white jeans, a blue-and-pink striped tee, and white leather sneakers. "I'll need time to come back here to put on my dress. It's more my style. I have a hunch casual dining means far more to *you* than it does to *me*." Her shot crossed the foul line. We were back to square one.

My plan to kill with kindness had backfired. I smiled, stifling a laugh at her pathetic antics, and wrote the restaurant's phone number on a scrap of paper. I handed it to her without a word.

Susan called us before her shift ended. "The grumpy twins informed me they are breakfasting tomorrow at seven a.m. sharp. I told them breakfast starts at eight, but they were insistent. I could tell from Chloe's tone that this is not a request. Thy will be done. I tried. Sorry; good luck."

"I don't mind special requests, but this is not an option," Jeff groused. "Who the fuck do they think they are?"

The kitchen team usually arrived at 7:00 a.m., unless we've made prior arrangements, and it was now too late in the evening to call an audible. We were used to serving twenty guests every morning and special requests were not unusual. But last-minute requests created a risk of allowing special situations to get out of hand. When guests see other guests dining early, it can cause a ripple effect of more special requests, which become unwieldy for the staff and risk upending regular breakfast service for the other guests.

So, under normal circumstances, with nicer guests, we would be happy to accommodate early birds with takeaway continental breakfasts. Instead, we surrendered ourselves to serve the continental breakfast in the dining room, just coffee, tea, fruit, and yogurt with toast. Period.

The next morning, 7:00 a.m. came too soon. I was bustling around the kitchen brewing early coffee, firing up the gas ovens, and prepping fruit courses. Jeff pivoted to front desk, checking the voice mail and email, switching on hallway lighting, and unlocking the doorways. He glanced up from his desk as Chloe and Daniel descended the staircase holding hands, dressed head to toe in matching trekking apparel as if visiting Balmoral Castle for a royal fox hunt. Daniel was carrying a quart of strawberries.

"Good Morning," I said, noting their nonresponse. The lights were still turned off in the dining room, and they took their seats in the east-facing windows while I turned on the lights. I didn't make a move to lower the blinds. Remembering their complaints about American tea the day before, I approached the table with a coffee carafe and handed them two menus. But Chloe wanted to shake things up. "You Americans make terrible tea, but I want it anyway!" Daniel nodded. "Go back to the kitchen and make sure the water is boiling hot—and I mean boiling," she hissed. "And don't forget to warm up the teacups and pot."

I took a breath, reminding myself to stay calm, unruffled, even if provoked by a guest.

Daniel reached over to the chair and picked up the quart of strawberries. He handed them to me. "We bought the strawberries in Southwest Harbor," he said, without making eye contact. "They are so much better than strawberries in Bar Harbor." Stunned by the stupidity of his comment, I knew I needed to carefully parse each moment. A new dining room drama was unfolding. "We'll be having these today," he said. "Find somebody in your kitchen to wash and slice them, and bring them back with our tea, two orders of toast, jam and butter. We'll skip the yogurt and granola."

I took the strawberries and reminded myself to breathe, while tempted to throw the fruit in the trash and not return. Instead, I retreated to the safe refuge of the kitchen, where I repeated the conversation to Jeff.

"What is wrong with them? Is there a language barrier?" he asked.

BOF vocabulary was limited, but effective. Fluent with the words *I, go, no, right now* and *right away*. They lacked nuanced and mannerly phrases like *please, thank you,* and *you're welcome*.

Jeff and I felt we were being pushed to the brink. "Keep me away from those jerks," he said. He'd hit his boiling point. I agreed to wait their table and check them out.

I returned to the dining room after completing my round trips from the kitchen with their tea and breakfast. "Would you like anything else?" I asked.

"I'll see you at the front desk. I want to talk about your false advertising."

I nearly choked on her accusation, then realized I'd lost the bet I'd placed with myself. I'd thought it couldn't get worse—but it did. I was relishing the fact they were checking out.

Chloe rang the bell at the front desk. "Yes?" I said.

"We didn't enjoy our stay. The room wasn't ready when we got here, and the trees are too tall, they're blocking the view. And the tea wasn't hot enough. How can you say you offer 'impeccable hospitality in Bar Harbor' on your website? It's false advertising."

I stood my ground, silently, resisting the provocation. A long silence lingered in the space between us. I gave her a copy of the invoice with the outstanding balance they owed. Chloe took a look at it, correctly deducing that we were no longer on speaking terms.

She unzipped her backpack, removed and opened her wallet, and selected a credit card which she waved inches from my face. I took the card and held it with three fingers, high in the air like an offering, before swiping it in the credit card machine. She stared at me quizzically. I feigned a smile and broke the silence.

"*Thank you. We earned every fucking penny.*" The first and only time I was rude to a guest.

"WHAT!? I'm going to roast you on Trip Advisor!" she snarled.

"Go ahead. We have more than five hundred five-star reviews. We'll let readers know how difficult you were. And don't call or try to book here again."

"What are you talking about? You can't stop me!"

I paused for dramatic effect. "Chloe, you forgot an important piece of information about this inn."

"Oh? What's that?" she huffed.

"The inn is our private property. You're not allowed to come back."

"Daniel!" she cried. "We can't come back?" He quietly ambled over and dropped the keys on the desk—PLUNK—and turned on his heel. Obviously, he'd seen the passion play before. He picked up their bags and walked away. Chloe stalked off in his wake.

Back in the kitchen, Jeff and I unanimously agreed that Chloe and Daniel's names would be added to the inn's exclusive DNB Club.

A club that takes a lot of effort to join, but once you're a member, you can never be kicked out.

DNB—DO NOT BOOK

Susan's Front Desk Note gave us a head-ups on the new guests who checked into Chloe and Daniel's room:

The new guests said, "We're foodies—and the breakfasts better be good!" Otherwise, they're a ho-hum, been there & done that sort of couple. They enjoyed the complimentary wine with the curried crab canapés. I'm not sure if on their honeymoon, but we might have another BOF on our hands, or déjà vu all over again. I hope not, but we'll see. More fun tomorrow!

I parsed Susan's note while waiting to greet the new guests and serve breakfast. Jeff read their reservation request, which spelled out the not-so-subtle threat about breakfast, a tactic to challenge innkeeper sanity. Jeff wondered if we'd recognize them without an introduction. I should have placed a bet. We heard Miss Déjà Vu and her companion before we saw them.

Clomp, clomp, clomp. We watched a thirty-something woman stomp down the stairs wearing shiny black patent leather riding boots, her arms folded in front of her. Her descent was dramatic, as if performing dressage on horseback, her head nodding side-to-side. Jeff whistled under his breath, "Here Comes the Bride." Her gait was stiff, tightly wrapped in an equestrian-style outfit; white shirt tucked into jodhpur-style jeans, a black, short-waisted jacket, red neck scarf, and a tight ponytail. Her groom was slight of build, wearing jeans, a carbon-gray turtleneck sweater, and a leather jacket. He followed behind her. They stopped by the front desk.

"Good morning!" I said.

"Hi, we're the foodies!" She smirked, trusting her Trip Advisor reputation had preceded her.

"Welcome to the inn. There's coffee in the pantry, please help yourself. Breakfast is served until 9:30."

They strolled past the piano, both of them running their hands over the leather settees and velvet armchairs. Onward to the theater of the dining room.

It was after 8:30 a.m., a busy time with few tables by the windows. I escorted them to a lovely spot with views of the fireplace and a large display of colorful tulips. "The menu is on the table. Please let me know if you have any questions."

Good Morning!
Croque Monsieur French Toast
Potato Latke, Smoked Salmon, Scrambled Eggs
House-Made Granola, Greek Yogurt, Seasonal Fruit

"We're the foodies," she said once again.

This was getting ridiculous, but since she mentioned it twice, I figured it was important to acknowledge it. "Oh, right, I read your reservation request. Thanks for reminding me. Susan said you prefer coffee; would you like some now?"

"I usually have coffee. But today I'd like matcha green tea latte with warm soy milk. Do you have it?" She shot me a look: *Well, do you?*

The question felt like a trap, and I didn't want to give a negative reply.

"We have green tea, but we're out of matcha. And yes, we serve soy milk."

"Good! We're foodies, and I'm really hungry. I read that you went to culinary school. Do you do all the cooking here?" she asked.

"No, but I have a wonderful team. Everything is fresh and made to order."

She arched one of her eyebrows. "Well, I'd like *you* to cook my breakfast today."

This request was a first. "I'm sorry; I'm working in the dining room today. But I expedite every meal that comes out of my kitchen. You'll be happy, I promise.

"Do you know what you'd like for breakfast today? The French toast, or the potato cake with smoked salmon and scrambled eggs?" I asked. I scanned the dining room, using body language to imply I needed to move along. We were at full capacity, servers were running dishes, clearing and resetting tables, and a few of the guests were flagging me down. They had questions or wanted to chat.

"I'm still deciding. Do you smoke the salmon here? And what about the eggs—do you raise your own chickens?"

"No," I replied, "we don't smoke the salmon or raise chickens, but everything is fresh." She seemed satisfied with my response.

"OK, we'll have both breakfasts, one of each. We're going to share. Can you bring extra plates?"

Spare plates were no problem, but I had eighteen other guests in the dining room. I placed their order and passed Vera, who had prepared their green tea with warm soy milk. She rolled her eyes at me. "I saw them at the restaurant last night. They send back everything."

"Maybe she's a little fussy and likes attention," I offered, giving Déjà Vu the benefit of the doubt. "And thanks for making her tea; I'll cover their table." Vera was relieved.

A short time later, the foodie breakfast orders were ready. My table was called out from the kitchen. I stood across from the stove watching Janine plate the potato cakes, smoked salmon, fluffy scrambled eggs. I topped them off with capers and minced chives from our herb garden. "Thanks, guys, the plates are perfect." I picked them up and walked back to the dining room.

I approached the foodie couple, glimpsing the sunlight glinting off the water glasses on the table, the warm interplay of firelight, fresh flowers, and beautiful breakfast plates. "Please enjoy your breakfast," I said.

No sooner did the plates hit the table, than the smartphones were out, clicking photos of the plates, the table, the innkeeper. I was feeling overexposed at this point, and I needed to tend to the other guests. Despite my dilemma, the questions kept coming.

"What is there to do around here?" she asked.

I thought it an open-ended question. "Well, you could go hiking or kayaking." Then I noticed her riding attire. "Are you going horseback riding?" I asked.

"I wear riding boots because they have good support—I have high arches. Which reminds me, do you have a nail file? I couldn't find one in the bathroom."

"Oh, sorry. Thanks for letting me know."

"And I want more lotion. I love the lemon verbena scent," she added.

"Of course, more lotion." I made a mental note to update the housekeeping report.

Finally, my exit path was clear, and I moved away from their table to visit with other guests. Vera had covered the other tables for me. She'd been busy chatting with all of the guests, so we decided to play tag-team, serving and refilling beverages at Miss Déjà Vu's.

"She's pretty nice, but keeps asking so many questions. Where are you from? Where do you go to college? Do you have boyfriend? It's too much! She wants you to talk to her before she finishes breakfast. I'm not sure why." We both shook our heads.

A few minutes later, I strolled past their table. "How was everything?" I asked.

"I loved my breakfast." I quietly sighed with relief.

"We really like the inn."

"Thanks!"

"But I have a special request. Can you make me sugar-free cookies today? I'm such a foodie."

As if I'd forgotten.

"I can never find cookies without sugar," she said.

I tried to be sensitive to her point of view, reminding her of the fruit in the pantry, the bowl of dark chocolates in the bowl on the piano, the wine and snacks that were offered each night. There were other options.

Maybe what she meant to say was that there wasn't much we could do to delight her. But trust me, we tried. I believe every hospitality worker in Bar Harbor tried. All the innkeepers, servers, bartenders, housekeepers, shopkeepers, and all the cookie bakers tried. Each of us dedicated to making all guests—even the fussy Brides of F*%kenstein and their companions—happy while on vacation. All of us embraced the hospitality practice of "killing with kindness" from time to time, which requires a lot of sugar, and occasionally large amounts of artificial sweetener. But if we were successful in satisfying the fussiest of customers, I believe all the villagers would happily put down their pitchforks and cheer.

CHAPTER NINE

Live life as if everything is rigged in your favor.
—Rumi

Innkeeping Academy Redux

The following spring, Roger, our former inn broker and innkeeping mentor, approached us to play host for one of his Innkeeping Academy seminars. Jeff and I happily accepted his invitation. Pre-season spring bookings were often light, offering plentiful opportunities to fill guest rooms by booking conferences and special events.

The events were a gateway for Roger to meet innkeeper wannabes (like us!), and to generate prospects for inns he had listed for sale in Bar Harbor and along the Maine coast. It was also recognition that the inn and our efforts had been successful, so successful we had a story worth telling others. It was our encore for a job well done. The inn was recognized as one of the finest small luxury inns in New England, with press coverage in *Down East* magazine, the *Boston Globe*, and *Maine Magazine*. The publicity had been good for business. And business had been very, very good.

Roger's personal style was laid back. His suave persona disguised shrewd business skills and exacting attention to detail. During our inn search, we had visited his town house in Portland. We were impressed with his stylish home, a mix of antique and modern furniture, sumptuous leather furnishings, and walls covered in art. His high standards for décor, food, and beverages, and his straight talk made an impression on us, as well as on his students. The irony, that he was no longer an innkeeper, was not lost on us.

Roger arrived before his students checked in. He'd booked the entire inn for the weekend, but preferred to stay with a friend nearby, which made for a nice separation between business and pleasure.

We'd worked on the breakfast and lunch menus, wine tastings, and snacks ahead of time, hammering out the daily agendas and aspiring innkeeper tours of the inn. The seminar event was a nice pre-season warmup for both the staff and us, a leisurely paced event with a few speaking parts for us each day.

While waiting for guests, Roger had a sidebar conversation with us on the front porch. "During the introductions tonight, I'd like you to provide some color on the innkeeping experience." We all laughed. Roger understood the road we'd traveled.

We turned to watch a silver Mercedes coupe convertible as it pulled into the roundabout, gravel spraying as the driver braked hard to a full stop in front of the inn. "Looks like another corporate second-act player, like us back in the day," Jeff said. We stood back and gave way, nodding our heads as our visitor confidently strode through the front door.

"I'm here for the inn seminar, and I like what I see. I'll take it!" he said. We thought, *Hey, buddy, not so fast.* We'd finally made our way up the success curve, and we weren't ready to walk away from our achievement. Yet.

Check-in was 3:00 p.m., and most seminar attendees arrived promptly. The Guest Pantry was stocked with chocolate-covered macaroons, coffee and tea, fruit, and other refreshments for guests to enjoy upon arrival. The wine event would kick off at 5:30, and Roger had reserved tables at a nearby restaurant for dinner.

Jeff and I took turns assisting the aspiring innkeepers during check-in, giving tours, and largely staying by the sidelines, similar to our normal routine of not getting overly involved with the guests, giving them space to settle in.

Our interactions with the innkeeper wannabes were limited to recording their names on the whiteboards in the office and kitchen, along with their early-morning breakfast beverage preferences. But several of the guests wanted to get right down to talking about the business of innkeeping:

"What did you and Jeff do before becoming innkeepers?"

"How hard was it to finance the inn?"

"What do you do after the inn closes for the season?"

But the seminar was Roger's show. We were happy to be co-stars in his play, so we kept to his script.

Admittedly, it was a relief to hand control of the event to Roger. It was unsettling to field innkeeper wannabe questions because our journey had not been easy nor typical due to the Restoration Vortex. Still, we blushed listening to the false narratives the students had constructed about innkeeping, just like we did.

"I love meeting people!"

"I love cooking and baking!"

"I love throwing dinner parties!"

Most of the students were unaware of the challenges of hosting new guests and delighting repeat guests with details or amenities they might not expect; welcome-back notes, flowers in their room, stocking their favorite cookies, and chocolate truffles for special anniversaries and birthdays.

Interestingly, our guest service strategy was exactly the opposite of what one wannabe had hoped. "You know, once they become repeat guests, they'll book for next year and send the money. It'll be less work because they know what to expect." Nothing could be further from the truth. Guests rightfully expected a 5-star stay every time, and it took the entire team to help the inn earn her stars. Everyone pitching in with creativity, consistency, and a caring attitude year after year, after year, after year.

This season's classroom of characters was fortunate. Roger had solid innkeeping chops, having been the owner of our one-time favorite inn. Strangely enough, we'd never met him during our many visits to his property. This spoke volumes about how absentee innkeepers differed from us. Maybe absentee owners knew something we didn't, or, more likely, we liked being hands-on, perhaps to a fault.

Most of the wannabes wanted to understand the complicated math of buying and operating an inn. They needed to hear about the significant sums of money, the enormous personal commitment to excellence, and to get an insider's view of the potholes along the way to better assess the opportunity. One of the students shared her financial leap of faith at check-in. "We're pledging our retirement accounts to finance the purchase of an inn. Both of us can cook, we love entertaining, we can't lose!"

Wow!

Yes, it all sounded easy, and familiar. We heard the echoes of our own hubris.

That evening, the students started arriving in the lounge, most having taken a rest before the wine event. Jeff queued up light jazz music while I arranged the wine glasses and finished garnishing platters of smoked salmon with fresh chives, alongside Camembert cheese, grapes, and slices of baguette.

Roger asked us to corral the students who had been taking self-guided tours of the books in the library and wandering around the dining room. Some were obviously impressed with the inn's modern yet classic style, and they were excited by the prospect of having their questions answered. While the students were assembled, drinking wine and chatting in groups, Roger kicked off the event.

"Teri and Jeff were both guests at my inn, as well as my inn brokerage clients. I represented them and sold them this inn. But I guarantee you it didn't look like this when they first saw it. Right, guys?" Jeff and I nodded our heads ruefully. "They walked into this inn with a vision and a dream, and you can have your dream, too."

Roger trusted us to keep the secret—that our dream turned into a full-blown nightmare before ultimately becoming a success. But we figured there were more than a couple of dreamers in this class, too, after bumping into a few of the students during the tour. It was clear many of them had read the Guest Information booklets in each room. We noticed many of the aspiring innkeepers were holding the booklet in their hands during the meet-and-greet.

Roger kept to his script. "For the next two days, you're going to get a crash course about the pros and cons of innkeeping, how to purchase an inn, inn operations and valuations. Then we'll take tours of several inns for sale in Bar Harbor and other villages on island." The students continued to help themselves to wine and snacks (which were going fast) as Roger reviewed the two-day seminar roadmap:

<u>Day One</u>
Meet your innkeepers
Self-assessment for aspiring innkeepers
Personal motivation, strengths and weaknesses
Day in the life of your innkeeper hosts
Innkeeping as a business, fact vs. fiction

<u>Day Two</u>
State and local visitor stats
Hospitably operating models: motels, inns, short-term rentals
Financial due diligence
Meet your bankers
Inns listed for sale in the area

Roger wrapped up the orientation by saying, "So before we get started tomorrow, I'd like to know if you have questions for me—or for Teri and Jeff."

Hands shot up all around the room. And since none of the questions had been provided to us in advance, it was open season. Roger pointed to one of the students. "Yes, go ahead."

A stylish, ample blond woman staying in Room 3 said, "I have a comment about my room—the robe isn't big enough; it hardly closes over my chest." Her chubby partner chimed in, "Yes, the robes are too small. The robes at our inn will be much, much larger."

Jeff said, "Here's a good example of one of the most valuable responses you'll need as an innkeeper, and you should write this down: 'Thank you for letting me know.'"

Roger took another question, and Jeff shot me a look as if to say, *OK, here we go!*

A well-groomed, modest fellow staying in Room 6 was traveling with his in-laws. "What's the hardest part of innkeeping?"

Jeff piped up, "Oh, that's easy! Avoiding death by ten thousand mosquito bites. You need patience to deal with the needs and expectations of the guests, staff, and vendors. Running an inn means staying ahead of the game, and the guests. We spend ninety-eight percent of our time worrying about the two percent we can't control. Trust me, it's impossible to control the weather, and occasional earthquakes."

Many of the students were puzzled to learn about ground-shaking events in a state best known for lobster, whoopee pies, and blueberries. "Earthquakes, here in Bar Harbor?" one guest asked incredulously.

"Yes!" Jeff said, recounting his experience last October, when there were two earthquakes in Bar Harbor on the same day. "The first quake struck before breakfast. There was a loud bang, followed by rumbling sounds. At first, I thought the furnace had blown up. Guests were startled and unsettled, but we assured them this inn was practically rebuilt from the inside out, so it's safe. Except, later that evening, there was another earthquake, which really rocked the boat. Martina, one of our student housekeepers, was up in the guest rooms doing turn-down. She came flying down the stairs in tears. 'Jeff, what was that?' I was trying to console her, and meanwhile, we had guests from California who marched up to me and began complaining, loudly, 'We didn't come here for earthquakes; we have those at home.' What could I say? This was an act of nature; it's not personal."

But some guests perceive sudden changes in plans or the weather as personal affronts. And it's difficult to predict Maine's unpredictable weather, which often surprises visitors by providing a three-season experience, sometimes all in the same day. Crisp, bracingly chilly mornings, hot sun-filled afternoons resulting in billowing blankets of cool fog, leading to cloudy, rainy afternoons best spent under a cozy throw in front of a warm fire. The temperature extremes can cause guests to get hot, or cold, under the collar, depending on their disposition. And of course, there are a few guests each season who preemptively quiz us about air-conditioning, special offers, and thread counts on the phone. Some guests are very particular, often booking their room months before arrival, requesting dinner reservations a year in advance, and seeking tips about packing. Our advice: Dress in layers, bring an umbrella, and pack a smile.

But during the summer, it's not unusual to have a few warm days along the Maine coast. And stretches of balmy weather are disappointing for visitors from hot spots like Arizona, Texas, and Florida, who look forward to cooler temperatures in Maine. Jeff gave me a look, my cue to chime in with one of my memorable guest stories. Who could forget Mr. Hot-n-Tot?

"Last August we had a crazy heat wave. It lasted nearly a week, and our guests from Arizona were prickly at breakfast," I said to get the story started:

"What should we do today? It's supposed to be 93 degrees. I didn't come to Maine for hot weather."

"How about going sea kayaking?" I figured it would be fun bobbing on Frenchman Bay and paddling to a nearby island on a warm, sunny day, the warm breezes tempered by the frigid ocean water. "Maybe you'll see a seal or two!" I suggested.

They loved the idea! I booked last-minute reservations for a tandem kayak excursion, and dinner at a sweet café on Cottage Street. A perfect day, problem solved. Or so I thought.

That night, the phone rang. Susan answered it. We were just starting to relax from our long day. "Jeff, it's Kurt; the chef at the café. He wants to talk to you."

Jeff picked up the phone and covered it with his hand. "I wonder what *he* wants?

"Hey, Kurt, what's up?" Jeff could barely hear the chef over the din in the restaurant. "Kurt, Kurt, I can't hear you. Can you speak up?"

"Listen, Jeff, this guest of yours from Arizona is a tool. I was doing you guys a favor squeezing him in without a reservation, but he's a real prick. He started complaining about the air-conditioning the minute he walked in."

The commotion of guests, kitchen staff, and servers was overwhelming; chef was slammed. "I'm in the shit tonight. I'm working a dozen salmon orders on the grill, one of my line cooks called out sick, and Mr. Hot-n-Tot is standing on the table cussin' at my wife and fussin' with the ceiling fan!"

More kitchen noise was pouring through Jeff's phone during chef's play-by-play.

"She just asked him to sit down, and he's refusing; now he's yelling! Goddammit! I have to go out there and deal with this jerk. I feel like punching the guy in the face." Clearly, chef was angry.

"Listen, Kurt, we had no idea he'd be a problem," Jeff said.

"OK, OK, but I'm so ticked-off. I don't have to take shit from anyone. Do me a favor, you guys, don't send dickheads like Mr. Hot-n-Tot to my restaurant if you can help it, OK?" And he hung up.

After breakfast the next morning, Kurt called back to repeat what had happened the night before, to make sure we knew that people like Mr. Hot-n-Tot would be 86'ed from his place of business in the future. I was also worried the troublemaker still hadn't cooled off, either. Servers were pouring coffee and taking breakfast orders. I passed by his table. "Good morning!" I said cheerily.

"What's good about it?" he snapped. "My room is unbearable. I can't get it under 68 degrees, and the A/C is going full blast! Why can't *you people* do something about it?"

I apologized for the inconvenience. "This heat wave is unprecedented; it was 103 degrees in Portland yesterday. Our HVAC systems are running full blast."

Not only were systems maxed out, but the staff, Jeff, and I were working overtime, too. Checking each guest room after the housekeepers finished service. Making sure room A/C controls were properly set, shades closed, ice water carafes topped-off, and the inn's complimentary bedtime chocolates prominently placed with a "Thank You for Understanding" note in the room. I guess Mr. Hot-n-Tot wasn't impressed.

I ticklishly inquired, "By the way, how was dinner last night?"

He hit his boiling point. "The place where you sent us was too hot! The chef was such an asshole, he asked me to step outside!"

"I'm sorry to hear that." Meanwhile I was thinking, *You were a nut, too bad*, so I changed the subject. "How was your kayak excursion?"

He shot me a look as he sarcastically ran his glass of ice water across his forehead.

"It was awful, like sitting in a cold bathtub with a hot furnace blowing in my face."

I nodded my head, filled their water glasses, and walked away. What more could I do? He was impossible.

Retelling this and other stories to wannabes, I shrugged my shoulders. "So, that's what sometimes happens—even good intentions can go wrong. So you put the difficult guest in imaginary isolation so they don't ruin another guest's day."

Another hand went up, the in-laws traveling with Room 6. "We're Jehovah's Witnesses. We don't drink and we don't plan on serving or permitting alcohol at our inn."

Jeff replied, "I think you might find some guests don't like conforming to house rules. Good luck with that."

The Q&A session was wrapping up, and one of the students called out, "What are your top innkeeper pet peeves?"

Jeff was fast on his feet. "Oh, that's easy." And he rattled them off our Top 10:

Number One— Late-night check-ins
Number Two— Makeup on the towels
Number Three— Repeat guests with bad attitudes
Number Four— Late laundry service deliveries
Number Five— Guests entering the kitchen
Number Six— Guests inviting non-guests for breakfast
Number Seven— Heavy luggage
Number Eight— Last-minute cancellations
Number Nine— Staff no-shows
Number Ten— Mean, implacable guests

Afterwards, hands were going up all around the room.

Jeff offered up an anecdote about our inn search to conclude the Q&A and return the podium to Roger.

"Teri and I scoured three states to find our inn. We looked at a small B&B in Vermont close to Mad River Glen ski area, thinking it might be a good destination for operating a year-round hospitality business. The property was listed for sale by owner, so we booked a one-night stay before showing our hand."

Jeff recounted our trip driving north from Boston along Route 89 in early April. The last vestige of snow was melting under a cover of road sand. With the weather suddenly warm, we opened the car windows for some fresh air, keeping a lookout for the place, which we read was tucked far away from the main route. We spotted more cows grazing, goats romping, and chickens pecking than we did people, and finally arrived at a modest clapboard farmhouse that was doing business as a five-room B&B.

The property had no curb appeal and badly needed paint. The B&B sign was dangling unsteadily from a hook, forlorn in the afternoon breeze. The parking lot was empty. Despite the unwelcoming condition of the property, we walked to the door and rang the bell. A fifty-something man answered the door casually dressed in shorts and a T-shirt. "Hey, how're you guys doing? You're staying the night, right?"

Jeff and I nodded.

He held the door open as we stepped into the small hallway, a space so tight the three of us could barely turn around. Our host handed us a key and pointed up the staircase. "Your room is at the top of the stairs. I'll be hanging around down here if you need anything."

We climbed to an attic room, passing the other four rooms which the owner said were No Vacancy. This surprised us, since there were no cars in the parking lot and no one else around. We pushed the door open, Jeff ducking his head to avoid hitting the rafters. The room was dark, even at 3:30 in the afternoon. I fumbled around for a light switch. Due to the sudden warm snap, the room was sweltering, hot and musty, and the windows were closed. The king-size bed was a futon covered in mismatched sheets, reminiscent of Jeff's college dorm room minus the lava lamp. The room looked as if it hadn't seen the light of day in quite a long time. We dropped our overnight bags and went back down the stairs to take a casual look around.

The innkeeper was sitting under a ceiling fan on a small brown corduroy sofa in the living room. There was only one other chair in the room, so if we'd planned on hanging out, one of us would have to sit right next to him on the couch. He patted the sofa cushion for me to sit down. "No, thanks anyway. We're going for a walk."

He reached for a cassette and put on a Grateful Dead bootleg concert. We both liked the group, which reminded us of our high school days, but we thought it was weird to play a pirated concert as a soundtrack for a hospitality business. We made a little chitchat while standing near the front door.

"So, how do you like being an innkeeper?" Jeff asked. We looked around the room, noting the skis on the wall and a few hanging plants that looked like they could use a drink.

"It's OK. It's a lot more work than I thought it would be."

"Well, business must be pretty good—the sign says No Vacancy!" I said cheerfully.

"No, my kids are visiting this week. They're staying in three of the rooms; there's you two, and other guests who aren't here yet. You'll probably meet them at breakfast tomorrow."

Jeff and I ambled around, wondering how this sad B&B could survive. No wonder he was selling it.

We drove back to a pizza parlor in town. Most of the restaurants were closed. It was the only option between the end of ski season and the arrival of summer tourists. After enjoying pizza and a few beers, we returned to the B&B, climbing the stairs to our attic room, which was hotter than a pizza oven. Not a hint of a breeze came in through the windows. We slept on top of the sheets rather than climb under the covers, tossing and turning all night.

The next morning we woke up sweltering from a fever dream. We dressed hastily, packing up our bags before heading down the stairs. In the dining room, the innkeeper had set the communal dining table for ten people. Apparently, his kids and the other paying guests had arrived while we were at dinner. A married couple in their early fifties was already sitting there. "Hi, we're the early birds," one of them said.

"Good morning," Jeff said.

Inn Mates

We took seats at the other end of the table, hoping they'd take a hint. We dreaded making small talk with strangers before having coffee. And we'd had a terrible night's sleep.

The wife asked, "Have you stayed here before?"

We shook our heads.

"We love staying here," she said. Now we were suspicious, wondering if the owner knew we were looking for an inn and had invited these two to influence us. "We love his cuisine," she said.

The "cuisine" was coffee in a paper cup, two microwaved pancakes, and a bowl of applesauce with cinnamon sprinkled on top. After filling up on applesauce and coffee, it was time to check out. We didn't have the heart to stick around and make small talk with the owner about our reason for visiting his B&B. We didn't want to get his hopes up, and we had no plans to write the next chapter for him.

Hearing this, the students nodded their heads.

"Moral of the story: If you're going to buy an inn, buy a going concern," Jeff said. "Make sure the inn is in good condition, has good cash flow, and a history of solid bookings." (He should have said, "Do as I say, not as we did," buying a distressed building with negligible business and dropping a hefty sum in the midst of a Restoration Vortex. But in fairness to ourselves, we had done our homework.)

Bar Harbor is a great place to be an innkeeper. Acadia National Park is a natural beauty and a magnet for tourists. But with all the visitors, campers, and cruise ship traffic, it can be hectic at times, especially on the Fourth of July.

Every year, the fireworks were launched from the town dock, mere steps from the inn, practically in our backyard. The previous year, the thundering fireworks finale shook the inn's windows, sending Riley running for cover. Hundreds of visitors wandered up and down Main Street, and small groups of people, not guests, walked into the inn dripping with melting ice cream cones and insisting on using the restroom. "Sorry, registered guests only."

While dealing with them, Jeff heard noises in the backyard and found three people, one man and two women, behind a Dumpster. One of the women was topless, changing her clothes next to it, and the others were watching, waiting for her. We thought we'd seen it all, but this was a first. Jeff asked, "Would you please put your clothes on and get off of my property?" Later that evening, we served our guests strawberry shortcake, ice cream, and champagne—shirts and shoes required.

At the end of the Q&A, Roger passed around the seminar materials for the next day. Jeff and I were first on the agenda after breakfast. Our answers to Roger's questions had been provided in advance.

Innkeeping Academy Agenda
What do Teri and Jeff like about innkeeping?

Innkeeping is a lens on life's rich pageant. For Teri and Jeff, it's also real income, psychic income, and rich emotional gratification from doing a job well for guests who are entitled to our best. But there are other reasons innkeeping rocks.

Owning an inn, you can:
- Be your own boss (guests can be your boss, too!)
- Live in a vacation destination
- Meet people from all walks of life
- Live where you work
- Work with your friend, family, spouse, or significant other
- Express your creativity
- Give to your community
- Work hard, then do nothing for a while
- Build equity for retirement
- Generate income during retirement
- Leave a legacy for others

Innkeeping Academy Agenda
Guest Amenities

Breakfast and Snacks
In addition to offering a pleasant environment, we specialized in breakfast. As a result, the kitchen was stocked with quantities of eggs,

cream, cheese, sugar, and flour. Not the ideal food pyramid for staying heart-healthy, slim, and energetic.

Beautiful, creative breakfast offerings were our pride and joy. Among the inn's luscious sweet and savory breakfast menu items, lemon ricotta pancakes, and rum-runner French toast, savory menus included hearty plates of lobster eggs benedict or sweet potato hash with poached eggs, all of which were daily temptations.

The inn guests are offered a full breakfast each day, plus a daily rotation of complimentary cookies, brownies, macaroons, fruit, and beverages in the Guest Pantry 24/7. Later in the afternoon, wine service and hors d'oeuvres were served at 6:00 p.m. When you're on vacation, there are no calories.

Each morning, Jeff and I sample small portions of food for quality control, and fight the urge to clean everything off our plates. Clearly, the resulting midday food coma from snacking on too many breakfast treats is a hazard. Naturally, the inn also served healthy meals and treats in addition to sweets. Fresh fruit, yogurt, oatmeal, and healthy vegetable omelets, spinach, kale, and sweet potato hash were among the offerings. But if you're working 7 days a week for 6 months straight, you feel entitled to a few treats. Every. Single. Day. There are no calories if it's work, right?

Jeff and I drink a few cups of coffee around 6:45 a.m. It was quiet time in the office and kitchen, both of us silently monitoring two kitchen timers that were set to go off—one in the office and another in the kitchen, the bakery equivalent of a belt-and-suspenders system, to be on the safe side. The strategy works wonders. In 15 years of inn operations, we served more than 50,000 meals, baked more than 200,000 scones, muffins, and cookies, and we had fewer than five baking disasters. Few…but memorable.

After the timer rings, one of us heads to the kitchen for a small muffin, scone, or whatever we were serving to the guests that morning. Again, quality control is very important. Zero calories.

The bakery treats for the Guest Pantry are baked after breakfast, plated and ready by noontime. Just in time for early check-ins, returning guests, or folks who skip breakfast. Here are a few of our guests' favorite treats:

Chocolate Cookies

The inn's delicious chocolate cookies are baked fresh daily, usually ready by 11:30 a.m. Guests often help themselves to two or three chocolate cookies, surreptitiously placing them in a paper napkin and eating them as soon as possible.

Coconut Macaroons

Our scrumptious coconut macaroons are dipped in heart-healthy dark chocolate. Guests often wait patiently until the chocolate has cooled, then sneak one to three macaroons into the palms of their hands. After the chocolate melts, the macaroons are ready to eat. Remember to provide napkins.

Brownies and Milk

Our guests liked nothing better than a warm brownie and a cold glass of milk. A few guests would buy ice cream and have two or more brownies, concocting ice cream sandwiches for lunch.

Housekeeping

The housekeeping team has designed fall-out drills and exercises to build strength, stamina, and endurance—a boot camp to replace the hours we would have spent at the gym. These are employee-only events. Memberships and coaching are not available to guests.

Staircase Medley Relay

This exercise is best performed at an inn that lacks elevator service. Like ours. Since there were 47 steps between the first floor and the fourth floor, the inn's staircases were perfect for building stamina and toning knees.

Starting in the basement, you'd hear your name called from somewhere in the inn. Then you'd quickly run up two flights of stairs to the second floor to figure out who's looking for you. Finding no one, you'd take a deep breath and run up to the third floor of the inn. The housekeepers would be glad to see you and would ask you to plug in the hall vacuum for them. It was also a good time for a few forward bends, followed by standing tall to take a few deep breaths.

Meanwhile, the innkeeper is staying alert and listening carefully for the front desk bell or telephone to ring, since one of us probably left our cellphone or walkie-talkie somewhere, and one of us would be running in circles to find it. Often when the phone or the front desk bell rings before 3:00 p.m., it will usually be a guest who's calling for early check-in. This is part of the "Innkeeper Spa Serenade," the simultaneous dinging and ringing of the land-line telephone, a cellphone, and the front desk bell or the front doorbell playing "Hail, Hail the Gang's All Here."

And since one of us probably forgot our phone at the desk, we'd draw straws to decide who'd have to run down the stairs, being careful not to trip over the vacuum on the second-floor landing. Once back on the first floor, we'd pivot to have a chat with the guest who'd called while they were walking to the inn, and who would now be standing at the front desk. It takes good aerobic stamina to act relaxed, not out of breath, when meeting guests for the first time. If they again request to check-in early, politely ask them to take a seat in the library.

By now, being somewhat winded, one of us would walk carefully up the first two flights of stairs, then break into a run up to the third floor to get a status and check the guest room on the fourth floor, being careful to unplug the vacuum on the third floor so the guests would not trip on it. After the sprint up, we'd let the housekeepers know the guests were waiting. Afterward, we'd take a breath to catch our breath, waiting for the housekeeping team to finish the room and lock the door, to indicate the room was ready for early check-in. Repeat several times daily.

Laundry Bag Kickboxing

This exercise is best performed by the strongest members of the housekeeping team, on a day when all ten guest rooms are being turned over.

Strip all bedding and towels from all ten guest rooms. Place the sheets and towels in large cloth laundry bags, tighten the drawstrings to ensure none of the linens fall out. Pick up or drag the 50# laundry bags to the top of the stairs, then push the laundry bags down the stairs. Chase down after them and give each a solid roundhouse kick to get the bags around the corner to the side exit door. Drag the bags to the back deck. Heave the bags up and over the deck railing to the driveway below. Take a water break while waiting for the laundry service to pick up. Repeat daily.

Bathroom Yoga—Downward Facing Dog

Yoga is a great exercise for staff and innkeepers who wish to maintain strength and flexibility. The downward-dog position is easiest to perform in guest bathrooms.

Remove all towels from the guest room. Spray disinfecting spray cleaner in the bathtub or whirlpool. Stand tall, make sure both feet are hip-width apart, then with hands on hips, stretch forward, bending at the hip, and place both hands on the floor of the tub. Be careful not to slip. Hold the pose for 5 deep breaths while scrubbing the tub, then rinse. Stand up to dry the tub completely. Combine the cleaning towels with other laundry from the guest room, and place in the laundry center on the second floor. Repeat 10x daily.

Cool-Down

At the end of the housekeeping shift, double-check the laundry area to make sure all linens have been stowed before locking the door. Be careful not to kick bundled laundry—you might find one of the student workers fast asleep under a load of clean robes. (Yes, this did happen!) At the end of the daily workout, rest quietly in the office while checking for guest voice mail and email. Call restaurants for guests to place dinner reservations as promised at breakfast. After wrapping up the morning activities, enjoy an afternoon nap.

Guest Services

The Assistant Innkeeper arrives at 2:00 p.m. Her first responsibility is to check the guest rooms, to provide a second pair of eyes with housekeeping, and to coordinate special guest requests, if any.

Check-in time is 3:00 p.m.

At 5:00p.m., the Assistant Innkeeper sets up the wine service, in between helping arriving guests. If she's very busy, both innkeepers jump in to help with check-ins, or put out the baked brie, or curried crab canapés, or hummus and spanakopita we prepped earlier in the day, along with wine for the guests. One of us will get busy making our own dinner.

At 6:00 p.m., we enjoy dinner. It's our relaxation in the evening, often taken on the back deck during the summer months. It's our private time. A time to visit with friends who drop by, like the laundry delivery guys who like to chat—"Hey, man, how's it going?"—while dropping off the clean linens and picking up the bags of dirty linens from the inn's laundry kickboxing event.

If it's raining, or if it's not possible to be outside, we enjoy dinner theater in our private dining room. Meanwhile, the guests who are providing the entertainment are enjoying wine in the lounge, chatting, singing, playing the piano, and laughing right over our heads. Afterwards, we amble out to the inn's common areas to show our faces, say hello, and check in with the office before getting ready for early bed. We set the alarm for 5:45 a.m. Enjoy a good night's sleep without worrying about the inn's fire alarm, guest lock-outs, or folks ringing the front bell to ask for a street map.

Wash—Rinse—Repeat

Lost and Found Policy

The Lost and Found Policy is not just best practice, it's a privacy protocol.

To an innkeeper, "lost and found" is translated into "a guest left it, we found it, and we hope he or she will call to reclaim it before we donate or discard it at the end of the season."

We learned a long time ago that the conventional wisdom is DO NOT contact the guest about something that has been found or left behind in the guest room. NEVER, EVER, EVER!!

Just imagine you stole away for a few days with a new significant other, and they leave behind their thong underwear. Then we call, text, or a leave a message: "*WE FOUND YOUR UNDERWEAR!*" and the receiving party has no idea their soul mate was traveling with someone else. No one likes a tattletale, especially an innkeeper tattling on a paying guest.

Not only could the guest rightly complain that the innkeepers were busybody do-gooders, but the guest might challenge the room charges paid by credit card out of spite. Proving the age-old axiom, *No good deed goes unpunished.*

Naturally, you may be curious, or wonder about what tends to be lost or found at the inn. Here's a sampling of items that were thrown away or donated to charity over the last decade:

- Enough charging cords and adapters to stretch from Maine to California
- Undergarments left in the bed, under the bed, in the closet, under the sink
- Personal care "enjoyment" items left in bedside tables
- Mite-infested travel pillows brought from home and left behind at the inn, posing a health risk
- Tote bags and travel umbrellas that were wind-lashed and broken
- Semi-finished wine and restaurant take-out containers guests think the housekeepers would like to finish
- Discarded clothing items, tattered and patched, which were replaced by new items you bought on vacation, because, really, who has time to shop anymore?
- A framed photograph of a golden retriever
- A lesbian porn video disguised in a 2004 Red Sox World Series DVD case

Frequently Asked Questions:

Why does the sun come up so early?
The birds like it.
Why are the birds so loud in the morning?
To greet the sunrise. We asked them to pipe down; they don't listen.

When is high tide every day?
> *It depends; it changes every day.*

Where can I find a REAL lobster?
> *A lobster pound. Fake lobster can be found at the toy store.*

What day are the Fourth of July fireworks?
> *Really?*

Can I use the inn's computer
> *No, sorry.*

Does my key open my room door?
> *Yes—it's very convenient!*

Can I help you cook breakfast?
> *No, sorry. You're on vacation, right?*

Can I open the windows in my room?
> *Yes, but please don't jump!*

Can I burn cardboard in my gas fireplace.
> *No. No. No!*

Can I sit on the fire escape?
> *No. No. No!*

Can I walk on the roof?
> *No. No. No!*

Does the inn have vegan mattresses?
> *Not sure. But they are ovo-lacto free!*

What do people do here in the winter?
> *Stay warm.*

Do Not Book Policy

Most innkeepers keep a list of the miserable minority of guests who have been bad actors while staying at the inn. It's called the Do Not Book list—a roster of shame.

There are sections of the DNB list devoted to grumpy, implacable guests who enjoy nothing more than spending their money insulting innkeepers, fellow guests, and staff.

Under the best circumstances, the innkeepers try to anticipate the grumpy guest before he or she enters the inn. Innkeepers are not savants, but we are at times clairvoyant. If the Assistant Innkeeper speaks words like "Room 8 was difficult at check-in," the innkeeper will become vigilant and will be on the lookout for guest bad behavior.

If we agree the difficulties can't be resolved, we will offer the grumpy guest alternative booking arrangements elsewhere, waiting for the right moment to inform them they are free to check out, as soon as possible. Here are actual examples when this technique has been used:

- Guest confronting the innkeepers at breakfast, insisting her diet is *sooo* meticulous she needs to cook her own food.
- Guests making rude, sexually explicit, or racist comments to other guests, staff, or innkeepers.
- Splashing a bottle of wine on the draperies, bedding, and carpet, and not telling us.
- Sneaking extra guests into the room.
- Inviting guests from other inns to breakfast with no notice.
- Smuggling newborn twins because grandma canceled babysitting to go on a cruise.
- Trying to bring three service animals to the inn.
- Stealing bottles of wine from the inn's refrigerator, drinking it, and passing out in the library.
- Beating the front door with a rubber mallet.
- Reservation no-shows demanding a full refund.
- Guests having loud arguments.

Innkeeping, like life, is a journey. No two days are the same. The guests come and go, and the parade of Life's Rich Pageant is complex and endlessly fascinating. So it's important to keep the doorways, exits, and chimneys clear and unobstructed.

Inn Maintenance

Hot water is not an amenity when you're an innkeeper. It's a requirement, like air, without which you might as well cancel your bookings, refund the deposits, close the doors, and walk away.

I never thought too much about hot water prior to becoming an innkeeper. In my experience, you turned the tap to call for hot water and it flowed. I didn't realize how vital chimneys were in the production of hot water. I didn't realize chimneys had bladders, vents, and spaces where hot air would get stuck. I did know the chimneys were in iffy condition when we bought the inn. Two were nearly collapsed, then removed. The remaining chimneys were cleaned, repointed, and placed into service.

So, after turning this inn inside out and putting it back together bit by bit, Jeff and I assumed all of the exhausted hot air would simply rise and drift right up the chimney. Except the air wasn't going up the chimney quite right. There was a problem.

It was mid-October, in the middle of nonstop full houses, our eyes fixed on the finish line of closing only a few weeks away. I was immersed in my habit of taking hot water for granted. Until one morning, I had to inform the guests that the water might not be hot enough. That's when I found myself in withdrawal, a full-blown panic attack. That's when I realized I was totally addicted to hot water.

The masons were scheduled to complete a minor job of repointing a few chimney bricks. One of the guys was astride the roofline; the other was hip deep in the chimney. He shouted out to report that the main chimney, which was connected to the boiler, had no flue. Water was raining in—condensed hot-water exhaust leaching out—a sticky situation, creating corrosion that could compromise the structural integrity of the chimney. To remedy this, a plan was hatched to send a rubber sleeve down the chimney and pour a new liner of concrete, which required a shutdown of the boiler for the procedure. The inn was booked, we were sold out, but we had no choice. If all went according to plan, the inconvenience would be minimal. If. Written notice to guests was placed in the rooms on the prior day to warm them up to the idea.

Inn Maintenance

Tomorrow, routine maintenance of the inn's boilers will take place between 11:00 a.m. and 3:00 p.m.
During this time, there will be no hot water.
We apologize for the inconvenience.

The next morning, while preparing coffee for the early risers, the scaffolding went up to the chimney. We'd asked the masons to work as quietly as possible while they ran bucketloads of concrete around a new bladder sleeve. In a couple of hours, the new flue would be perfectly set, in time to restart the boilers.

The bladder operation was a success! I baked extra oatmeal raisin cookies as a thank-you to the chimney guys (as well as the guests), and they were on their way.

Hours later, Jeff and I nervously hovered around the scene, fingers crossed, as Rick, the plumber, went to the basement to light the enormous boiler. Minutes passed, and he climbed up from the basement. "Hey, guys, this thing is not venting. There's too much negative pressure. It won't draw the exhaust up the flue." This harsh reality was evidenced by his eyes tearing blood-red from the boiler exhaust that was filling the boiler room and our apartment with noxious fumes. Imagine stepping aboard a jumbo jet and finding your seat is located in the engine compartment. At this point, we were feeling pretty negative, too, about the afternoon guest arrivals because right over our heads, we could hear Susan padding around upstairs, charming registered guests who were aware of the hot water issue, and welcoming twelve new guests who'd rushed into the inn from a driving rainstorm. The floors on the porch and in the hallway were slick with rain. The hall mirror fogged up from the moisture dripping off the guests. Likely half of them were planning to take a warm, relaxing shower or whirlpool bath.

Jeff and I were kicking ourselves for deciding to undertake this "minor" project in the midst of one of the busiest times of year—Columbus Weekend, the ultimate holiday of the innkeeping season, coming after nonstop full houses for nearly six months. The success of the inn—solid bookings, waiting lists, and back-to-back full houses—left no room for downtime, errors, poor hot water, or chimney leaks. Period.

"I think we can kick the system on for hot water, but it's going to be tight," Rick said. "I'm going to open all the basement doors and windows to bring in fresh air, and get an industrial fan to vent the exhaust outside."

Like a miracle, his hunch worked! Despite our good luck, our spirits were still dampened. All of this was happening in the middle of a thunderstorm, and the basement was wet, damp, and smoky. "This is OK for tonight, but it's a temporary solution, Plan A," he said.

"What are the other options, Rick?" Jeff asked cautiously.

"Plan B, I'm going to send a camera up the chimney to see if the blockage resulted from the concrete pour. Plan C is the worst-case scenario—the chimney comes down and will have to be rebuilt." He shrugged his shoulders.

I thought, *Rebuild the chimney while we're open for business? You must be kidding!*

It was only four o'clock in the afternoon, but it was starting to seem like a good time to start drinking.

Fortunately, Plan D was devised, and an updraft booster fan was installed to push exhaust out of the boiler immediately after it was fired up. Just in the nick of time.

Resting in bed that night, our thoughts drifted. After owning the inn for more than a decade, the clicks, buzz, and night music of the Dream had gotten familiar, like heartbeats or a pulse. You instinctively know when things are humming right along or if something is not quite right.

We hope the inn has many healthy years ahead of her in the macro sense, but the micro tweaks are emerging here and there. Next year, a new roof. Paint a side of the building each year, ensuring it will look younger than its age. Fortunately, the inn's medical team, the vendors and repairmen-in-waiting, are close by with calculators working. These guys know us, they know the inn, and they know we pay on time. Yes, after fourteen years, we're still paying our dues.

PART SIX

CHAPTER TEN

I know you're tired, but come, this is the way.
—Rumi

Front Desk Notes

Susan,
I've been running in circles all day, and we're not even open. A stream of pre-season tourists came to the inn this afternoon, knocking on the doors and windows despite the No Vacancy sign hanging outside. I taped a new sign to the front door:

OPENING SOON
PLEASE CALL FOR RESERVATIONS

Jeff's hip replacement surgery is scheduled for tomorrow. He'll be back on April 30th, staying in Room 1, the ADA-compliant room with handrails and supports in the bathroom. I've taken it out of service for three weeks. By then we hope he'll be well enough to walk up and down the stairs to our apartment. He thinks he'll be in fine shape within one week. I'm not sure about that, but "hope springs eternal."

We picked up the medical supplies Jeff will need after surgery. A walker, cane, and raised toilet seat, which Jeff regarded quizzically. His physical therapy sessions will be held here while he's convalescing, and he'll need rest and privacy, so please don't knock on the door if you have calls or questions from vendors, contractors, or issues with guests. Forward all calls to me. I'll be responsible for opening and closing the inn, oversight of front desk, kitchen, and dining room operations, and housekeeping. A special All-Hands Meeting is scheduled for tomorrow.

Have a nice Evening!

Teri Anderholm

Innkeeper Wellness Program

Innkeepers often joke, "No one can get married, get sick, or die when we are working!" So what started out as an inside joke eventually grew into hospitality gallows humor, and later became reality. We had to strike a balance between being convivial hosts, enjoying the inn and guests, managing the staff and property, and adhering to healthy habits to get through the season. Especially in a popular destination like Acadia National Park.

With more than four million visitors each year, the tourist season in Bar Harbor is a six-month-long marathon, not a sprint. Pacing yourself is important, and it's a good idea to rest during the off-season because being an innkeeper is different from being a guest on vacation. Still, there was a comforting mind-numbing monotony that took over when working seven days a week.

In May, it's easy to jump the starting gun and run too fast when you're feeling fresh and rested, succumbing to the notion that running a hotel, inn, or B&B is a piece of cake. A walk in the park as the first few weeks roll by effortlessly. But if you start the work season ragged, or tired, you're at a disadvantage right out of the gate. June melds into July. Mental fatigue starts to set in. The guest interactions become rote, as we're asked and answer the same questions day after day. "When's low tide?" "Where can I get a 'real' lobster?" and by August, you've forgotten the day of the week and you crave sleep. It can be a grueling month, between warm weather, large crowds of tourists, and mornings staring at tables of guests, unable to remember their names or the menus. Fortunately, the mood was usually upbeat, especially when we were surrounded by friendly guests who remembered to pack a sense of humor. But sometimes they didn't.

At one of the impromptu innkeeper midseason mixers, a colleague had a confession to make. He mixed up a double gin and tonic and took a long drink. "I had the worst guest this week. She was a witch, unreasonable, demanding more padded hangers and stacks of hand towels. She called me after midnight to complain the blow-dryer wasn't hot enough, then the housekeepers told me she left mascara all over the pillowcases. I lost it!" he said sheepishly. "I couldn't wait to get rid of her. When she came to check out and gave me guff, I threw her American Express card out to the sidewalk. Good riddance!" His confession fell on sympathetic ears.

The marathon required consistency and steadiness while running the race. Streamlining work processes to ensure that each morning, evening, and weekend would be blessedly the same for six straight months. With no extreme events, like hurricanes, power outages, staff shortages, or health problems. Of course, all of these things happened, but we managed, often relying on our homemade brand of "hospitality gallows humor," a collection of smartass quips and bad jokes we improvised. Like the phrase, "Guess what I don't have to do today?" which everyone repeated nearly every morning when we were closed for the season.

Innkeeper jokes and puns were a coping mechanism, more fun than griping about the disappointment of missing out on attending family celebrations, summer BBQs, graduations, and the occasional funeral. We surrounded ourselves in a cloak of mirth to ward off the likelihood that any one of us would get sick or have a medical issue. And despite our preoccupations with guests, staff, and personal health matters, innkeepers stuck together, helping each another if one of us had an emergency or needed a ride to the hospital, pitching in to help one another with breakfast or a turn on front desk.

Still, every evening felt like a Sunday from childhood, fraught with the night-before-school anxiety, a sense of foreboding and dread, fretting about bedtime while watching *60 Minutes* on TV. Every morning felt like Monday—the alarm clock ringing early, when it was still dark outside. The darkness smoothing over middle-of-the-night fretting, wondering if the front desk bell, a fire alarm, or a locked-out guest would need assistance. But the rewards for running the hospitality marathon were worth it once you crossed the finish line at the end of October. Because from November through March, every single day felt like Saturday.

Just after Labor Day, Jeff and I, our colleagues and staff, were limping along, inching day by day toward the season's seventh-inning stretch. But when the back-to-school vibe of September took hold, I detected a change in the weather and in myself as summer slowly shifted to autumn.

Jeff and I would sneak away to go apple picking, getting fresh apples for the guests to enjoy. Traveling down country byways, we'd pause by the side of the road to watch stands of daylilies and cattails waving in the breeze. Then we'd return to the car, bouncing along a dirt road until we turned into the orchard. The car door opened, and Riley jumped out, tail wagging.

The first thing we noticed was the quiet. Monarch butterflies silently fluttered in the goldenrod. Then the feel of the soft ground underfoot as our shoes sank into the deep grass. Windfalls of fruit were squashed here and there as we carefully negotiated the slippery spots around and under the trees. Bees buzzed haphazardly, drunk on apple mash. The peace and quiet of the outside world was magnificent, but also disquieting. We took in several deep breaths of freedom. For a few moments, we forgot about our responsibilities for the inn, staff, and guests.

Jeff picked up the handle of a red wagon, and I grabbed an apple pole. He gazed around and took in the view, then tugged the wagon down a well-worn path, the little wheels squeaking behind him.

"This is the most relaxed I've felt in weeks," he said.

"You said it, I'm exhausted."

We meandered between the bountiful trees laden with fruit. Small wood signs pointed us in the direction of vast fields of juicy Macintosh, tart Macoun, and shiny Cortland apples. We had to step carefully around the bees and wasps who were busily indulging themselves in pools of sweet pulp. The aroma of wood smoke gave way to the sweet smell of cider donuts and cinnamon-dusted apple crisps that were offered for sale. We took turns taking bites of the apples while we stumbled around the uneven ground, feeling drunk from the juice. We held hands and kissed under an apple tree. Our field trip to the Garden of Eden, savoring the arrival of autumn, our fall appetites were now whetted. Instinctively, we knew summer was almost over, and we'd soon turn the corner to October. From the apple orchard, we could see a light at the end of the tunnel. The off-season was in sight.

By late October, the weather became cooler, which ignites new energy and a second wind. We started ticking off the days on the kitchen calendar until closing day. Surprisingly, the countdown made us feel as though we could run the marathon forever, all of us picking up steam as we approached the finish line. We were unstoppable! The exhilaration was palpable, our pulse strong and steady, until the adrenaline started to drain away a few hours after closing. By nightfall it was nearly impossible to resist the urge to sleep for three days straight. A week later, we flew to St. Croix, USVI, for a long winter's nap.

Medical Leave

The next season's spring opener was going to be tricky. The stiffness and pain in Jeff's left hip and leg became unbearable. He decided it was finally time to have that hip replacement surgery he'd been trying to put off.

Jeff had recovered so completely from his car accident 30 years ago, he sometimes forgot about it. Still, after being an innkeeper for more than ten years, it was inevitable one of us would have a health issue. We knew there would be medical or family leave down the road for one or both of us, which would require planning and coordination with staff to make sure all of the wheels at the inn remained on the track.

Jeff thought it would be a good idea to wait until the snow melted, so surgery was planned for late spring, before we opened for the season. Our thinking was that the daily exercise while working would serve as a convenient, familiar rehab to help him regain strength, range of motion, and stamina.

We expected the surgery would go without a hitch, performed without delay, complications, or unnecessary pain. It was scheduled for April 27th. Pre-season startup was under way as we worked according to a detailed punch list. I was serving as player/coach. Jeff was upbeat, happy about our well-laid plans for the season, grateful for a seasoned team of players who were on their game, and a solid book of reservations. Still, he was apprehensive about getting a new hip. He had a good night's sleep before being admitted to the hospital.

Early the next morning, after he was admitted, I returned to the inn, double-checking the front door to ensure the new No Vacancy sign was clearly displayed, the windows and the doors locked. I bought a box of donuts at the grocery store and made a few pots of coffee. After flipping on the kitchen lights, I wandered to the back door to open it as the staff came in, grabbed coffee, and took their donuts for the meeting in the lounge. My All-Hands Meeting was scheduled at the very moment Jeff was being wheeled into surgery at the hospital. I passed around the agenda and opened the meeting.

"Welcome back!" I looked twice around the room to make sure everyone knew one another. "As you know, Jeff was admitted for surgery today. He's asked that we pull together this season, like always. He really appreciates all the hard work you've done already. Thank you."

I pulled out the maintenance report Jeff had prepared for the meeting. Someone once said God is in the details, and as all innkeepers know, it's ALL about the details.

"The painters have finished up the exterior painting on the east-facing side of the inn. Please use the back entrance this week. It's still chilly at night, and the paint takes longer to dry. Don't make the same mistake I made, check me out—"

I pointed to the front leg of my jeans, which were smeared with paint after I'd accidentally brushed past the front door. "Thank God I wasn't a guest."

Heads were all nodding.

"The handyman will be here later this afternoon to dig out the front storm drain. How many of you remember the basement flood from a few years ago?"

Lincoln said, "Ohhhh, yes!" All the other hands went up, too.

During a winter nor'easter, the water runoff had inundated the town's storm sewer. Rip currents of flood water knocked over a hundred-year-old granite wall, forcing wastewater into the basement. The sump pump didn't stand a chance. The building alarm sounded when the water rose thigh-high in the basement. The fire department arrived to pump it out of the building, and the resulting damage was significant. It was a nightmare, which we hoped never to repeat.

As the repairs were performed, we wanted answers: *What happened* during the storm that sent wastewater up through the sump pump, toilets, and shower drains? Jeff got to the bottom of it, sending a camera down into the pipes to figure out the root cause. A crushed outflow pipe was buried beneath the asphalt parking lot of the hotel next door. It was dammed up. And because their parking lot was private property, the hotel was not obliged to repair the problem. We were merely gnats on the shoulder of an 800-pound gorilla.

Next up, housekeeping—one of the most important aspects of inn operations. We had had top-notch standards for cleanliness and loveliness for guest room comfort, and our extraordinary team treated the inn like their own home. The pride of ownership was in evidence every single day.

"This year, we're moving to a new triple-sheet system. Jeff and I liked the look and feel of the 'heavenly beds' at other hotels." Bedspreads were out. Duvets were in. A couple of the housekeepers started clapping. They loved the new linens and were excited to learn a better way to take care of guests. This would lead to larger guest tips and thank-you notes, which were perks the staff loved.

"The plumbers were here to service the A/C units. So housekeepers, please check the systems by turning the units on and off. Double-check and clean all the remotes, and make sure they all have fresh batteries."

The agenda moved to kitchen operations.

"The kitchen training meeting will be held tomorrow to review the new menus, food allergy concerns, hand-washing, proper food handling, plus daily cleaning checklists. We also have new kitchen equipment...wait for it...a Hobart high-temperature dish sanitizer that has a two-minute wash cycle." Cheers went up among the kitchen crew and servers.

We were getting down to staff scheduling, which was being changed to accommodate Jeff's absence. While no one was indispensable, we were a team, and we functioned as an integrated unit. All of us were cogs in a hospitality wheel. As one shift ended, another started; the hand-offs were tricky, requiring good timing and communication, like Front Desk Notes. The goal was a seamless flow of activities to ensure guests were happy and comfortable. "Let's remember our guests are on vacation, and they want to have a good time. When you see them in the morning, say 'Good morning' and offer a smile, make eye contact." Which I was trying to do just then, but I became distracted, wanting to call the hospital to check on Jeff. But there was one last thing that needed to be said. "Let's have fun this season!"

Meeting adjourned.

After the meeting, a nurse called to report that Jeff's surgery went well. I was relieved—until told she told me The Doctor wanted to talk to me and asked that I come to the hospital. During the short walk, I wondered why we would be meeting outside the recovery room.

He took a seat across from mine and shook his head. "I don't know how stable Jeff's going to be."

My blood ran cold. "What do you mean, he's not stable?" I cried.

"We tested his range of motion in the operating room. Something doesn't seem right."

The puzzled look on my face told him I was confused. He slowly got to the crux of the matter. "When we were in the OR, I needed an extra-large ball and socket joint. We didn't have the right size today." I took a deep breath, thinking to myself, *What are we going to do now?* As if reading my mind, he said, "I'm going see how he does when he gets of out of bed later today."

I secretly crossed my fingers. Jeff had not been informed about any of this, but he would soon find out.

The Doctor and nurse tried to help Jeff stand up, and the hip ball-joint popped out. He was asked to lie back down, and it popped out again. Jeff was jangling like a skeleton on a string and covered in a cold sweat. The Doctor wanted answers ASAP and found a portable X-ray device to take a closer look. When we met outside Jeff's room the next morning, he said, "I've been up all night worrying about Jeff's hip." He wasn't the only one. The physical therapist confirmed that Jeff was unable to stand, sit, or walk. No surprise: The hip wasn't stable, and Jeff would need a second surgery before the wound healed up.

This was a harsh pill to swallow. Jeff was not only in pain, he was anxious, worrying about functioning during the season. I tried to console him, bringing him coffee and almond croissants during my daily visits with him at breakfast, lunch, and dinner. My heart broke watching him hobble with an unstable hip. He was bedridden and miserable, waiting for his new surgical date to roll around, four days hence.

I bumped into The Doctor again in my new role of patient advocate. "We have complete faith in you, but what are we going to do?" He reviewed the possible complications from the upcoming surgery, and worst-case scenarios, dissuading me from transferring Jeff to Mass General in Boston. "Jeff is in good hands," he said.

The Doctor took my place as Jeff's best advocate, treating his case as a personal crusade and arranging hip replacement hardware from four regional hospitals who expedited the prosthesis cavalry to deliver the cargo. The next day, four overnight couriers arrived at the hospital, each driver wheeling six-foot-high stacks of surgical bins into the hospital, STAT. I took photos on my phone to share them with Jeff. Finally, we could relax—a little.

Back at the inn, painters, plumbers, kitchen crew, housekeepers, and suppliers were making progress on the punch lists for opening day. A teeming hive of activity. We were on a tight schedule for opening day, booked for the entire season. Jeff would be the first check-in.

Jeff's second surgery was short and sweet. He felt more secure and looked forward to his normal routine. But recovery from major surgery was painful, and rehabilitation was slow, not to mention it was taking place in a public setting.

The Doctor and the physical therapist made house calls. "Hey, this place is really nice!" they said. Yes, it *was* really nice, but despite the praise, it was difficult for Jeff to rest when the business was up and running. His ears and eyes were tuned to every click, buzz, and hum of the hotel's life systems outside his room door, sounds that were as familiar as his pulse. He could hear the comings and goings of every guest, the sound of footsteps back and forth in front of his room, the commotion of chatting guests on the front porch.

After the first week, Jeff emerged from his room on his walker, then a cane, which he nicknamed HURRY. The crew got a kick out of the cane name; only later would we learn how prescient the name would be.

Still, it was difficult getting back on your feet when you couldn't lift your leg, put on your socks, or tie your own shoes. Jeff handled his challenges by changing the focus from himself to others. And he rallied. Within three weeks, he was working in his office, walking around, acting pleasantly attentive, seemingly nonchalant about his recuperation.

By June, Jeff and I were finally able to sleep together in our bed. I was softly tracing circles on his back while he was becoming drowsy. I noticed a small pink spot, and almost didn't have the heart to ask.

"Jeff, do you remember something happening to your back in the hospital?" I was hoping a sensor or patch had been removed, and the spot was still healing.

"No." He was half asleep.

I persisted. "Did you have a something removed by a dermatologist?"

"I'll check it tomorrow."

The next morning, Jeff checked his back and phoned the dermatologist, who was able to examine him due to a timely cancellation. A skin check and biopsy were performed. "Doctor, do you think it's serious?" he asked.

"Don't know Jeff, let's find out. We'll send the tissue sample to the lab and get back to you with the results. My office will call you."

Days later, both of us were immersed in our work and had forgotten about the tissue issue. Until the phone rang. It was the dermatologist's assistant. "Good morning, Jeff! The doctor said you have melanoma!" she said cheerily. Jeff nearly choked on his coffee. "You're being scheduled for surgery in two weeks. Have a nice weekend!" she chirped.

Jeff was stunned. "I can't believe what I heard! They gave me this news on the *phone?* Teri, I'm scheduled for surgery right after the Fourth of July weekend."

The Fourth of July is still early days in the hospitality marathon, with many, many more months until closing in October. Jeff and I had once joked, "No one can get sick or die when we're working." But this time, it wasn't at all funny.

Just after the Fourth of July, Jeff was back in the hospital, still hobbling around on his new hip and skittish about a third surgery within a ninety-day period. But unlike the hip, the skin cancer surgery went smoothly. The cancer had been detected early, but wide margins were taken, leaving a large incision across his upper right shoulder to match the incision in his left hip.

Jeff returned to the inn the same day and took off only a day or two before he returned to work full-time. His work routine was good low-impact exercise that brightened his mood even though he was wearing a J-drain attached under his shirt with safety pins. Jeff was a selfless team player. His courage and work ethic impressed the staff, who pitched in to make sure he was comfortable and cared for. We were a family, taking care of our own. We made sure the guests were none the wiser.

At the end-of-season dinner, we celebrated Jeff's recovery and recognized the staff who had made the season a success. Everybody was a hero. Still, we felt Jeff had earned a hospitality purple heart for his meritorious service and sacrifice in the line of duty.

Teri Anderholm

Family Leave

Despite the innkeeper's golden rule, "No one can get sick or die while we're working," Jeff's sister Liz called with bad news just before Mother's Day.

"Mom fell and broke her hip. She was alone when I found her, and I'm not sure how long she was on the floor. She's going into rehab; I'll keep you posted on her condition."

We were hopeful Jan's condition would improve, but she'd become weak from her fall, and her condition wasn't improving. On Mother's Day, Liz texted a photo of Jan in her hospital bed, and her situation was not looking good.

Jeff reminded me of his mom's prank telephone calls:

"Hello, I'd like to talk to one of your guests."

Meanwhile, Jeff knew it was her. "What's the guest's name?" he asked.

"His name is Ralph Slice," she said petulantly.

Jeff said, "Slice, like the soda?" No reply. "OK, Mom, thanks for calling." And he hung up. Her telephone call was recorded in the phone log: "Mosquito bite—ten thousand and one."

Still, somewhere in the back of my mind, I thought of the poetry of Jan passing away on Mother's Day. She was a colorful character, a feisty redhead, stubborn, proud, at times a terribly provoking mother and mother-in-law. Passing away on Mother's Day would be a fitting punctuation mark to her life. Motherhood defined her, despite her unique style of nurture which defied definition. She died the following day. Arrangements were made for Jeff and his siblings to gather at later date.

Later that week, Janine and I were preparing breakfast for the guests. I cranked up the oven to bake maple oat scones, reaching over the sink to open the windows for a cool breeze. Janine was sautéing shallots.

"I hope you had a nice Mother's Day," I said.

"Yes, it was nice, quiet," she said.

"I have some news—Jeff's mom died the day after Mother's Day."

"I'm so sorry to hear it," she said.

"Me too." I had Jan in mind when I was making chitchat during breakfast.

Jeff was standing ready in the office. We expected Sunday-morning check-outs to be brisk. He hung up the phone, as guests from Room 4 stopped by the front desk. Dressed head to toe in L.L. Bean trekking apparel, they cut a neat figure reminiscent of the cartoon Canadian Mountie, Dudley Do-Right, and Nell.

"I heard chirping sounds when I was in the shower. I think it's coming from the fan light."

Jeff thought, *Oh, great.* "Thanks for letting me know."

He picked up the phone to schedule a pest control specialist. We had played host to unwelcome families of squirrels, bats, and stray mice from time to time.

Jeff reported back to Dudley. "I think there's a nest of hatchlings in your bathroom's fan ductwork. Unfortunately, we're booked, so I can't offer you another room. We'll offer you a discount for your trouble."

"No problem, Jeff. We love birds. Maybe we'll be here when they fledge."

We loved guests who were affable and understanding. Life happens...

Back in the kitchen, a few minutes later, "*CHIRP*" came from the back window. I turned, spotting a cardinal on the deck railing. I'd not seen any bird life on the deck before, and I was fascinated by songbirds, especially cardinals and blue jays. Grandma Doris had told me about their symbolism. "Cardinals are messenger birds, a reminder of deceased loved ones." A shiver passed through me.

"Janine, did you see the cardinal?"

"Yes, I saw it; it flew away."

I returned to get a few more scones from the cooling rack. "*CHIRRP, CHIRRP, CHIRRP!*" A red-and-brown female cardinal was sitting pretty in the herb garden among the early green leaves and buds on the golden chain tree.

"There it is again!" I said. "I think it's my mother-in-law." It then began chirping madly, and began flying in figure eights, back and forth between the kitchen windows and the back deck.

Jeff wandered into the kitchen. "Hon, did you see the cardinal?" I asked. He gave me the woo-woo eye roll.

"I think it's Jan," I said.

"Right, maybe she's come back to get in a last word."

We named the inn's new mascot Jan, and it spent the entire summer at the inn. We became used to Jan's chirping and swooping from the roofline down to the porch and back deck. Bird wings flapped in front of the kitchen windows as if waving to us, then followed Jeff and me to the dining room windows, as if to say, "Hey everybody! Look, it's me!"

We smiled at the sightings, retelling stories of Jan and her antics: a family trip to San Francisco wearing her signature flowerpot hat; flicking cigarette ashes into a pristine trout stream before kissing the Blarney Stone in Ireland. Sometime later, Jeff and his siblings sifted her ashes over the waters of Mother's Beach in Kennebunk.

Work/Life Balance

Innkeepers often said, "Happy guests, happy innkeeper." I kept telling myself I should be living the innkeeper lifestyle, easygoing, fun-loving. Even though most of us admitted to falling asleep the minute our heads touched the pillow. But I'd lost the ability to relax and enjoy life, often waking up in the middle of the night in a doom loop, worried.

One night, I rolled over in bed and looked at the clock—3:10 a.m. I still had three hours to sleep. But the middle of the night was the only time I had to think and reflect. Was it insomnia, too much work, not enough rest? Or was it the stress of performing my smiling role day after day after day? Was being an innkeeper making me sick? It was scary to have these thoughts.

Like my staff, friends, and colleagues, it was nearly impossible to read or indulge in personal hobbies during the work season. I occasionally read a little poetry, but I'd abandoned attempts at writing, thinking it was frivolous. Being creative felt like a second job. But I knew I had to make room for *my* life while working. I reached over to my bedside table and switched on the lamp. I dimmed it lower. The glow from the mica shade bathed me in a warm pool of amber. I picked up a book of poetry written by Rumi, my spiritual companion, reading a passage that seemed like it had been written just for me.

> The Bird Wings
> Your grief for what you've lost lifts a mirror
> up to where you are bravely working.
> Expecting the worst, you look, and instead,
> here's the joyful face you've been wanting to see.
> Your hand opens and closes, and opens and closes.
> If it were always a fist or always stretched open,
> you would be paralyzed.
> Your deepest presence is in every small contracting and expanding,
> the two as beautifully balanced and coordinated as birds' wings.
> —Rumi

I slowly read the words: I *was* grieving, and I *was* bravely working. Not just working at the inn, but working to avoid burnout, but it wasn't working. My hand was always open; I was giving too much. I needed to close it, to say "not right now" or "just a minute," or even "NO" on occasion. And I needed to start saying *yes*, mostly to myself.

That morning after breakfast, the van from Queen Anne's Flowers pulled into the roundabout. The delivery man strode up the granite stairs with a bouquet wrapped in newspaper. A bundle of floral surprise. I savored the perfume of the flowers and fresh greenery, and fell into a quiet joy. While sorting the flowers, I was mindful of each one, arranging them in the vases on the porch, piano, and dining room tables. When I was done, I took a couple of steps back, took a few photos, and then a few moments to smell the flowers.

A few days later, I bought a spiral notebook and a flower-topped pen, and rededicated myself to writing in a journal. Soon, writing was one of the highlights of my day. My meditation, a sacred time to slow down and sit with my emotions. Sometimes I'd write early in the morning before making coffee, or while hanging out at the front desk, or if I was waiting for late-night guests. I took time each day for a personal check-in, and started thinking about writing a memoir, a book that would tell the story of our journey...but it lacked an ending, since we were still living the life. Still, I had a hunch the inspiration would come one day. And yes, one day inspiration did arrive, and I wrote about it. After that night, I began to sleep like a stone.

Holiday Letter

Dear Family and Friends,

Despite Jeff having hip replacement surgery weeks before opening this season, all went smoothly. Guests were great, the team outstanding. But we had one small glitch on July 5th. His name was Tropical Storm Arthur.

Arthur arrived after midnight—3:20 a.m. to be exact. A thunder crack jolted us out of bed. We went back to sleep but the smell of burning wood awakened us. Holy smoke—was the inn on fire?

Jeff set off running with his cane, out into the pouring rain, and saw that a lightning bolt had taken out a nearby tree, which had fallen on a power line. A lively, smoky fire and live wires were sizzling. The fire department arrived at the scene, and kept an eye on the fire, but didn't spray water. When we asked why, they told us they couldn't do anything until the power was shut off.

"What should we do?" we asked. "There's smoke blowing into the building."

A fireman said, "Shut the windows."

At 6:45 a.m., the scones came out of the oven, then we lost power. The backup generator didn't start. Uh-oh. No emergency lighting or refrigeration. Jeff called the power company: "Thank you for holding. There are sixty-two calls ahead of you."

He called the police: "We don't know what's going on, but most of downtown is without power."

He called the Chamber of Commerce: "We don't know anything."

Meanwhile, our guests were relaxing calmly, disappointed by the weather, but good-natured.

As it rained buckets, we saw storm drains overflowing in the streets, and then we remembered: no power—no sump pump! Water was ominously filling the basement. As the staff served an impromptu breakfast to good-natured guests, Jeff tried in vain to use a hand pump to stop water from flooding the basement. This exercise is akin to bailing a two-square-foot area of a swimming pool…as the water kept filling in.

Jeff contacted Rick, the plumber. Got his answering service and called again. Then we realized the phone system was not working properly. So we had a trifecta: No power. A basement filling with water. And we learned something about the inn's phone system. Somehow, all incoming calls were forwarding to one of the guest rooms. The nice guests were answering reservation calls: "We can't take your reservation, but we're staying here and it's nice!"

Luckily, Rick showed up with a gas generator. Jeff hustled down to the dark basement to meet him. In the dark, he misjudged a step and took a header into the staff shower room. Ow! New hip OK, nothing else broken! We got the sump pump operating, but there was still no power, and the refrigerators and freezers were full of food and getting warmer.

When the telephone system was finally restored, Jeff called the power company; a recording said to expect power to be restored by four p.m. or seven p.m., but didn't say which day. Jeff called back a few minutes later: "There are forty calls ahead of you." Finally, he got someone on the line and was told, "We don't know."

Jeff and I huddled, thinking that if the power wasn't going to be restored, we couldn't have guests staying at the inn without lights, safety systems, food, or hot water. We informed the guests and gave them the option to leave if they wished. No one wanted to leave. They remained good-natured, so we decided Wine O'clock would start early—2:00 p.m.

One of the guests broke out a guitar and performed a wonderful, impromptu two-hour concert. Teri visited the larger hotels. They were in tough shape, worse than us, and were simply closing. Therefore, there was nowhere to send guests.

Dusk started to gather. Guests didn't want to leave, and there was nowhere for them to go, so we decided to purchase even more flashlights at the supermarket, which still had no power but was running on generator. As you'd imagine, we were not alone in our need to keep the lights on, and we looked wistfully at the empty pegs that used to hold flashlights.

A check of the power company's website showed they expected to restore power…three days hence, *ON TUESDAY!!!* We conferred with our inn neighbors about a common plan should we all not have power the next day. We agreed that we'd have to shut down and send everybody home.

Rick returned on his own volition and somehow got our commercial generator fired up. With power for hallway lights and refrigeration, and the phones working, things were looking up. Jeff decided to get take-out Chinese food—none of us had eaten all day. "Hi, we'd like to place an order."

"I'm sorry, we can't take order. We have big business problem," and she hung up. I guess we weren't the only ones. Around nine p.m., miraculously, the power came back on. We were exhausted, and went to bed. All was back to normal. Power to the People!

And to all, a good night.

CHAPTER ELEVEN

As you start out on the way, the way appears.
—Rumi

Front Desk Notes

Susan,
You may remember John and May, the guests from a few years ago. The ones who went AWOL from the cruise they were on. They'd never been to Bar Harbor before and rang the front desk bell looking for a 5-night reservation. We only had single-night vacancies here and there. They didn't care; they checked in anyway, and switched rooms five times during their stay. John just sent a six-page email. I printed it out, and it's hanging on the kitchen wall-of-fame. I've titled it: "The Best Guest Review of All Time."

> *It seems like only yesterday when we walked the plank from the cruise ship, landing at your inn. It seemed too good to be true. We were in thrall to serendipity. Your place is indelibly etched into the narrative of our life in a very unexpected way. We cannot believe what an incredible direction our lives have taken. Guess what we did?!?*

They bought an inn in Bar Harbor!

Exit Ramp

Bar Harbor's winter landscapes are quietly majestic and picturesque. But coastal storms have been known to wreak havoc. Frigid weather systems swoop down from Canada, or come up the coast as nor'easters delivering heavy snowfalls held in the clutches of gale-force winds, with an ever-present threat of deadly ice. Such worrisome weather can fell tall trees, collapse roofs, and down power lines, knocking out electricity and disabling travel, leading to costly repairs and inconvenience for inn owners.

Jeff and I were busily taking guest reservations at the remote office on St. Croix. Fortunately, the inn remained safe and dry despite more than eight feet of snow and the perennial mystery roof leak. And we were on schedule to reopen smoothly, and on time. The roof replacement project, which we had expected to complete the prior year, had been deferred because roofing crews were running months behind schedule. We figured as long as the building stayed dry, we could wait it out.

Newly returned to Bar Harbor, we were catching up with friends and fellow innkeepers at the post office and grocery store. We learned there had been a few mild squalls of the business sort around town. The Bank rang in the new year with a flurry of organizational changes. Veronica, the commercial lending officer, with whom we'd done business for a decade, was out. Stan, the new loan guy, was assigned to our account. He called to schedule a meeting. "Hmm, probably a meet-and-greet," I said to Jeff. We didn't think twice about it. I gathered up our business and personal tax returns. Jeff whipped up an overview of the inn's annual forecast and operating budget. Easy. With fourteen years under our wings, we were soaring, flying high.

Stan arrived promptly for the meeting. We shook hands at the front door and gave him an informal tour, stepping over the drop cloths and blue tarps that protected the wood floors from leaks during the winter. He was circumspect, seemly armed with an agenda, but we didn't get it right away, as he looked around, taking note of the paint cans, ladders, and rollers. Jeff and I cleared space in the library, and we settled in.

Stan's reputation was already well known among other business owners in town. Rumor had it he was a sharp-witted pro, bringing big-bank experience to small-town Maine. He leafed officiously through the forecast and expense commentary, which included information about the $18,000 roof replacement, an expenditure we'd normally cover out of operating income. "The Bank would prefer it if you financed the work." He startled us—this was an eye-opener.

"Why is that?" Jeff asked quizzically.

"Well, you have untapped lines of credit, and we'd like to see you keep your ratios in compliance with the loan agreement."

Loan agreement? Compliance? My ears pricked up. "Are you saying we're in breach of our loan agreement?" Even a whiff of noncompliance was repellent to me.

"No, not technically, but you're paying all of your accounts in full, which reduces cash and net income. It brings down your ratios. You should be using lines of credit instead, and I think you should you raise your rates."

After fourteen years of innkeeping, we'd never had a conversation like this with a lending officer, nor had we received instructions on how to operate our business.

Apparently, we didn't understand the purpose of the meeting and had no clue where the discussion was headed. Jeff asked him straight out, "Have we done something wrong? We've never missed a single payment or had a late obligation since we opened for business." Jeff shot me a look that told me he was as perplexed as I was. "We're doing well, blowing away our forecasts, five-star reviews, and industry awards."

Rather than getting to the point, Stan was focused on his questions. "What are your plans for the inn?" he asked.

We thought, *Plans for the inn? What is he talking about?* Our plans were to stay true to a course that had taken us a decade to get right. Both of us were laser-focused on charting, setting, and double-checking our sailing coordinates, at times trimming our sails, our lifelines, and our lives to steer away from the rocks. It was beginning to look like Stan hadn't done all his homework. He had sweated the math exercises, but either forgot or didn't have time to study for the emotional intelligence multiple-choice exam. He could tell by the stunned looks on our faces that his questions had caught us by surprise. He rifled through papers on his lap.

Jeff took back the helm in an effort to steer the conversation back on track. He took a few moments to recount the pitiful saga of the inn's million dollar–plus Restoration Vortex. Building revenue and reputation from a cold start. And my return to my former career in Boston for five years to help keep us afloat. I tried to lift the mood. "Yeah, you know the old cliché. A tale of two corporate escapees who went AWOL, then chaos ensued."

He listened and took it all in. It was clear he hadn't been briefed about our account, experience, or trajectory of success. He apologized. "I'm sorry for thinking innkeepers' lives were easy. Like Bob Newhart was on the TV show."

Still, we wondered, *What was the purpose of this meeting?*

Stan riffed on his experience with regulators and the ongoing challenges of managing risk at a small, regional bank. Jeff and I looked at each other thinking, *Aha!* We'd finally solved for X. The Bank's loan portfolio was under internal review. And as we read between the lines, we learned he was meeting with all of the small inn owners up and down the coast in an effort to stress-test the hospitality portfolio. Who could they thin from the herd? *Now what?* we thought.

Stan's stress test worked wonders. We were now stressed, and a little paranoid, despite the fact that we understood every financial institution has their issues to worry about. Still, the meeting put us off, much like the political winds of change blowing hot, left and right, in the months leading to the highly contested presidential election of 2016. We became further concerned about the potential for uncertainty in the coming years, since we were still catching our breath after riding out the rough years. We felt lucky to have survived a tumultuous decade sailing the inn through deeply troubled waters. But the navigation had been taxing; it was starting to make our legs feel weak, our stomachs queasy. Was it time to actively manage against uncertainty and risk that might lie ahead? Was it time for us to plan our exit from innkeeping?

Stan was back at the helm. "How long do you plan to operate the inn?"

The discussion again drifting into unfamiliar waters. Jeff and I were knocked off course, again, and started looking for a lifeline in the midst of the opaque discussion. "Are you saying we should sell?" Jeff said, edgily probing to get to the heart of the matter, and the purpose of the meeting.

Stan said, "Well, I don't think you can right now. And it'll probably take more than five years to sell it." He briskly wrapped up the meeting and rushed out to his next appointment.

Jeff and I were a little shell-shocked. Jeff was agitated. "Wow, it's a throwback to the corporate world, when a guy comes to a meeting just to whack his fist on the table."

Up to this point, Jeff and I had been all in. We were Inn Mates. The inn was our life. But after the meeting, we decided it might be time to start looking for a life preserver, in case we might need to swim rather than float to the nearest exit.

Mid-May arrived, and we opened without incident. We enjoyed a record-breaking season. In the final days of October, we were running with the wind, sailing crisply past the six-month flag that signaled the end of the hospitality seasonal regatta.

Steady as she goes, it was smooth sailing as we crossed the finish line and brought the inn home to port. We were euphoric from successfully completing the race. It was time to batten down the hatches and close for the season. Still, we had energy to spare for closing weekend and celebrations with staff and guests.

Many of our repeat guests and special friends booked rooms for closing weekend. A few guests brought along their guitars and lent their voices to perform impromptu concerts around the piano, in the library, and on the sunporch. Jeff and I served snacks and wine as a thank-you, later making dinner for ourselves and close friends who joined us in the kitchen. Jeff took off his innkeeper hat and took a turn sautéing beautiful mussels and clams in garlic and olive oil, for a pasta dish that was perfect with a lemony escarole salad and Italian biscotti.

During dinner, the closing weekend guests left to attend the Halloween screening of *Rocky Horror Picture Show* at the Criterion Theater. Jeff and I called it an early night, and we were "lights out" before the movie curtain went up.

Sunday morning, the final breakfast of the season, the team was poised to make the last operating day in October as wonderful as opening day in May. We were running on adrenaline after the blockbuster year, but even so, the early-morning coffee was piping hot at 6:30 a.m.

Before breakfast service, I leisurely strolled through the dining room. The autumn's low morning light was shining on the bare branches and shaggy bark of the river birch trees. The table flowers had been replaced with small orange pumpkins and gourds. A seasonal tribute stood alongside the final breakfast menu for the season:

Closing Day Menu
Cinnamon Apple Cheese Danish
Blueberry Buttermilk Waffles, Maine Maple Syrup, Bacon
Eggs Benedict w/Citrus Hollandaise
Thank you for a memorable season!

While waiting for guests to arrive in the dining room, we baked four dozen chocolate chip cookies for farewell treats. Grateful to the guests who had spent their time and money at the inn during the quietest time of year, helping us make our numbers for October: 91% occupancy. The inn was sold out nearly every single day for six months straight, and we still had a wait list.

Earlier in the week, The Bank's CEO stopped by. "What more can we do for you?" he asked solicitously. Perhaps Stan had reported that his initial visit was awkward, or maybe he was inquiring about the construction they'd undertaken and the Dumpsters lining the abutting parking area.

"Well, it would be nice if the demo crew could hold off slamming debris into Dumpsters at 6:25a.m.," Jeff replied, glancing out the windows of the sunporch. "A couple of our guests complained about the noise. It's bad for business."

Yes, the construction debris was an eyesore, but we were still raw after the uncomfortable meeting with the loan guy, who seemed to be pushing us out of our business. So we had put the awkward encounter out of our minds. It was the end of the season. We were tired, well beyond tired, and overwhelmed with bittersweet feelings saying goodbye to our staff and friends. We also had a yard-long punch list to complete before closing for the season.

Like most innkeepers, we loved our jobs, but there were times it was loathsome. In our case, it was mostly the lingering result of the hard knocks we'd sustained from the Restoration Vortex. We were lucky to have survived. But our success wasn't simply good luck. It was also the dedication of our staff and ourselves sweating the details to ensure that each guest felt acknowledged and appreciated while staying at the inn.

During Innkeeping Academy, fourteen years earlier, we'd learned there are several types of innkeepers; mom and pop innkeepers who rented rooms for a lark; investor innkeepers who were mostly focused on "heads in beds"; and small inn owners, like us and many of our colleagues in Bar Harbor, who considered ourselves community ambassadors. Most of us were fixated on ensuring guest comfort and being helpful. We welcomed guests from every corner of the world. People who went the distance to visit Bar Harbor and Mount Desert Island, easily a five-hour one-way drive from the closest urban centers of Montreal, Boston, Quebec City, and Halifax, Nova Scotia. Many arrived on overnight flights from California, Europe, Mexico, Argentina, Thailand, and points in between.

We trained our crew and ourselves to remember the names of our guests. Infrequently, we might never learn their names, but we knew it was better to have a handle on who was staying at the inn, rather than engage in hosting a parade of nameless and anonymous strangers who exchanged their money for a bed.

So, on this closing morning, the staff and a few friends celebrated after guest check-outs with a special breakfast of mango smoothie shooters, waffles, and eggs benedict. Jeff and I placed thank-you cards on the table before the team took their seats in the dining room. The envelopes included notes from the guests, and generous tips. Some of the staff shed a few tears as they read the notes and cards at the table. It was easy to be kind to the people who cared for the guests: Without them, we were nothing.

Lincoln opened his card and a photo fell out. He passed around the picture we had taken of him at his birthday party where he received a stiff frozen red snapper, one of his favorite island foods, and a fun surprise. "Thanks, guys. I love working here, we a family," he said. "I had only one baby picture of myself growing up in Jamaica." He paused for a minute. "It burned up when my house burned down." We all shook our heads. There were no words.

I was clearing the dining room while the last guests checked out. "Thanks for an amazing experience!" they said. We thanked them and locked the front door as they left. The inn was closed for the season.

DJ Jeff queued up the tunes. Bob Marley. Exodus. Full-Blast. And as soon as the front door was closed, the team jumped to begin shutdown. Not a leisurely letdown, but a full-on hustle to get the job done, and move on their winter jobs in Florida. The tune of the natural mystic rang in our ears as we shared the leftover contents of the kitchen's four refrigerators with the staff. All of us were much too tired to cook. That night, we gathered at a local restaurant for dinner to celebrate closing day. But our personal idea of heaven on earth was a home-cooked meal when we were back home on St. Croix.

A week after closing, on election day 2016, Jeff and I greeted sunrise at the top of Cadillac Mountain. We stood shivering in the shimmering darkness as the sun slowly colored the sky in shadows, then striations of deep rose and pale pink. And we had plenty of company. We admired the silhouettes of our fellow travelers who were wrapped in silence, respectful of the early morning hour and the precious moment. A hush clung in the air as a brisk ocean breeze kicked up pinecones that scuttled across the granite boulders. We were silent witnesses to the birth of a new morning. A stillness we felt no one would ever want to disturb.

Driving down from the mountain, Jeff and I gazed out the windows to endless views of the Atlantic Ocean and the tree cover surrounding Eagle Lake, quietly taking stock of the year we'd been through, and the years before it. The restoration debacle. The joys of innkeeping. The stress and physical demands of the inn. And the march of time. The reality of getting older. We figured it was high time to start planning ahead. To get out while we were standing on top of the mountain, rather than crawling out from under it.

We initiated early-stage discussions about selling the inn with our eyes wide open, and with solemn hearts. Fortunately, our friendship, love, and marriage had endured, and we were lucky we didn't land in Chapter 11 bankruptcy court after the early financial slip-ups, spills, and falls. We saved Chapter 11 for the pages of this book! We called our broker, and the inn was listed for sale.

Paradise Tossed

What do you call 363 days of perfect weather,
and the two days when the weather wants to kill you? Hurricane Season.
—Jeff

During 2017, I was away from Maine caring for our elderly dog Riley on St. Croix. His arthritis rendered him slightly lame, and he couldn't make the trip back to Maine. We wanted him to remain comfortable at home. This meant Jeff would return to Bar Harbor to run the inn by himself—once again. I was able to land the manager gig with Pat and Mark at Sweet Lime Furnishings. Jeff and I hatched a plan: We'd switch places during the month of September for two weeks. Jeff would fly to St. Croix for a break. I would take the helm at the inn.

It was my first time being alone on island, and my risk management tendencies kicked in. I had a bad feeling about hurricane season. I saw local islanders planning, stockpiling batteries, lanterns, canned food, rice, fruit cups, crowbars, and tools. I got busy researching NOAA's hurricane readiness advice, creating a list of additional tools and supplies I might need: dog food, medication, paper towels, toilet paper, and solar charging units. Jeff, back in Maine, thought I was overdoing it. "Once a risk manager, always a risk manager," he joked.

Every Friday afternoon, after closing the store, I filled a shopping cart with supplies at the hardware store in Gallows Bay. The store clerks gave me odd looks, a fledgling survivalist on a spending spree.

I worried about what I didn't know, over-preparing to calm myself down. I bought everything on the NOAA list: band-aids, water jugs, battery-powered fans, radio, solar charging units, and an axe—*What will I need that for?* But into the cart it went. The last item on the list, a chainsaw, was a tool that was not in my wheelhouse. Jeff said, "I'll take care of it, don't worry about it." That's what he usually said. But I did worry—it's my nature. And I wasn't the only one.

Our neighbors along the ridge had premonitions, too. "Hurricane season is going to be active this year," they said. "NOAA says seventeen storms; you should get busy trimming the brush and trees along the driveway, cut down the coconuts and give them away on the side of the road. When a hurricane comes [notice *when*, not *if*] they'll be bouncing off your walls like cannonballs."

I looked around at the magnificent coconut palms, avocado, papaya, and mango trees, all heavy with fruit, and wondered, *Is this garden carnage necessary?*

I got my answer on July 5th.

BANG! The transformer on the power pole by our house blew out. It was smothered by overgrowth. Now I was in the dark. All the household systems were shut down—lights, water pumps, and air-conditioning—and the generator was finicky. I double-checked the refrigerator temperature and contacted WAPA, the utility company. A truck came the next day, but the towering bucket truck could barely clear the driveway, and it couldn't turn around due to the tree cover. The driver said, "You need to cut this stuff down. When a hurricane comes [again, *when*, not *if*], we won't be able to help you." I hired a yard crew who worked weekly from July to September, hacking away brush, trimming fruit trees, and hauling the fruit away. I told Jeff about the preparations, but honestly, I don't think it really registered with him. He was immersed in the daily drama of running the business.

The days passed quickly, and suddenly it was September, the heart of hurricane season. The air turned still and dry, there'd been very little rain, since it evaporated before it could fall. The Sahara dust that blew east over the Atlantic Ocean and Caribbean Sea sifted across the horizon, creating hot, cloudless days, and magnificent sunsets.

Meanwhile, drought-loving plants like desert rose and bougainvillea were in full flower.

Pat, Renate, my co-worker, and I took a break. We decamped to our listening post at Sweet Lime, sitting in a mix of sun and shade under the flamboyant trees.

Renate was sweating out the last days before her exodus, moving off-island to reunite with family in Germany. She hadn't been home in 37 years. She'd moved to St. Croix after having been field-tested working in remote villages in the Middle East and Africa. She was now looking forward to a change of scenery, German bread, pastry, pickles, and beer. And perhaps wishing her timing could have been better. She'd earlier sold her home and was now scrambling to pack her shipping container as the season's first tropical storms gathered in the Caribbean.

"Paradise is a lot of work," she said, recalling her brushes with Hurricanes Omar, "wrong-way" Lenny, José, and Marilyn. She taught us that a 50-pound bag of rice keeps you in food for 180 days, three cups per day. Keep your generator tuned up and fueled. Have plenty of bleach on hand to purify drinking water, and learn to use a chainsaw. She also taught us compassionate wisdom.

Renate smiled wanly as we drank coffee and passed around chocolates kisses. She was faced with a dilemma. Her family of elderly rescue dogs couldn't travel, and she couldn't find anyone to care for the brood. Her vet gave her sensitive and practical advice, lovingly transporting them over the rainbow bridge. The journey broke our hearts. But the timing of the sale of her home, closing mere days before Hurricane Irma's arrival, turned out to be prescient. And two weeks later, Renate's courage would be revealed as gifts of love and mercy.

On August 31st, I left Riley with a trusted friend and returned to Bar Harbor. Our original plan, drawn up under sunnier skies in May, called for Jeff to take a two-week vacation in St. Croix during

September. When my connecting flight touched down in San Juan, NOAA had upgraded Irma to Cat 3.

I called Jeff. "Hon, I can turn right around to ride out Irma."

"No, Teri, let's stick to the plan. I'll be OK. When the hurricane hits, I'll be home to take care of Riley. But please, do not call this trip a vacation."

I was sad about his decision, but relieved to step back from the terror of an approaching hurricane.

The flight to Boston was uneventful. As the plane circled the airport, I looked down over South Boston, Fan Pier, and the financial district—the view reminding me of homecomings from past business trips in my former life. On the drive to Bar Harbor, I felt the joy of heading to the comfort of my inn family and friends, miles away from the hurricane angst.

Jeff called. "On your way to the inn, can you pick up the weed-whacker at the lawnmower shop?"

"Will do," I said, thinking, *I wonder if they sell chainsaws* as I drove along Route 3 and read the sign, "Lawnmowers and Chainsaws for Sale."

I walked into the store to shop for the final item on my hurricane prep list. Now there were dozens of chainsaws right in front me. I could buy one for each hand if I wanted to. I spoke with the store owner. "Can you recommend a chainsaw that can travel as checked luggage?" He gave me a look, perhaps wondering what I had up my sleeve.

"Uh, yah, sure, here it is. It has a short bar, a battery pack, and it comes with a jug of chain oil."

Check, check, double-check. "I'll take it."

I arrived at the inn late afternoon, and Jeff met me at the back door. His smile and warm hugs filled my heart. "Jeffie, I don't know where to begin," I cried. My pent-up feelings of loneliness, fear, and isolation finally let loose. We had 36 hours together before he would leave to catch a flight back to St. Croix in the shadow of Hurricane Irma.

Jeff packed lightly since he had most of what he needed back at the house. But he was exhausted, having worked 109 days without a day off. We had hoped his trip to paradise would be a welcome break from innkeeping. Instead, he reminded me, "Please don't call this trip a vacation." He zipped his suitcase and checked around to make sure he had everything: keys, passport, a round-trip ticket to paradise, a major hurricane brewing, and a brand-new electric chainsaw.

The next day, I drove Jeff to catch the airport bus. I pulled into the parking lot. We got out of the car and kissed goodbye. I hugged him tight, overwhelmed with tears and tugs of remorse and sadness. I was afraid of us being alone—again. But soon I would be surrounded by the somewhat comforting responsibilities and trappings of the inn.

It was Labor Day weekend, the inn was full to capacity with twenty guests, seven staff, and 24 nonstop hours of hurricane coverage. I had never felt so alive, so terrified, so anxious and sleepless.

Jeff was in the air somewhere over Miami when I got the text from Pat's husband Mark, who was golfing in Ireland.

> Pat's fallen and broken her hip. I'm flying back to St. Croix ASAP, as soon as I can book a flight.

Mark and I were busy sending texts to connect all the dots.

> How did Pat get to the hospital?
>> She crawled across the floor to her cellphone and called 9-1-1. An ambulance picked her up.
> Mark, do you think the store and house are closed up?
>> That's a good question! I can't get anybody on the ground!

We calculated Jeff's flight trajectory and figured he would be landing within a few minutes. Pat was being wheeled into X-ray at Juan Luis Hospital on St. Croix as Jeff's flight approached the airport. He landed, turned on his phone, and it started pinging as if he'd won the jackpot at a casino. Lots of messages, alerts, and calls. Meanwhile, Hurricane Irma was upgraded to Cat 5, destination US Virgin Islands.

Jeff, Pat's had an accident. She's at Juan Luis Hospital.

What do you need me to do?

Can you check on Pat's house and lock up, then go to the hospital. We need to find out how she's doing.

OK, I'll head to the hospital as soon as we land.

Jeff collected his checked baggage (with chainsaw) and located the car where I had left it in the airport parking lot with the key sitting on top of the tire, a standard island practice. He jumped into the car, on his way to the hospital to find Pat. Fortunately, she was in stable condition and getting excellent care. Twenty-four hours later, Hurricane Irma arrived with winds topping 100 mph.

Hurricane Irma battered but didn't break St. Croix. Her wrath was saved for the islands of St. Thomas and St. John. On those neighboring islands, there was a direct hit that caused catastrophic damage. Streets were flooded, roofs were blown off the hospitals and airports. And all of the Virgin Islands were without electricity.

In the midst of sweeping up debris, local Good Samaritans on St. Croix collected drinking water and canned goods for her sister islands. And no one would have guessed that Irma was simply the warmup act for another hurricane forming off the coast of Africa. A new unnamed storm was traveling briskly and gaining strength over the warm waters of the Caribbean Sea—it was later named Maria.

The relief efforts ended abruptly. NOAA gave Virgin Islanders a heads-up. Hurricane Maria was on the way, just two days away. Everyone needed to urgently prepare for her arrival. People rushed back to the stores to stock up on batteries, water, and fuel for the generators, then battened down the hatches—again. Ten days after dodging the buffet from Hurricane Irma, Hurricane Maria was barreling directly for St. Croix.

Within hours of becoming a named storm, Hurricane Maria developed a tight eye at the center, tightening her squeeze and concentrating the tropical-force winds into faster and faster rotations, becoming a Cat 5 hurricane in record time.

Jeff hurried to close up our house, opting to shelter at a lower elevation with Pat and Mark at Sweet Lime. He knew it would be safer to ride out the storm there, rather than riding a whirlwind at six hundred feet above sea level. After finishing his storm preparations, he sent me a selfie. The anxious look on his face had me wondering if we'd ever see our home again. Say hello to the growing realities of climate change.

Back at the inn, it was business as usual: breakfast at 8:00 a.m.; guests checking out; afternoon baking; guests checking in; wine and snacks at 6:00 p.m.; except my phone was going off nonstop.

"How's Jeff doing?"

"Can he travel back to Bar Harbor?"

"How's Riley the inn dog?"

I'd fretted my way through the day, relieved to have had the camaraderie of guests, fellow innkeepers, and neighbors for support. Helene, next door, knew I was worried, and suggested we return to our yoga mats. I checked in with Susan before heading out, and she reported, "We have guests from the UK. They told me they're not fond of air-conditioning. I checked with them after they got settled in their room. They said they're fine." Susan had a knack for dealing with touchy guests.

A strong onshore breeze wafted across Main Street as Helene and I climbed the stairs to the yoga studio. Hurricane Irma had weakened and was churning north, stirring up the jet stream and the waters of the Atlantic Ocean off the coast of New England. Hurricane Maria was preparing for her debut in the vicinity of the US Virgin Islands, her winds strengthening as she swept across the Caribbean.

My bliss in the yoga studio was replaced by intermittent hammer blows of guilt as the lights were dimmed. Helene and I chanted along with our yogi, David, leading the group... "*Ommmmmmm, shanti, shanti, shanti*"—the Sanskrit chant for peace. I closed my eyes, hoping Hurricane Maria was listening.

Afterward, the calming effects of the yoga practice helped, but hours later I was still unable to sleep. I was glued to NOAA coverage of Hurricane Maria. St. Croix had shut down the power grid. The monster storm was imminent, and Jeff was in the path of a direct hit.

RING! RING! RING! RING! RING! The front desk bell startled me back to reality. I jumped up, taking the stairs to the office. I opened the door labeled "Privacy Please" and met one of my new guests. He was in a huff and stood braced against the doorjamb with a miserable look on his face.

"The ventilation system in this hotel is driving us crazy. There's too much air blowing into the room through the vents! What are you going to do about it?"

I said to myself, *This guy must be kidding. My husband's in the middle of a hurricane!* I found my composure. "Tonight's weather is unsettled because of coastal storms. I'm sorry if it's too humid in your room."

"The room's not humid, it's fucking freezing. Turn off the air-conditioning," he snapped.

"I'm sorry to hear that. How about opening a window if you're too cold. I'd rather not shut the system down; it will affect the entire wing," I replied.

"I don't want to hear it! Turn the system off, for fuck's sake!" His face flashed crimson as he stood by at the door. I had to squeeze sideways to get past him on my way to the office. He followed me to be sure I turned off the HVAC system. Then he stormed back to his room. I was too worried about Jeff and Riley to get pissed off.

I returned to NOAA's storm reports. The hurricane continued to gain strength as it picked up speed. It made landfall, walloping the US Virgin Islands, then Puerto Rico with drenching rains and tornados. Despite sustained wind speeds of more than 175 miles an hour, the storm tracked slowly, becoming a slow-motion catastrophe.

Then I got some good news. Somehow, St. Croix's broadband network was operational, and Mark had a generator, enabling us to communicate via internet. He began to issue real-time hurricane play-by-play to a broadcast audience of his family and friends in

Bar Harbor, San Francisco, Singapore, and Virginia. We hung on his every word.

Mark:
18:30
We are hunkered down at Sweet Lime.
We ordered in Chinese Food; who wants to cook at a time like this?
20:00
The utility company shut down the grid. Moved to generator. Will update you later.
22:00
Winds picking up. Howling sounds like a jet engine. Lights out all over the island.
22:30
Maria, this isn't funny anymore. I just looked outside, there's metal roof material flying through the air. Uh-oh, I think we lost the roof.

That was the last communication.

At breakfast the next morning, I was busy fielding questions from guests and answering phone calls from family and friends.

"How's Jeff doing after Hurricane Maria?"

"Is he OK?"

"How's Riley the inn dog?"

All were excellent questions. Unfortunately, I had no answers, and I was more than worried. Still, I had to maintain my well-practiced innkeeper composure. "I don't know. I hope they're OK. We lost communication. I'm waiting for an update."

RING! RING! RING! I was summoned to the front desk by the late-night guest who had stormed the office the night before. "I just heard about your husband's plight from another guest. I'd like to offer an apology," he said. Apparently, he'd had a change of heart, but it was small consolation. I still hadn't heard a word from Jeff.

Sometime later that day:

Jeff:
Hi, Teri, I'm OK, but Maria whacked us. The roads are impassable. Mark and I drove as far as we could on Scenic Drive to check on our house. The driveway is inaccessible; there are downed trees everywhere.

We parked and walked to the house. Can't see structural damage, and the roof looks OK. The doors and windows held, but many were on the verge of bursting. The panes and doors have loosened from the concrete casements and are vulnerable. All of the fencing is gone, and many of the solar panels are MIA. We lost all the coconut palms, the mango trees were ripped out by the roots, and the papaya trees were snapped like toothpicks. It's a war zone.

Four days later:

Jeff:
The airport lost the control tower. People are swarming around the airport to get information. I'm trying to book a flight to get back to Maine, but I'm having trouble. Right now, only military aircraft are flying. There're a few mercy ships off the coast transporting injured people to Miami. I'm running out of my medication. You gotta help me. Please work to get me a flight!

Jeff's urgent SOS message seemed like the result of PTSD. So my part-time job, in addition to running the inn, was calling to book flights from the Caribbean region. During the day, all of the phone lines were jammed. So I set my alarm to 3:00 a.m., thinking it might be easier to get through to the reservation services in the middle of the night. It was a good idea.

"Your hold time will be forty-five minutes"—which was an improvement. I reached a reservationist who quizzically reported there were daily flights despite FEMA reporting the airports in the Virgin Islands were closed. "Yes, planes are flying, we have seats available." I booked four flights, and each one of them was canceled the day of departure.

Nine days later, Jeff got creative and booked a seaplane from Christiansted Harbor to St. Thomas, with a connecting flight the next day on an Atlanta-bound flight. The pilot deftly dodged floating palm trees, rigging, and broken dock planks during takeoff. The Caribbean Sea was chock-full of filthy debris and waste from storm water runoff. As the plane landed in St. Thomas harbor, the pontoons nearly collided with fallen logs and floating shopping carts. As in St. Croix, there was no electricity, no taxis, no streetlights, no people on the sidewalks.

Jeff had a fitful night's sleep in a hotel with no roof. He arrived at the St. Thomas airport five hours early for his flight. He sent me a text:

> When we're wheels up, I'll believe I'm finally coming home.

Many hours later, Jeff's plane touched down in Boston. He collected his bag and took a shuttle to a hotel. There he enjoyed hot and cold running water, electricity, and a full night's sleep for the first time in weeks. The next morning, he was on an express bus bound for Bangor. I spotted it when it was approaching the station, looking for Jeff in the windows. He saw me and waved. Shaking slightly, he stepped down from the bus. We hugged, and fought back the tears. We were back together. It was such a relief, but we were one short—Riley had been staying with Jeff, but had to remain on island with friends until I came back. Despite the temporary respite from stress and our impromptu reunion celebration, Jeff and I suspected our snowbird life would probably become a thing of the past.

It took more than two weeks to book a flight back to St. Croix. I returned to the island to reunite with Riley, begin remediation of our home, and assist Pat and Mark to reopen the store. All the airlines were overrun with "continentals," people like me who were returning to the island to check on family members and assess damage to homes and businesses. Jeff briefed me on what to expect back on the island. We had a punch list for repairs to the house, and a tentative plan to stay with Pat and Mark until the three of us could move back home.

Prior to my flight, I stayed overnight at the same airport hotel where Jeff had recently checked out., enjoying a late supper of fresh green salad, grilled salmon, and a glass of cold white wine in the cool quiet of my room. After dinner, I ran a warm, soothing bath to unwind before going to bed. It would be one of the luxuries I wouldn't have again for months—running water, electric lights, no bugs. I swished the water in the tub, added bubble bath, and watched the suds float to the surface. I told myself, *Don't get used to it.*

Four hours of sleep was all I could manage. At 4:15 a.m. I turned on the lights and put on the clothes I had taken off the day before. I hadn't packed another outfit. Instead, my two 50-pound suitcases were both a traveling hardware store and a drugstore, each crammed with canned food provisions, OTC medicine, and hygiene kits with bug repellent wipes, soap, shampoo, tissues, toothpaste, and hand sanitizer.

The Miami departure gate was the final leg of the trip. The passengers were sharing information on their personal situations, hopes, and fears. As the plane gained altitude, my attention was fixed on the placid blue water. I was on the lookout, waiting to see if or when there would be evidence of the destruction from Hurricane Maria.

The plane took us over Puerto Rico and descended to 10,000 feet, en route to the St. Croix airport. At the lower elevation, evidence of massive damage was obvious. Miles and miles of blue tarps, and glittering metallic flakes that looked like Christmas tinsel were in reality thousands of destroyed aluminum roofs, which were strewn in all directions. The flight slowly glided over the western side of St. Croix, running parallel to the Frederiksted Pier. Among the cruise ships at anchor, some were being used for mercy transports. Others provided temporary housing for FEMA workers, many of whom had just left Houston after helping victims of Hurricane Harvey.

The plane seemed to defy gravity as it moved low and slow on a glide path to the runway, making it possible for us to get a bird's-eye view before the plane touched down. Passengers huddled to catch glimpses out the windows. A collective gasp rose up, followed by grief-stricken cries and shouts of disbelief. The air traffic control tower was gone, a temporary one standing in its place. "I can't believe it!" "It's a mash-up down there!"

And the closer *we* got, the worse *it* got.

Metal roofs hung from the trees, cars were overturned, homes and shopping areas were flattened. Rooftops were blanketed in blue tarps. The electrical grid, usually dicey at best, had been ripped apart. The poles were scattered on the ground like pick-up sticks. No electricity. Blocked roadways. No cars. A vision of hell.

The plane landed with a thump and taxied to the gate. The cabin doors were opened, and hot, humid air rushed in to greet us. Travelers jammed into the aisles and made tracks for the exits. The metal gangway above the tarmac heaved as crowds of people were packed together on the stairs, taking in the view of the palm trees, stripped and headless. We stumbled together, a mass of the walking dead, looking around to catch our bearings. The earth had shifted underfoot. It took effort to remain upright, to resist the human urge to fall to the ground and beg for mercy.

I followed the crowd to baggage claim and got my bags, flagging down my friend Kathryn, who had circled the airport in her car as she waited for my flight. Riley was in the backseat of the car. He was hot, but safe, and very glad to see me. Jeff and I had missed him like crazy. Kathryn, a perennial optimist, was in pretty good spirits. "Let's take a drive to your house before going to Pat's." she said. That's when the feeling of nausea began. It wasn't air sickness, or car sickness. I was heartsick; I'd seen enough.

The drive though the stripped orchards and farms of Estate Mon Bijou leveled off at Scenic Drive on the ridge of our neighborhood, Estate Betsy's Jewel. My mood darkened as I watched the debris roll past the car windows in slow motion. The tree canopy was gone, the branches were bare. And for the first time ever, I actually could see our house from the road.

Our driveway was still inaccessible due to fallen power poles that blocked the road. We drove in the car as far as we could. I left my luggage in the car, which we parked by the side of the road, and walked up to the house. The mango trees were ripped out at the roots. From the look of things, I could tell Jeff had used his new chainsaw to clear a few doorways. The hurricane shutters were intact, yet many of the windows and doors were jarred from their frames and sagged on the sills. The hurricane's low pressure and the strong winds had nearly blown the doors and windows inside out. The exterior paint had been scoured off in wide swaths as debris swept past the walls. Mold was beginning to accumulate. Our old diesel generator had dropped dead. I bumped into my neighbor for a quick chat, and he said he'd clocked wind gusts over 225 miles an hour. "It felt like a twelve-hour tornado up here." he said.

Kathryn took me to Pat's, and Riley and I moved in. A few days later, I dropped off the supplies we'd bought at a few nonprofit organizations. Many families needed provisions due to shipping delays to the island, and it is very important to maintain good hygiene after a hurricane. There were numerous physical and biological hazards—broken glass, sheared metal debris, unsafe foodstuffs, and unclean drinking water. Most people were living on hurricane provisions: Spam, peanut butter, mac & cheese, canned veggies and tuna, dry milk, boiled water, and rum.

Pat, Mark, and I reopened the store. Business was brisk. Some people were rebuilding. Scores of families were in shelters, and many homes had no roofs.

Yet the St. Croix spirit was upbeat and positive. Virgin Islanders worked hard to put their lives back together, patiently, one day at a time, despite the hurricane-induced stress that tinged the air.

Most peopled were compassionate and patient, but a few "continentals" lacked empathy and resented the inconvenience from the storm, irritated by delayed furniture deliveries due to impassable roads and driveways.

"I need furniture right away!"

"Why does everything take so long?"

"Harrumph, I've had it with island time!"

I learned that grumpy guests and stressed retail shoppers had much in common.

Jeff returned to the island in early November, moving in with Riley and me temporarily at Sweet Lime. We'd lost our home generator, our solar panels were damaged, and the island still lacked electricity, so we stayed with Pat and Mark until Thanksgiving. But we were homesick, as was sweet Riley. When we returned to our place, he snuggled on the couch, then on his bed and our bed. He played ball like a puppy, and slept in the shade of the covered gallery. He'd survived Irma and Maria, thanks to lots of love, good friends, medication, and tasty dog treats. Until the hurricane stress and the adrenaline finally wore off. And then one morning, he woke up and he couldn't stand up. He looked lost, miserable, and defeated. It was his way of telling us he'd had enough. He had waited for us, and now he wanted some final rest.

Four days after Christmas, Riley gently nosed us after refusing his favorite breakfast of scrambled egg. We carried him into the vet's office with hot tears running down our faces. We whispered to him and smoothed his fur during his final moments. A candle was lit, and it flickered in the darkness. Jeff and I sat with him and said goodbye. We knew how he felt: Both of us were exhausted from hurricane stress and the added pressure of operating the inn's remote office while living without electricity or running water for more than one hundred days.

Teri Anderholm

Holiday Letter

Dear Friends and Family,

On September 3rd, inn mate Jeff kissed inn mate Teri goodbye and headed down to the St. Croix home of the inn's winter reservations office, landing right in the path of Hurricane Irma. Then, 10 days later, Hurricane Maria—a Cat 5 monster—scored a direct hit on St. Croix, creating destruction and chaos in its wake. The recovery will take months.

On October 2nd, Jeff finally made it back to the inn. Teri did a great job running the show for four weeks while worrying like crazy about her husband, dog Riley, and their island home. Many thanks to all of you who reached out to check on us during this trying time.

Jeff wants to especially recognize the dozens of old friends who called to check on Teri, and our wonderful supportive guests, who followed events during their stay. Even former guests here in town stopped by. Thanks, also, to our good friends and fellow innkeepers from Bar Harbor who stopped in to comfort her. We even had a few St. Croix friends, who happened to be visiting Bar Harbor, who reached out to share news—and a glass of wine—in the hurricanes' aftermath.

Thanks also to the Bar Harbor business community, who hosted relief efforts to help island families in need. Your generosity is appreciated and will never be forgotten.

Teri and I plan to wrap up our successful 14th season at the end of this month. Do a couple of projects in anticipation of the 2018 innkeeping season; and return to St. Croix to put our house in order.

We kept the holiday letter's postscript to ourselves. Given the uncertainty of events, Jeff and I had roughed out a couple of options:
+ Due to no power, leave the debris in St. Croix.
+ Return to Maine, move in with friends.

Or,
+ Sell the inn to the highest bidder.

CHAPTER TWELVE

One of the marvels of the world is the sight of a soul sitting in prison with the key in its hand!
—Rumi

Swan Song

The aftermath of hurricanes taught us sobering lessons. Even the best laid plans can't prevent calamity, and control is an illusion. And now, with our life's work and treasure on sale to the highest bidder, it was time to take stock of our life. We felt under siege.

A Downeast newspaper wrote about Jeff's firsthand account of Hurricane Maria, and local businesses held fundraisers to raise money for needy Caribbean families. The publicity was good for St. Croix's plight, getting the word out that it was time to help others. Some people, it seemed, wanted to help themselves. A local buyer caught wind of our predicament and thought it might be a good time to add another inn to his portfolio: *They're under duress; maybe I can strike a deal.*

We weren't under duress, exactly, but we were living in the midst of a State of Emergency without electricity or running water. Under those circumstances, we considered it a time of hardship. Still, the buyer hoped to drive a hard bargain, but we were in no mood to haggle. Jeff put the broker on notice: "If we don't get our number, we'll happily operate the inn for the rest of our lives." Eventually, a fair price was hammered out, and the closing was scheduled for mid-March.

Days before closing, Jeff flew to snowy Bar Harbor to sort out our personal property, mostly artwork, clothes, and books, and a few pieces of furniture which he put in storage. For Jeff, it was cold and lonely working within the freezing hulk of an unheated inn, the frigid cold seeping into his bones and numbing his fingers, his toes, and his feelings. I stayed warm in St. Croix, overseeing home repairs and watching over the store for Pat and Mark. We both wondered how it would feel when the deal was sealed. Would there be an epiphany, or would it pass as any other day?

Jeff called while sitting in a lawyer's office. "The inn's closing is happening right now; I'm sitting here with two attorneys. The brokers couldn't make it."

I was heartsick imagining Jeff sitting by himself during his swan song, his final performance as an innkeeper before retirement.

A few minutes later Jeff texted:

> You are now an ex-innkeeper.

After signing the papers, he treated himself to a solemn, not celebratory, dinner, raising his wine glass in a farewell toast to the inn: "Here's to fifteen years," he said, questioning if it had been worth it. Or whether fate had held us captive, as the events which shaped our lives during those years seemed to have had a life of their own.

I was sitting on the patio at Sweet Lime as tears trickled down the face of a bronze Buddha fountain. A cooling Caribbean breeze ruffled the bougainvillea, amid the cooing of mourning doves. I re-read the text. I was numb.

I glanced around for a distraction and strolled past a carved Balinese table that held a tall vase of glorious bird of paradise flowers. I picked up the vase and poured out the stale water. Nicking a finger while trimming the stems sent tears streaming down my face. I refilled the vase and replaced the flowers, thinking that rearranging flowers was an easier task than the work ahead to rearrange our lives.

Jeff flew home the next day. We hugged at the airport, both of us shell-shocked after selling the inn. "What have we done? Now what do we do?"

Before the hurricanes, life had been in balance at long last. The inn was successful, and we'd realigned the needs of our business, friends, family, and personal interests. But after the Cat 5 winds of change, the only thing we could do was hang on and plan ahead. We asked ourselves and each other about how we would feel if another hurricane came our way. We'd weathered Hurricanes Sandy, Irma, and Maria. Would we have the energy, heart, and youthful enthusiasm to rebuild our lives yet again?

After searching for answers, we traded our beautiful island home and returned to a safe harbor in Maine. But our hearts remain full of the memories of our days living in paradise, when we were warmed by the sun and the pleasant company of friends, and a community of compassionate folks who pulled together when life, nature, or other circumstances warranted.

Since returning to Maine, Jeff and I have been knitting our lives back together. Revisiting the road we traveled, renewing friendships that were on hold for over fifteen years of innkeeping, and wondering what the universe may have in store for us. But every year, when the month of April rolls around, it hits us—hard.

"Oh, yeah. Right. We are not innkeepers anymore." Remembering well our innkeeping life; waking to bedside alarms, front desk bells, kitchen timers, and once or twice, the inn's fire alarms. Basking in the memories of so many mornings, too numerous to count, full of fun and anticipation for the warm smiles of our staff and guests.

But these days, there are no morning alarms. We're not in a hurry. We rest easily and let thoughts of the past percolate and bubble away. It's usually the time when one of us looks at the other and says, "Guess what we don't have to do today." Yes, our hospitality gallows humor is still alive and well. Some habits are hard to break.

When I woke up this morning, I looked at the clock—6:40 a.m. I reached for a book on my bedside table. A literary classic, a book I'd always wanted to read. The page seemed to open itself.

> No, no, no, no! Come, let's away to prison:
> We two alone will sing like birds i' the cage:
> When thou dost ask me blessing, I'll kneel down,
> And ask of thee forgiveness: so we'll live,
> And pray, and sing, and tell old tales, and laugh
> At gilded butterflies, and hear poor rogues

> Talk of court news; and we'll talk with them too,
> Who loses and who wins; who's in, who's out;
> And take upon's the mystery of things,
> As if we were God's spies: and we'll wear out,
> In a wall'd prison, packs and sects of great ones,
> That ebb and flow by the moon.
> —*King Lear*

The words conjured images of butterflies, high tides, and waxing crescent moons. Thoughts of the inn—it was our passion, and, at times, a prison of our own making.

First there was the introduction and chemistry. We assessed whether we were a match. Then we were inspired by our dreams, we made goals and plans for the future. Then there was reality, occasionally a bad day or a bad dream, but we had found a purpose in life. Our work was an expression of loving kindness, a form of redemption from past disappointments. But we knew we wouldn't always be part of the beautiful space we had created. We were only stewards of the inn. And someday, it would go on without us. And so, it does.

Years ago, well before we moved on, I sat in the inn's library with a pencil hovering over a page. I promised myself I'd write a memoir, a bookmark in the story of our life. A reminder of how we felt spending our days creatively, performing acts of kindness for mostly perfect, and occasionally imperfect, strangers.

When I told Jeff I wanted to write this book, he said sarcastically, "Well, then, maybe it would have all been worth it." And I've asked myself: Was it worth it? Where did the years go? How did we get here?

Well. Gravity brought us through the trees on shredded golden parachutes. After hitting the ground, we took the road less traveled and found an old inn destined for the wrecking ball. We fell in love with our inn-dreams, and we were swept up in a Restoration Vortex. Then we got a wake-up call and we rallied ourselves, becoming Inn

Mates in the process—two people who shared a calling and who vowed to stay together on a steep uphill journey, not knowing where it would lead.

Along the way, we met thousands of travelers, some of whom became friends. We greeted them at the door smiling, and we invited them in. Some of the visitors were unexpected, a few were unpleasant, but we welcomed them, too. Life's Rich Pageant.

After many years, we reached the summit of our innkeeping success, stumbling on an earthly paradise and we couldn't believe our luck. Until we were rocked by hurricanes that threatened to blow our house down and left us in the dark to contemplate our lives. We learned several lessons—about undue attachment, acceptance, and the sweet surrender and necessity of letting go—lessons better learned later, rather than never. And we finally discovered we held the keys to our freedom all along, but we just didn't know it.

There were times we cursed being Inn Mates, wishing someone, a friend or fortune-teller, would have said, "You two may not be ready to play with that toy." But I doubt we would have listened. Still, buying a once-grand, dilapidated inn wasn't the best ticket to avenge corporate wolves, fix broken homes, or mend our broken hearts. But I do know I would do it all over again, if we had to, but if there is a next time, Jeff and I will know better.

After the sale of the inn, Jeff and I got back on the road of life. It's now paved with simplicity and gratitude—but we were still one short. We flagged down a furry transport and fell in love with a mocha-colored schnoodle we named Theo, *a divine gift*, and now we are three.

Jeff and I still have moments of heartache, times when we need a guiding star to light our way. During such times, I turn to Rumi, my muse, who always seems to have the answers I'm looking for. He put it this way: *"You have to keep breaking your heart until it opens."*

So, after a safe landing, and with open hearts, we begin again.

ACKNOWLEDGMENTS

I started writing *Inn Mates: An Innkeeper's Memoir* in 2016, although I didn't know it at the time. What started out as a cookbook project for guests turned into something completely different, and the first sixty pages seemed to write themselves. It was a story I needed to tell, and I'm grateful I've had an opportunity to tell it.

Thank you, Helene Harton, Susan Sassaman, Fayelle and Michael Anderson, Annie Shaw, Hamish Blackman, Karen Sale, Mark David, Michael Saunders, Kenn Chandler, Randy Spraque, and David Walker for your friendship, which grounded us in difficult times. Thanks also to Claudia Johnson and Pat Sellergren, lovely sisters, my first readers who encouraged me to write this book, and who pushed me along when I stalled. Your friendship, too, is a precious gift in my life. Then, I struck gold a third time when I was introduced to a new friend, Barbara Gilbert, a fine editor and reader who offered the writerly discipline I lacked, reading my draft manuscript to help me smooth the edges. I do hope you'll share your biscotti recipe with me someday.

I've tried to listen carefully to the voices of so many friends, family members, and former guests who were in my thoughts and kept me company during the writing of this book. Sadly, some of the people who live in my heart are no longer with us and will not be able to hear my words of appreciation for the love and inspiration they have given to me. Thank you to my loving father, Joseph Waltner, and to our dearly departed friends Richard Kreisman, Roy Kasindorf, and Richard Sassaman, whom we lost far too soon.

I'm humbled by the talent and hard work of the more than 100 people who played a role in the inn's restoration and operation. I'm also thankful for our families, friends, former staff, and all of the guests who passed through our lives, leaving us with memories and experiences which helped me to write a few new chapters of our own. I remain forever grateful.

Be not forgetful to entertain strangers:
for thereby some have entertained angels unawares.
—Hebrews 13

Inn Mates

March 1983, rooftop in Brighton section of Boston. Two kids at the start of their careers...with no inkling of becoming innkeepers.

Inn for sale in Bar Harbor. Lots of potential for the "right buyer."

Between careers…a break at the shore during the renovation. Smiles and naïveté.

Ghosts in the attic. Soon to become our penthouse suite.

A creepy attic becomes Room 10, our penthouse suite. Forty-seven stairs from the front desk.

In the middle of the Restoration Vortex with the sign we rescued from the bushes. Worried and overwhelmed as the invoices piled up.

Before: A multi-bed family "suite" just off the main parlor.

After: The inn's library, where the idea for Inn Mates: An Innkeeper's Memoir *originated while waiting for late guest arrivals.*

Teri and Jeff—inn mates at work in the kitchen. From executives to line cooks!

Early in the morning at the start of the innkeeping day. The dining room is serene, awaiting our guests.

Inn Mates

The art of hospitality—"Life's Rich Pageant." Teri, inn guests, and Riley the Inn Dog.

High style in high season. The inn at twilight.

Teri Anderholm

And now we are three...

ABOUT THE AUTHOR

Teri Anderholm hails from Ann Arbor, Michigan. She is a graduate of Boston College. Later she earned her professional chef diploma from the Cambridge School of Culinary Arts. After a lengthy investment career, she enjoyed a stint at a top-rated restaurant in the Boston area. In 2004, Teri and her husband, Jeffrey Anderholm, became innkeepers at the Bass Cottage Inn, located in Bar Harbor, Maine. Teri is a member of the Maine Writers & Publishers Alliance. Teri and Jeff Anderholm and their dog, Theo, live in Saco, Maine.